Dimensions of Social Welfare Policy

Dimensions of Social Welfare Policy

Neil Gilbert

Harry Specht

University of California, Berkeley

Prentice-Hall, Inc. *Englewood Cliffs, New Jersey*

Library of Congress Cataloging in Publication Data

GILBERT, NEIL.
    Dimensions of social welfare policy.

    Includes bibliographical references.
    1. Public welfare. 2. Public welfare—Finance.
3. Public welfare—United States. I. Specht, Harry,
joint author. II. Title.
HV41.G52   362'.973   73–20430
ISBN 0–13–214486–7

© 1974 by Prentice-Hall, Inc.
Englewood Cliffs, New Jersey

10 9 8 7 6 5 4 3 2

Printed in the United States of America

Prentice-Hall International, Inc.,   *London*
Prentice-Hall of Australia, Pty. Ltd.,   *Sydney*
Prentice-Hall of Canada, Ltd.,   *Toronto*
Prentice-Hall of India Private Limited,   *New Delhi*
Prentice-Hall of Japan, Inc.,   *Tokyo*

To Allan, Ida,
and Lynne

Contents

Preface

In writing this book on social welfare policy analysis we encountered many opportunities to take sides and to argue the authors' point of view. There was also strong temptation to allow prescriptions to sneak into analysis because the subject matter deals with compelling issues of human well-being. Moreover, we recognized that proffered solutions to the weighty problems of social welfare would be comforting to many readers, whether or not they agreed with our views; for if they agreed they might congratulate their wisdom and if they disagreed they would have the chance to reaffirm their own position by dissecting the authors' biases and faulty logic. In either case, a book that gives firm and sure direction to social welfare policy is likely to provide more immediate gratification for the student than one that analyzes the terrain and debates the values and costs of different paths that might be taken.

Nonetheless, we offer few explicit and firm prescriptions for specific social welfare policies. (In the few cases where we do prescribe, it was less by design than from an inability to resist temptation.) We thus forewarn the reader who is looking for specific answers to questions of social welfare policy that he will not find this book very comforting. One of our objectives in this text is to share with the reader the real intellectual challenge and the discomfort that are confronted in the making of social welfare policy choices. "Good" and "righteous" answers to the fundamental questions in social welfare policy are not come by easily. Addressed seriously, they require a willingness to abide complexity, an ability to tolerate contradictions, and a capacity to appraise empirical evidence and social values critically, which is to say that professionals who are engaged in the business of making social welfare policy choices will require patience, thought, and an intelligent curiosity to fulfill their commitment well.

To speak of policy choices implies the existence of plausible alternatives. Our second objective in writing this book is to present and illuminate these alternatives. The book is organized around what we consider the basic dimensions of choice in social welfare policy, dimensions of choice we have placed in a framework that provides students new to the field with an intellectual set, a way of thinking about and analyzing social welfare policies that is applicable to a wide range of specific cases. Using this framework, we explore the choices, the questions they raise, and the values and theories that inform different answers. Ultimately the purpose of this book is to help students come to grips with some of the complexities of social choice in the hope that it will equip them to appraise and further develop their own thoughts on social welfare policy.

This book was written over a period of years both at the expense of and for the benefit of our students. We are pleased with whatever benefit they may have derived from exposure to the developing ideas for the book, but mostly we are grateful for the tolerance and critical comments they offered in response to our ruminations. We would like to express particular thanks to Paul Terrell for the many useful questions he raised. We also thank the editors of *Social Work* and *Welfare in Review* for permission to use material that originally appeared in these journals and is now incorporated in Chapters 1, 5, and 8.[1]

We owe special appreciation to Wayne Vasey of the School of Social Work, University of Michigan; Wyatt Jones of the Florence Heller School for Advanced Studies in Social Welfare, Brandeis University; Eveline M. Burns of the School of Social Work, Columbia University; and Riva Specht. Each read the manuscript and provided us with thoughtful criticisms and constructive suggestions. While their good advice helped us to clarify and improve this work, we must, of course, claim exclusive responsibility for whatever deficiencies remain.

It will become quickly evident to our readers that we, like other contemporary students of social welfare policy, have been considerably influenced by the writings of Eveline M. Burns and Richard M. Titmuss. Their impact on this field is of such magnitude as to be pervasive and footnotes are an inadequate means of recognizing how much they have done to illumine social welfare policy.

Finally, we must acknowledge our debts to those who bore the brunt of the moments of strain and weariness that all authors inevitably experience. Our wives and children demonstrated remarkable perseverance and good humor in supporting us as we tried to find our way through the dimensions of choice. To Barbara and Evan Gilbert, and Riva, Daniel, and Eliot Specht, mere thanks is not enough to express the extent of our gratitude and affection.

[1]Harry Specht, "Casework Practice and Social Policy Formulation," *Social Work,* Vol. 13, No. 1 (January 1968); Neil Gilbert, "Assessing Service Delivery Methods: Some Unsettled Questions," *Welfare in Review,* Vol. 10, No. 3 (May/June 1972); and Neil Gilbert, Armin Rosenkranz, and Harry Specht, "Dialectics of Social Planning," *Social Work,* Vol. 18, No. 2 (March 1973).

*Dimensions of
Social Welfare
Policy*

The Field of
Social Welfare Policy

*"I don't think they play at all fairly," Alice began, in rather
a complaining tone, "and they all quarrel so dreadfully one can't
hear oneself speak—and they don't seem to have any rules in
particular: at least, if there are, nobody attends to them—and
you've no idea how confusing it is all the things being alive: for
instance, there's the arch I've got to go through next walking
about at the other end of the ground—and I should have cro-
queted the Queen's hedgehog just now, only it ran away when
it saw mine coming!"*

LEWIS CARROLL
Alice's Adventures in Wonderland

1 Students entering the field of social welfare policy quickly come
to feel somewhat like Alice at the Queen's croquet party. They
confront a landscape that, for many, is puzzling and complex.
The vast territory that the field covers has constantly changing
internal features and outer boundaries that are not readily comprehensible.[1] The knowledge base of social welfare policy is fragmented and less
immediately related to the realities of day-to-day practice with individuals, families, and groups than other knowledge areas that students of the
social services must master. Yet the study of this subject matter is central
for those who practice in the social services because, to a large extent, it
shapes the forms of practice that professionals are called upon to use and
determines the client systems to be served. Thus, the relative demand for
social casework, for employment counselling, for liaison and advocacy

1

services, and for community development, among other forms of practice, in part results from the choices that frame social welfare policies at a given point in time.

The objectives of this introductory chapter are to provide a general orientation to the field of social welfare policy and to illustrate the inter-relatedness of practice and policy analysis. We expect that when the nature of the subject matter is clearer, students will be less easily intimidated by it and more likely to recognize the importance and power of policy studies.

The purpose of this book is to develop an operational understanding of social welfare policy, as the title suggests, through becoming acquainted with the dimensions of choice which the subject matter allows. However, to provide students with an overview of social welfare policy, in this chapter we explore three major contexts that illuminate the subject matter from different angles. These contexts are: (1) the institutional focus, (2) the patterns of analysis, and (3) the professional functions in the developmental stages of social welfare policy. The institutional focus defines what social welfare policy is about and delineates some of its boundaries. The patterns of analysis indicate the different perspectives from which social welfare policy is studied, the types of questions generally asked, and the ways that knowledge so obtained feeds into professional functions. The developmental stages describe the process of social welfare policy formulation and the roles of professionals in this process.

Policy and Social Institutions

Social welfare policy is an elusive concept used frequently as a synonym for social policy and public policy, both of which are broader in scope and more inclusive than the concerns of this book. Social welfare policy is identified with public policy because enactment of most social welfare policies involves expenditure of the public dollar. Government spending in this area (see Figure 1-1) has been increasing, and amounted to 71 percent of the $268 billion spent for social welfare activities in 1972. Total social welfare expenditures in 1972 accounted for 25 percent of the gross national product. Even when private dollars pay for program support they are often augmented by public funds (the details and implications of this will be discussed in Chapters 6 and 7).

However, public policy includes more than just social welfare activities. It encompasses the broad range of goods and services supported by public funds, such as defense, aerospace research, and transportation.

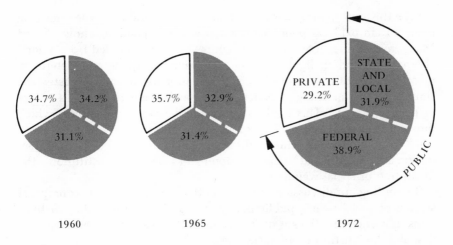

1960   1965   1972

FIGURE 1–1
Percent Public and Private Social Welfare Expenditures in Constant Dollars,
Selected Fiscal Years 1959–60 through 1971–72.

From Alfred M. Skolnik and Sophie R. Dales, "Social Welfare Expenditures, 1971–72,"
Social Security Bulletin, Vol. 35, No. 12 (December 1972).

Similarly, the term social policy is often used to designate a more extensive range of activities than we would subsume under the heading of social
welfare. For example, Gil defines social policies as

> Elements of a society's system of social policy, a system of interrelated,
> yet not necessarily logically consistent, principles and courses of ac-
> tion, which shape the quality of life or level of well-being of members
> of society and determine the nature of all intrasocietal relationships
> among individuals, social subsystems, and society as a whole.[2]

According to this definition, social policy includes all the courses of action
that impact on human relationships and the quality of life in a society. T.
H. Marshall's definition, though somewhat more circumscribed, comes
closer to what we would designate as social welfare policy.[3] For him it is
"the policy of governments with regard to action having a direct impact
on the welfare of citizens by providing them with services or income."
Specifically, the "central core" of programs included under this definition
are social insurance, public assistance, health and welfare services, and
housing. At the periphery, but still within bounds, are programs dealing
with education and delinquency prevention.[4]

Even the term "policy" has several nuances.[5] For Kahn it is the "standing plan";[6] Rein explains policy as the substance of planning choices;[7] and Mangum describes it as "a definite course of action selected from among alternatives, and in light of given conditions to guide and determine present and future decisions."[8] On this matter we defer to Webster and simplicity. The meaning of policy that we will use is that it is "a course or plan of action." This book is about the decisions and choices which inform the course or plan of action in public and private voluntary agencies. What binds and delimits these decisions and choices is that they inform action addressed to the functioning of a particular institution—the institution of social welfare.

By limiting our discussion of policy in this way we skirt the conceptual swamp of social policy, public policy, and social welfare policy distinctions, but enter the thicket of institutional delineation as we attempt to describe the "institution of social welfare."

All human societies organize life into enduring patterns that carry on essential social functions.[9] "Institutions" are networks of relationships that are generally accepted as the way of carrying out these essential social functions.[10] "Essential social functions" are human activities such as child-rearing and the production, consumption, and distribution of goods. For example, all societies develop institutions for socialization that are networks of relationships within which responsibilities and expectations for raising and training the young are distributed. Socialization, of course, is not limited to children. The function has meaning for all stages of the life cycle.

One primary institution seldom exhausts the patterns a society uses to deal with any particular essential function. While the primary institution for socialization in our society is the family, it is by no means the only one. Religious and educational organizations and social service agencies also assume some responsibilities for socialization, but this is not the primary or core function of these institutions.[11]

For our purposes, there are five social functions around which the major institutional activities of community life develop: (1) production-distribution-consumption, (2) socialization, (3) social control, (4) social integration, and (5) mutual support. These functions represent the organization of basic human activities necessary in day-to-day living. We shall comment on each of them briefly, paraphrasing from both Johnson's and Warren's descriptions.[12]

> 1. *Production-consumption-distribution* has to do with the processes of producing, distributing, and consuming those goods and services re-

quired for living. This includes the modern business corporation which is the principal provider of such goods and services as well as other institutions, whether industrial, professional, religious, educational, and governmental, which provide goods and services. For the individual these institutions affect his way of earning a living and providing for family needs for goods and services. For the community, the ways in which these functions are carried out will determine the extent to which its members are self-supporting and in receipt of what is required for healthful functioning.

2. *Socialization,* which we mentioned above, involves those processes by which society transmits prevailing knowledge, social values, and behavior patterns to its members.

3. *Social control* refers to the arrangements by which a society influences the behavior of its members to achieve conformity with its norms. Formal government, which has coercive power to enforce universally applicable laws through the police and the courts, is a primary institution of social control. However, many other social units, including the family, the school, the church, and social agencies assume responsibilities for carrying out this function.

4. *Social integration* has to do with the relationships among units in a social system. Members of a particular institution or of the system-as-a-whole must be loyal to one another and the system must achieve some level of solidarity and morale in order to function. Socialization refers to mechanisms for teaching people how to behave; social control functions have reference to the means for governing or coercing that behavior; and social integration refers to the means of getting people to *want* to behave, e.g., to value and to abide by the rules of the system of social control, socialization, and so forth. The social agencies which carry out these social integration functions are those concerned with the development of social values and norms and include the church, the family, and the school.

5. Finally, *mutual support* functions come into play when individuals are not able to meet their needs through the major institutions which operate to carry out the other social functions we have described. This may occur for a wide variety of reasons such as sickness, loss of a wage earner, or inadequate functioning of the economic institutions. In technologically underdeveloped societies, mutual support activities are carried out primarily by the family. As societies have become more complex, other groups, organizations, and agencies develop which carry out mutual support activities, such as the church, voluntary agencies, and government. *The institution of social welfare is that patterning of relationships which develops in society to carry out mutual support functions.*

The Institution of Social Welfare

In the very simplest of societies, all of the functions noted above are carried out by one social institution, the family. As societies become more complex, individuals and groups specialize in these social functions, and with this specialization other institutions evolve, such as religious, political, and economic institutions. These four types of institutions—familial, religious, political, and economic—are generally recognized as the major social institutions of society.[13] Each institution serves more than one function; at the same time each is closely associated with a primary or core function (see Table 1–1). The institution of social welfare is, by comparison, more functionally diffuse than the others. That is, family, religious, political, and economic institutions intersect at the periphery but contain primary functions which can be defined in fairly discrete and independent terms, while the primary function of social welfare—mutual support—is defined in terms that are relative to and dependent upon the other institutional functions. Mutual support activities come into play only when human needs are not being met via family, political, religious, or economic activities. This is clearly expressed in the literature where various efforts to describe and conceptualize the distinctive features of social welfare policy tend to emphasize objectives concerning integration,[14] distribution[15] and social control.[16]

Functional diffusion is the quality that complicates efforts to delineate the institution of social welfare as a separate and distinct entity. Indeed, it lends weight to the conception that social welfare serves mainly a residual function wherein its activities are perceived as necessary only when those who are served by the "normal" institutional channels are unable to benefit, either through personal failings and exceptional needs or when these "normal" channels fail to perform appropriately. Viewed as a residual, temporary substitute for the failures of individuals and major institutions, social welfare is seen as a rather negative and undesirable set of

TABLE 1–1
Institutional Functions.

Institution	*Primary Function*
Family ⟶	Socialization
Religion ⟶	Integration
Economics ⟶	Production–distribution–consumption
Politics ⟶	Social control
Social welfare ⟶	Mutual support

activities. Supporters of this view argue that it is inappropriate to place social welfare alongside of and on equal standing with the major societal institutions of Table 1–1.

Speaking at the Conference of Charities and Corrections in 1915, Dr. Abraham Flexner expressed this residual conception of social welfare in comparing social work with the recognized professions:[17]

> A good deal of what is called social work might perhaps be accounted for on the ground that the recognized professions have developed too slowly on the social side. Suppose medicine were fully socialized; would not medical men, medical institutions, and medical organizations look after certain interests that the social worker must care for just because medical practice now falls short? The shortcomings of law create a similar need in another direction. Thus viewed, social work is, in part at least, not so much a separate profession as an endeavor to supplement certain existing professions *pending their completed development.* [Emphasis added]

Competing with this conception is the "institutional" view of social welfare as a distinct pattern of activities serving not as a safety net to catch the pieces after all else has failed, but as an integral and "normal 'first line' function of modern industrial society."[18] Perceived thus, as a basic social institution, social welfare carries none of the stigma of the "dole" or "charity." Rather, it is seen as the normal and accepted means by which individuals, families, and communities fulfill their social needs and attain healthful living.

Whether the institutional or residual conception of social welfare prevails depends in large measure upon how we comprehend both the causes and the incidence of unmet needs in society. In both conceptions, the major institutional structures are viewed as ineffective to some degree in meeting people's needs. The fundamental issues are: To what extent is this an anomaly reflecting mainly the deficiencies of some individuals and a small margin of institutional malfunctioning? To what extent is it a regularly anticipated consequence reflecting the inherent limitations of both institutional adaptations to change and individual efforts to deal with the exigencies of life in modern industrial society? In other words, is it the workman and a few of his tools that occasionally may be faulty? Or, are both inherently imperfect given the complex and uncertain demands of the job? An answer of "very much" to the first question and "very little" to the second relegates social welfare to the status of a residual activity which, as Figure 1–2 suggests, serves as a safety net for the basic institutional structure. Reverse these answers and social welfare emerges as a basic social institution.

RESIDUAL (Safety Net Function)

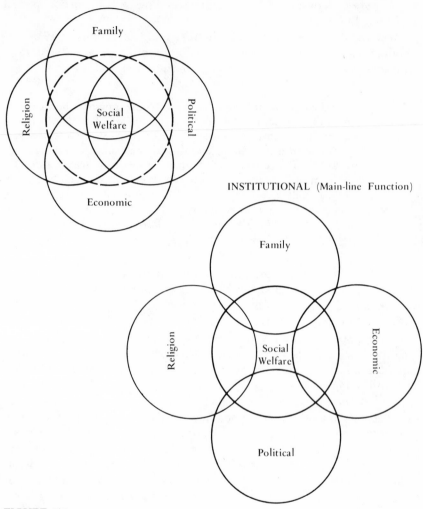

INSTITUTIONAL (Main-line Function)

FIGURE 1–2
Conceptions of Social Welfare.

The answers to these questions, however, remain equivocal. In this regard, Wilensky and Lebeaux's assessment of the status of the competing conceptions of social welfare in the United States is still accurate.

> While these two views seem antithetical, in practice American social work has tried to combine them, and current trends in social welfare present a middle course. Those who lament the passing of the old order

> insist that the second ideology is undermining individual character and the national social structure. Those who bewail our failure to achieve utopia today, argue that the residual conception is an obstacle which must be removed before we can produce the good life for all. In our view, neither ideology exists in a vacuum; each is a reflection of . . . broader cultural and societal conditions. . . . With further industrialization the second is likely to prevail.[19]

In sum, social welfare may be characterized most accurately as an emerging institution whose core function is mutual support. Historically, mutual support activities are secondary functions of other institutions, mainly family and religion. Modern times have brought increasing demands on such activities as our conceptions of need and standards of well-being have changed. The limitations of existing major institutions to meet these demands as well as individual vulnerabilities to the forces of change in urban industrial society are becoming more apparent. However, the extent to which these limitations and vulnerabilities are perceived to exist varies greatly among segments of society. An elaborate system of public and private agencies has developed for the express purpose of providing mutual support. Thus, the relative importance of this activity as a distinct pattern begins to emerge, a pattern of activity comprising the major set of relationships and programs to which our discussion in this book is addressed.

Finally, while social welfare is described here as an emerging institution, there are certain eligibility requirements for social welfare benefits that lend credence to the residual conception. Because it is unlikely that these eligibility conditions will be eliminated entirely from social welfare concerns, it seems that the residual conception will linger even as social welfare approaches institutional status. We will discuss this phenomenon in greater detail in Chapter 3 when we examine the basis of social allocations in policy design.

Analytic Perspectives
on Social Welfare Policy

Considerable insight, knowledge, and speculation, products of diverse research perspectives, are encompassed in the social welfare policy field. Though there are no clear-cut domains, analysts tend to approach this field of study in several different but interrelated ways. The different approaches to social welfare policy analysis can be characterized as studies of the three "p's": *process, product,* and *performance.* Each perspective examines social welfare policy with reference to a particular set of questions, primarily relevant to the professional roles of planning, administration, and research. Professionals engaged in these roles will devote the major portion of their resources and energies to questions concerning the process, product, and performance of social welfare policy. In actual practice in agencies, sometimes all three roles are performed by the same worker. In such a case he would tend to draw equally on the knowledge and insights generated by all three modes of study. However, in most large agencies and programs the tasks of planning, administration, and research are specialized, and practitioners tend to be more interested in the insights of one analytic approach than in others. Though even when the roles of planner, administrator, and researcher are highly compartmentalized, requirements for handling "outside" tasks seep into the job.[20]

Similarly, it is important to underscore that what we distinguish as three analytic perspectives in reality are overlapping and interrelated. This is a shorthand way of stating that conceptual distinctions tend to capture the core qualities of a phenomenon, but by their very nature (since concepts are themselves a form of shorthand) concepts do not portray subtle and relative characteristics. Frequently, policy analysts may employ different combinations of approaches in their investigation. Thus, for example, Sar Levitan's study of the War on Poverty traces the *process* of development of the Economic Opportunity Act of 1964, describes the various programs that were *products* of this act, and evaluates their *performance.*[21]

Whatever the practice, though, it is theoretically useful to distinguish among these analytic approaches to the study of policy because at the core they address different types of questions and the knowledge and insights generated are differentially applicable to major practice roles related to social welfare policy. At the conclusion of this section we will describe what we believe are the policy-relevant tasks of the direct-service practitioner. And in the final section of the chapter we will tie the process of policy formulation to these professional tasks, illustrating how they are related to one another in practice.

Studies of Process

The study of process in social welfare policy is based on an analytic perspective that focuses upon the dynamics of policy formulation with regard to sociopolitical and technical-methodological variables. Political science and history are two of the major academic disciplines on which the study of process is based. Process study is most concerned with understanding how the inputs of planning data and the relationships and interactions among the various political, governmental, and other organized collectivities in a society affect policy formulation.

Studies of process are employed as points around which policy assessments are organized, usually in the form of case studies of the political and technical inputs to decision-making. Because process studies may vary in respect to the time dimension with which they deal, they can include analysis of current programs such as Meyerson and Banfield's study of decison-making processes in planning for public housing and various investigations of citizen participation in the development of community action programs. Historical analyses that provide a more long-range perspective, as in Lubove's study of factors influencing the development of welfare legislation, are included here too.[22]

Regardless of time perspective, though, process studies generally deal with such questions as the societal context in which policy decisions are made, the behaviors, motivations and goals of various actors who participate in the process, and the stages of the process of policy development. Process studies help illuminate how social context, the actors, and stages of development contribute to policy outcomes.

Studies of the Product

The product of the planning process is a set of policy choices. These choices may be framed in program proposals, laws and statutes, or standing plans which eventually are transformed into programs. The analytic focus of such studies is upon issues of choice: What is the form and substance of the choices that comprise the policy design? What options did these choices foreclose? What values, theories, and assumptions support alternative choices?

Although widely employed in a variety of academic disciplines, product study is the least systematically developed perspective on the analysis of social welfare policy. Analyses of choice usually focus upon one or another issue of choice that is germane to a specific policy, but there is no systematic framework for placing the generic issues of policy design in a broad context. Examples of these issue-specific studies are cited in the following chapters, as we attempt to explicate a generic view of social welfare policy from this analytic perspective. In the next chapter we will address the development and utility of this approach in greater detail.

Studies of Performance

Performance studies are concerned with the description and evaluation of the programmatic outcomes of policy choices. Studies of program outcome are more amenable to objective, systematic observation than studies of process and product because program boundaries are more sharply delineated. Performance can be measured through the collection of quali- tative and quantitative data and through the application of a wide range of methodological tools of various academic disciplines. Research method- ology as taught in the social science disciplines and in professional schools provides the major technological and theoretical knowledge and skill for these kinds of studies.

From this perspective, investigators ask two types of questions: How well is the program carried out? What is its impact? With regard to the former, programs are monitored to see what they consist of, whether they are reaching the target population, how much they cost, and so on. Impact is measured in "the difference between pre-program behavior conditions and post-program behavior and conditions which can legitimately be at- tributed to the intervention."[23]

Why Policy Analysis Is Relevant to Practitioners in Direct Services

We have observed that from various perspectives the study of social wel- fare policy may serve the interests of planners, administrators, and re- searchers. There is also another group of professionals responsible for carrying important policy-related functions. However, most of the people in this group can exercise these functions only because they devote the major portion of their energies and resources to direct-service activities. This is particularly true in the case of practitioners such as caseworkers, probation officers, and group workers who are engaged in the direct provi- sion of services to clients.

The practitioner directly involved in the provision of services to clients can play an important role in the formulation of and is instrumental to the execution of the policies that guide social service organizations. Indeed, it is well recognized that in practice the separation of policy formulation from execution is a delicate division, more characteristic of a porous mem- brane than of the solid line of bureaucratic hierarchy. Aware and experi- enced practitioners often exercise considerable discretion in executing broad directives, and so shape as well as discharge the requirements of organizational policies.

The importance of the direct-service practitioner's discretion for policy interpretation increases as organizations grow larger and more complex. Too frequently, though, with regard to influencing social welfare policy, the charge to the practitioner is delivered in oversimplified clichés instruct- ing them to "get into the political arena" or to learn to deal more effectively with the "community power structure."[24] However, this demand can be demoralizing to professionals, particularly to practitioners whose major functions and energies are devoted to dealing with problems of individuals and families. At best a general call to arms without more specific instructions about which arms to use or how to use them is only temporarily inspiring, and at worst it is likely to leave many feeling inadequate.

A second reason for the direct-service practitioner's sense of inadequacy in dealing with social welfare policy formulation is that it is not as well defined as other professional tasks. In casework or probation work, for example, the actual doing (counseling) and the units with which one does it (cases) are relatively clear. Many of the methods used in direct practice allow professionals to work within a series of fairly well-defined roles that usually have a high degree of consonance and frequently can be filled by one person. However, the process by which policy is formulated involves a wide range of roles that often strain against one another and must be filled by several people.

In addition, the transmission of knowledge and skills in the field of social welfare policy is neither well organized nor sharply defined. Participation in social welfare policy formulation requires expertise in a major area of service, and a comprehensive and extensive knowledge of a field. But it also requires certain general analytic skills that may be taught to all in the helping professions. If policy formulation is seen as a process that entails many different tasks, roles, and transmissible analytic skills, then all professionals can learn to utilize the process and contribute to it in the most appropriate ways.

The fact that the direct-service practitioner's major functions are remote from the final decision points in the process of policy formulation tends to make many students feel that the requirement to take courses in social welfare policy is somewhat of an affliction. The direct-service practitioner is more inclined to concentrate on the development of interactional skills, on learning how to conduct himself as a professional, and how to engage himself with clients, colleagues, and community leaders and groups. The study of social choices and social values seems, to many students, too abstract and theoretical. But the professionals who give insufficient attention to social choices and social values in order to devote exclusive attention to development of their practice skills will be like musicians playing background music to a melody that seems to come from nowhere. Like musical themes, the directions and goals which are reflected in social welfare policy are neither accidental nor aimless—they develop because men make choices. One has to understand what the range of choices is, what values are implied in the alternatives, the framework within which these choices are made, the various means by which these choices are implemented, and the methodological tools that can be used to assess the consequences of these choices.

While the direct-service worker may be less engaged in and concerned with designing social welfare policy, he is affected by it in important ways. In the long view, policy choices affect the kinds of technology the direct-service worker will use and they determine how his knowledge and skills are valued by society. For example, the 1962 amendments to the Social Security Act placed great value upon the provision of supportive casework services to welfare clients and this choice was supported with substantial financial resources. By 1967 social welfare policy had changed. Along with the push for the separation of income and services, a significant policy shift resulted in the de-emphasis of individualized therapeutic interventions and withdrawal of resources to support them. We will examine these choices in more detail later and assess some of the values, theories, and assumptions underlying them. At this point we merely want to stress the fact that the direct-service practitioner who has the conceptual tools to analyze the dimensions of social welfare policy is more likely to be a participant in these changes than a product or victim of them.

Whether the direct-service practitioner is interested in or conversant with social welfare policy, the public *assumes* that those who are engaged in the provision of services will be able to provide information and knowledge that can be used in making choices about social welfare programs. Legislators, politicians, and community groups turn to caseworkers and probation officers to ask for advice about planning and developing programs; and their advice will be treated seriously, whether it is ill or well informed, largely because of their status as professionals. There is, then, a professional obligation to be knowledgeable in this area.

Finally, many students who are now training as direct-service practitioners will, later on, become planners, administrators, and researchers because these ranks are frequently filled by agencies from within on the basis of seniority. Direct-service professionals who will ultimately perform these primary policy-related roles would be wise to link some part of their formal education to the elements of the curriculum for training planners, administrators, and policy analysts.[25] From a career point of view, it is essential that the direct-service practitioner have at least an appreciation of the dimensions of the field of social welfare policy if not an intimate knowledge of its specializations.

The Process of Policy Formulation

Many authors have developed models of policy formulation that are similar to the one we will offer.[26] These models of process are usually presented as a series of unfolding stages, the number of which vary according to the author's purpose. In most cases the neat sequential ordering of the process is qualified by the recognition that in reality these stages are in a state c_ dynamic readjustment, feeding back data that alter the ones preceding while forming the groundwork for the ones to follow.

For students new to the field of social welfare policy these models are sometimes confusing because they vary not only with regard to the number of stages and the terminology used to describe these stages, but also with regard to the headings or general labels under which they are presented. Nevertheless, there is much similarity. Briefly, to illustrate this point, in Table 1–2 we compare three process models found in the literature. Model A contains six stages under the heading of "planning process";[27] Model B contains five stages under the heading of "problem-solving process";[28] and Model C contains three stages under the heading of "social policy development process."[29]

As Table 1–2 suggests, whether the stages are divided into six categories, three categories, or somewhere in between, these models correlate directly with regard to the substance and rational progression characteristic of the process being described. The models differ simply in regard to the levels

TABLE 1–2
Comparison of Models of Policy Development.

Model A (Kahn) Planning Process	Model B (Perlman & Gurin) Problem-Solving Process	Model C (Freeman & Sherwood) Social Policy Development Process
1. Planning instigators	1. Defining the problem	1. Planning
2. Explorations		
3. Definition of the planning task	2. Establishing structural and communications links for consideration of the problem	
4. Policy formulation	3. Study of alternative solutions and adoption of a policy	
5. Programming	4. Development and implementation of a program plan	2. Program development and implementation
6. Evaluation & feedback	5. Monitoring and feedback	3. Evaluation

of generalization employed. And this is where the model we will use differs from those in Table 1–2—it contains eight stages.

The purpose of dividing the policy formulation process into eight stages is not, as some might suspect, to go one up on our colleagues. Rather, the objective is to provide a sense of the rich variety of tasks and professional roles that enter into and which are primarily associated with different points in this process. Five social welfare related roles are identified: practice of direct service, research, community organization, administration, and planning. As indicated earlier, these various roles are often filled by the same worker; for example, a planner may do research and community organization.

The policy formulation process, as outlined in Table 1–3, functions to uncover incipient and unmet needs and to blaze a trail of advocacy toward new methods of meeting those needs. It might take place in a variety of settings—in a small private agency, in one department of a large agency, or in a nationwide bureaucracy. The model does not reflect the complex feedback interactions among stages nor does it take into account the question of who generates the initiative for carrying the process forward.

Identification of Problem

The basis for institutional policy change is sometimes an unrecognized or unmet need in the community, a need the originator of the policy goal believes the institution is responsible for meeting. The perception of the problem and the institution's responsibility are related to the political, economic, social, and institutional forces that the originator perceives. What people define as problems is related in part to their institutional

TABLE 1–3
Professional Roles and Policy Formulation.

Stage	*Professional Roles*
1. Identification of problem	1. Direct service
2. Analysis	2. Research
3. Informing the public	3. Community organization
4. Development of policy goals	4. Planning
5. Building public support and legitimation	5. Community organization
6. Program design	6. Planning
7. Implementation	7. Administration and direct service
8. Evaluation and assessment	8. Research and direct service

positions. So, for example, it is possible that concerns for organizational maintenance might guide the perceptions of administrators more than their feelings of responsibility for providing better service to clients.[30]

Tasks that must be completed during this stage are case-finding, recording examples of unmet needs, and discovering gaps in services. These are tasks that direct-service practitioners are singularly well equipped and positioned to perform. It is in their functions as advocates and social brokers for their clients that they will most likely be involved in the policy formulation process. Scott Briar has discussed these functions as part of the direct service worker's professional role, noting that they bring to the task "a substantial body of knowledge with which to understand the dynamics of the welfare system and its constituent agencies."[31]

However, to use such knowledge in this process requires a professional orientation that views service to one's client as the foremost professional responsibility, beyond even that of organizational loyalty. For the practitioner, a major dilemma of contributing to policy formulation emerges when (as we will discuss in Chapter 5) the requirements of bureaucratic conformity clash with this professional value of service.

Analysis

Having identified a problem, it is necessary to develop some factual data about the number of people who are affected by it and formulate a clear-cut statement of how the problem is actually being measured. The kind and quality of information-gathering at this stage may change as the process evolves. For example, consider the following hypothetical case. A probation officer observes that children are being physically mistreated in the county probation department's residential institution. Unable to make headway with the agency's administrator (who is defensive and unwilling to recognize that the requirements of order in his institution can be met without occasional physical punishments to keep the youthful inmates in line), the probation officer brings this problem to the attention of a group of concerned citizens who have been organized through the county community action program. This citizens' committee sets up meetings throughout the county and invites all youths who have been at the institution and want an opportunity to speak of their experiences.

In this case a fairly informal procedure, the community meeting, is used early in the process to generate much of the raw data for the citizen committee's work. As these meetings progress and some of the issues become clear, the committee might direct its energies toward bringing in a professional standard-setting agency or research unit to examine systematically the community's probation program. Whatever the specific method, the basic task at this stage is to move from an expression of concern about unmet needs to an organized (frequently complicated and expensive) program of information-gathering and analysis. Research skills are primary to this task.

Informing the Public

The *public* is the various subsystems in the agency or general community that must be informed of the problem if the process is to proceed. The size of the public—as big as the community-at-large or as limited as the administration of an institution—depends on the nature of the problem. The task is to present the problem in a form that will capture the interest and attention of the relevant parties. These tasks require organizing skills and use of the appropriate media.

As in the stage of analysis, there is no clear-cut time frame that divides information-gathering and informing the public. Through the use of testimony at community meetings, efforts made to inform the public are interwoven with information-gathering and analysis. The neighborhood survey by resident volunteers is a similar method for simultaneously uncovering unmet needs and informing a segment of the public (the resident volunteers). Both research and organizing skills are required to implement such a survey.

This step precedes the next stage—developing policy goals—because while parties who are initiating change may have specific policy goals in mind, they will have little meaning to the relevant public until it is aware that a problem exists.

Development of Policy Goals

The preceding stages have stimulated public awareness that some problem or unmet need exists and information was provided concerning its dimensions. Now the point has been reached where discussion turns to solving the problem and meeting the need. At this stage many solutions will be offered for dealing with the problem, all of which must be sifted, analyzed, and shaped into a general policy goal. For example, in the case of the probation department, some of the goals might be to change the attitudes and behavior of staff in the residential center, to move residents out of the probation center facility into halfway houses in the community or other facilities, or to attack the basic causes of delinquency.

The primary professional function at this stage is closely associated with what Kahn describes as the definition of the planning task.

The planner's most serious decision and major contribution is what may be called the *formulation or definition of the planning task.* The "task" is formulated through a constant playing back between an assessment of the relevant aspects of social reality and the preferences of the relevant community. Each of these two factors affects and modifies the perception of the other. The task definition appears as an integration of the two. Much else in social planning follows from the outcome of such integration.[32]

The outcome or product of this stage is a general statement of the broad-based objectives or goals to be achieved.

Building Public Support and Legitimation

During and after the process of goal formulation, efforts must be made to involve the relevant public and to gain their support for the general course of action being proposed. Those who are initiating the policy will have to find groups in the broader system that can lend support and legitimation to the policy objectives and can assist in translating them into instruments for action.

Major tasks at this stage are the cultivation of leadership, coalition formation, and negotiation of a consensus among the potential supporters. Compromises may be made at this stage that modify the goal statement. Here the organizer's skills of bargaining, exchange, and persuasion are essential to forge the support base. The culmination of this stage is the creation of a platform containing the goals and objectives of the supporting groups, which may consist of political parties, professional associations, citizen organizations, agencies, clients, and so on.

Program Design

Once the general direction has been set, the tasks of actually drafting a program design are generally considered to rest on the drawing boards of the social planner. At this point goals and objectives are transformed into a set of operational guidelines for action—whether in the form of statutes for consideration by some legislative body or program proposals to be considered by an agency board of directors.

The plans of action or policies that are products of this stage describe the allocation of responsibility for the proposed program and deal with organizational structure, financing, and facets of program operation. These elements of program design vary in regard to the amount of detail and specification which they contain. Frequently, the program is designed at a level that leaves considerable room for interpretation by those who will administer and implement its services.

Implementation

Depending on how detailed the program design is, a large part of the process of policy formulation may be left for this stage, when the concrete translation of action principles to programmatic elements may be accomplished through practice, precedent, and experimentation. A good illustration is the Economic Opportunity Act of 1964, in which the guidelines requiring the "maximum feasible participation" of the poor were quite vague; the practical details of implementation were left to the program administrators. In Chapter 4 we will discuss some of the different ways this policy design was interpreted and their implications for program development.

The chief tasks at this point, getting the program organized, clarifying policy, producing the service or benefit, and delivering it to the client group, relate to administrative and direct-service functions. Also, the courts may enter the process at this stage and play a major role in the clarification of policy. It is by establishing a system of rights and guarantees through appeals and judicial precedents that a body of administrative procedure and law evolves for any social program.

Evaluation and Assessment

In a sense the goals of social welfare policy are always receding. New programs create new expectations and needs and uncover additional unmet needs. Programs themselves become a major element in the "demand environment" of policy. As we shall see in Chapter 4, this continuing process is based in part on faulty assumptions of policy design concerning the availability of resources and supportive services in the external system.

This stage requires an assessment of the impact of policy, an evaluation of how the policy meets the problem, and how the program implements the policy. Actually it is the first stage all over again, for the process of policy formulation is ongoing and has neither a discrete beginning nor an end.

Summary

In this chapter we have sought to introduce the field of social welfare policy by discussing it in three different contexts. The results of this discussion may be summarized briefly as follows:

1. *Institutional focus*—the field is characterized as consisting of policies related to the emerging institution of social welfare; an institution that has mutual support as its core function.

2. *Analytic perspectives*—the field is studied by various academic disciplines from viewpoints that tend to coalesce around three perspectives; these perspectives deal with questions of process, product, and performance.

3. *Professional functions*—the development of policy in this field involves a series of practice roles including administrator, planner, community organizer, direct service practitioner, and researcher; each of these roles may serve primary functions at different stages of the policy formulation process.

In general, the purpose of this overview is to illustrate via the "big picture" some of the breadth and depth of the field. Also, we have suggested why the study of this broad and complex field is of central importance to students training for professional positions that serve the institution of social welfare. Effective participation in this institution requires certain basic knowledge about social welfare policy. Such knowledge includes an understanding of the process of policy formulation and the technical tools and sociopolitical savvy required to move it along. It also includes the methodological techniques of descriptive and evaluative research required to assess performance. Finally, this knowledge entails insight into the abstract entity—those principles or guides to action that constitute the social welfare policy—which is the culmination of process and the prelude to performance. The development of such insight hinges on obtaining a grasp of the fundamental choices that inhere in the design of social welfare policies.

Notes

[1]For some valuable insights into boundary definitions of social welfare policy, see Martin Rein, *Social Policy* (New York: Random House, 1970), pp. 3–20; Kenneth Boulding, "The Boundaries of Social Policy," *Social Work*, Vol. 12, No. 1 (January 1967), 3–11; Richard Titmuss, *Essays on 'The Welfare State'* (London: Unwin University Books, 1963).

[2]David A. Gil, "A Systematic Approach to Social Policy Analysis," *Social Service Review*, Vol. 44, No. 4 (December 1970), 411–26.

[3]This distinction between "social policy" and "social welfare policy" is discussed by George Rohrlich, "Social Policy and Income Distribution," *Encyclopedia of Social Work*, Vol. II, ed. Robert Morris (New York: National Assn. of Social Workers, 1971), pp. 1385–86.

[4]T. H. Marshall, *Social Policy* (London: Hutchinson University Library, 1955), p. 7.

[5]See Chapter 2, pp. 00–00, for discussion of distinctions that are made between policy and program.

[6]Alfred Kahn, *Theory and Practice of Social Planning,* (New York: Russell Sage, 1969), p. 13.

[7]Rein, *Social Policy,* p. xiii.

[8]Garth Mangum, *Emergence of Manpower Policy* (New York: Holt, Rinehart and Winston, 1969), p. 130.

[9]For a probing, in-depth examination of functional analysis, see Robert Merton, *Social Theory and Social Structure* (2nd ed.) (London: The Free Press of Glencoe, 1964), pp. 19–84.

[10]Harry M. Johnson, *Sociology: A Systematic Introduction,* (New York: Harcourt Brace, 1960), p. 22.

[11]The term institution is commonly used on two levels of abstraction. For example, there is the religious institution (such as St. John's church) and the Institution of religion. In the former sense this concept implies an organization or agency that performs a social function; in the latter it reflects the sum of organizations and agencies with the primary responsibility for performing this function.

[12]Roland Warren, *The Community in America,* (Chicago: Rand McNally, 1963), pp. 9–20; and Johnson, *Sociology,* pp. 51–66.

[13]For a detailed discussion of these institutions, see William Ogburn and Meyer Nimkoff, *Sociology* (Cambridge: Houghton Mifflin, 1940), pp. 553–740; Robin Williams, Jr., *American Society* (New York: Alfred A. Knopf, 1951); and Francis Merrill and H. Wentworth Eldredge, *Culture and Society* (Englewood Cliffs, N.J.: Prentice-Hall, 1952), pp. 462–82. In some cases education is also included on this list, though we consider it within the larger institution of social welfare.

[14]For the emphasis of integration see, Kenneth Boulding, "The Boundaries of Social Policy."

[15]For the emphasis of distribution see, Richard Titmuss, "The Role of Redistribution in Social Policy," *Commitment to Welfare* (London: George Allen and Unwin, 1968).

[16]For the emphasis on social control see, Martin Wolins, "The Societal Functions of Social Welfare," *New Perspectives: The Berkeley Journal of Social Welfare,* Vol. 1, No. 1 (Spring 1967), 1–17.

[17]Abraham Flexner, "Is Social Work a Profession?" Presented at the Conference of Charities and Corrections, May 17, 1915.

[18]Harold Wilensky and Charles Lebeaux, *Industrial Society and Social Welfare* (New York: Russell Sage, 1958), p. 138.

[19]Wilensky and Lebeaux, *Industrial Society and Social Welfare,* p. 140.

[20]For example, in Robert Perlman and Arnold Gurin, *Community Organization and Social Planning* (New York: John Wiley & Sons, 1972), an entire chapter is devoted to various ways the administrator of a direct service agency is engaged in community organization and social planning tasks.

[21]Sar Levitan, *The Great Society's Poor Law* (Baltimore: Johns Hopkins, 1969).

[22]These are only a few examples of studies from the process perspective: Martin Meyerson and Edward Banfield, *Politics, Planning and the Public Interest* (New York: Free Press, 1955); Roy Lubove, *The Struggle for Social Security* (Cambridge: Harvard University Press, 1968).

[23]Howard Freeman and Clarence Sherwood, *Social Research and Social Policy* (Englewood Cliffs, N.J.: Prentice-Hall, 1970), p. 13.

[24]Alan D. Wade, "The Social Worker in the Political Process," *Social Welfare Forum 1966* (New York: Columbia University Press, 1966), pp. 52–67.

[25]For a more detailed discussion of these curriculum issues see, Neil Gilbert and Harry Specht, "The Incomplete Profession: Commitment to Welfare vs. Commitment to Services," *Journal of Education for Social Work* (forthcoming).

[26]See for example, Elizabeth Wickenden, *How to Influence Public Policy* (New York: American Association of Social Workers, 1964); and Robert E. Agger, Daniel Goldrich, and Bert E. Swanson, *The Rulers and the Ruled* (New York: John Wiley & Sons, 1964).

[27]Kahn, *Theory and Practice of Social Planning,* p. 61.

[28]Perlman and Gurin, *Community Organization and Social Planning,* pp. 58–74.

[29]Freeman and Sherwood, *Social Research and Social Policy,* pp. 3–16.

[30]Organizational maintenance and direct service needs frequently make competing claims on social welfare administrators which leads Etzioni to suggest that this type of position constitutes a case of institutionalized role conflict. Amitai Etzioni, *Modern Organizations* (Englewood Cliffs, N.J.: Prentice-Hall, 1964), pp. 82–85.

[31]Scott Briar, "Dodo or Phoenix? A View of the Current Crisis in Casework," *Social Work Practice 1967* (New York: Columbia University Press, 1967); see also, Gordon Hamilton, "The Role of Social Casework in Social Policy," *Social Casework,* Vol. 33, No. 8 (October 1952).

[32]Kahn, *Theory and Practice of Social Planning,* p. 61.

A Framework
for Social Welfare
Policy Analysis

Even when armed with this much greater scientific knowledge,
contemporary societies will, of course, face difficult choices be-
tween simultaneously held but competing values or objectives . . .
The precise balance between adequacy and equity in the determi-
nation of social insurance benefits, between equal access to mini-
mum security and retention of the principle of local autonomy,
between the interests of different social classes in allocating the
costs of social security measures, or between the claims of family
obligation and responsibilities to the wider community illustrate
the nature of these ultimate and difficult value choices. Yet while
there is no guarantee that democracies will act rationally in
formulating their social policies, it is also abundantly clear that
they cannot even be expected to do so unless they are made aware
of the full implications of the choices available to them.

EVELINE M. BURNS
Social Security and Public Policy

2 Traditionally, courses in social welfare policy have emphasized the study of process and performance. In courses organized around process, students learned about social, political, and technical processes in policy formulation, and in courses organized around performance they learned about the details of social welfare programs in operation. A major advantage to the study of performance is its focus upon factual and substantive material—it describes and evaluates *programs*. Here too lies its major shortcoming—the substance of social welfare programs is continually changing. Moreover, the programs are so numerous that one or two courses can cover only a segment of the field.

A third approach to the study of this field, as indicated in Chapter 1, is to focus upon the product or set of policy choices that evolve from the planning process. From this perspective the analytic task is to distinguish and dissect the components of the structure of policy design rather than to examine the sociopolitical processes through which policy is developed or to evaluate operational outcomes of policies. The components of the structure of policy design to which this task is addressed are dimensions of choice. In this chapter we present a framework for analyzing the generic choices inherent in the design of social welfare policy.

With this analytic approach to the field of social welfare policy, we will use program descriptions as examples to concretize and substantiate general concepts. Since we are interested mainly in the common elements of social welfare policy rather than in the details of specific programs, there will be a certain eclecticism in the selection of these examples which include large and small programs, pieces of programs, existing programs, and proposed programs, some of which may never leave the drawing boards and others which have not yet arrived on the public agenda.

As Eveline Burns has suggested, the major advantage of this approach is that it equips students with a convenient and meaningful set of concepts that are applicable to and provide insight into a wide range of policies.[1] To accomplish this, however, we must simplify reality somewhat, the price of any effort to cull and distill certain essential elements of complex phenomena. If the effort is successful, it is well worth the price.

An analytic framework is an intellectual tool to order and simplify reality by directing our attention to certain elements in a field while filtering out others. (Shortly we will elaborate the analytic framework around which this book is organized.) But first let us say a few words about certain features of the field of social welfare policy that our framework tends to screen out. These features have to do with the "levels of comprehensiveness" and the "realms of policy." This brief detour into "levels" and "realms" is taken to underline some complexities of the reality we are dealing with. To some extent the analytic framework shields us from these complexities without, we hope, doing great violence to reality. Nevertheless, these are facets of the field of which students of social welfare policy analysis will want to remain cognizant.

Levels and Realms

Although social welfare policies are formulated at different levels within society, much of this field is identified with the more comprehensive policy choices made by public and private agencies at the national or macro-level. However, we should not forget that policy making also includes activities of agencies at the local or micro-levels. The director of a neighborhood settlement house planning to have his agency offer, for example, a premarital counseling service to local residents, as well as the task force member assigned to help draft national strategy for a war on poverty, are engaged in designing social welfare policies. This view of policy as pertaining to micro- and macro-level program development, though widely held, is not universal.

Occasionally the term *policy* as found in the literature designates an overall strategy or master plan focused on a geographic or functional sector of society. Moynihan's observation that "programs do not a policy make," reflects this point of view, distinguishing program from policy according to levels of comprehensiveness.[2] But the point at which program ends and policy begins is inexact, and the question of what constitutes comprehensive policy rather than fragmented program development is open to a wide range of interpretation. For a quick sampling, there is the macro-/micro-system distinction wherein policy formulated at the macro-level, usually national in scope, is identified as "comprehensive."[3] But there is also the American Institute of Planners' Committee on the Restatement of Institute Purposes which defines comprehensive planning as efforts to identify and order the physical, social, and economic relationships implicit in development programs *within a delimited geographic area ranging from a neighborhood to an international region.*[4] And, finally, to spice up the issue a bit there is the view that at whatever level it is preached comprehensive planning is rarely practiced. In this view, as Lindblom argues, most policy formulation is achieved by "muddling through" via successive limited comparisons between what is and a series of incremental alternatives of what might be.[5]

In this book we make little effort to sort out or distinguish social welfare policy in terms of comprehensiveness. Our treatment of policy is impartial to this issue; it includes analyses of designs to guide implementation of programs of limited scope at the micro-level as well as broader scope national-level strategies. While many of the specific examples we employ focus on the macro-level, the concepts and issues are equally applicable to policy choices addressed by planners and administrators in local agencies.

In addition to the different levels of comprehensiveness, the literature also contains distinctions regarding the various realms of social welfare policy. Titmuss, for instance, discerns three systems of welfare: social, fiscal, and occupational. "Social services" are commonly attributed only to the system of social welfare. But Titmuss argues that if "social services" are defined according to their aims (i.e., collective interventions to meet certain needs of the individual and society) rather than on the basis of administrative methods used to achieve these aims, then in fact they also obtain in the systems of fiscal welfare (e.g., tax exemptions for dependents) and occupational welfare (e.g., fringe benefits such as pensions and health insurance).[6] Whether the latter legitimately qualify as social welfare rather than simply as one of the conditions of employment, a substitute for wages, is ambiguous. Wilensky and Lebeaux offer the following guidelines: "The degree to which an industrial welfare program may be considered social welfare varies inversely with extent of emphasis on contractual relationship between two parties seeking a mutually rewarding arrangement, and directly with the extent of social sponsorship and control."[7]

From another angle, social welfare policies are often classified in terms of functional fields (e.g., health, education), problem areas (e.g., juvenile delinquency, unemployment), population groups (e.g., children, the aged) or some combination thereof.[8] There is considerable overlap among these realms. The line between functional fields and problems is rather fuzzy; it appears to be less substantive than definitional. A perusal of the Department of Health, Education and Welfare's classification of social welfare expenditures indicates a functional division in terms of social insurance and public aid (income maintenance), health, education, and medical programs. There is one special classification based upon group affiliation (veterans' programs) and a residual category of "other" social welfare which includes the problem area of juvenile delinquency and group classified programs of child welfare.[9]

If we attempt to chart the various viewpoints concerning the levels of comprehensiveness on a vertical axis, and the realms of policy on a horizontal axis, a singular fact emerges from the matrix about the field of social welfare policy: It does not lend itself to a conceptually neat and orderly mapping. It is a field where what one person may consider a comprehensive policy in a functional area another person may perceive to be a fragmented program in a problem area.

Aside from providing a sense of the amorphic quality of the field of social welfare policy, where does all this leave us? The answer is that with a heightened respect for some complexities and facets of the field, which we will not attempt to explore in depth, we begin to move closer to setting the boundaries of an analytic framework. Moreover, we can sufficiently appreciate the major question with which those who take an analytic approach to the field of social welfare policy must grapple: Apart from the levels of comprehensiveness and realms of policy into which they may conceivably be cast, what are the common elements in social welfare policies?

Elements of an Analytic Framework

There is no exhaustive answer to the question posed above with which everyone engaged in policy analysis will agree. Obviously, the apparent commonalities in the design of social welfare policy vary according to the plane of abstraction on which the analysis is conducted. In this respect an analytic framework is somewhat like a microscope in that it provides a conceptual lens through which the phenomena under investigation may be studied. Unlike the microscope, most analytic frameworks do not have a wide range of focus. Rather they tend to lock on some level of abstraction that magnifies and draws our attention to the phenomena being examined within the context of a distinct conceptual set. Along these lines, our analytic framework places social welfare policy in the context of a *benefit-allocation mechanism functioning outside the marketplace.* As Marshall has observed:

> In contrast to the economic process, it is a fundamental principle of the Welfare State that the market value of an individual cannot be the measure of his right to welfare. The central function of welfare, in fact, is to supersede the market by taking goods and services out of it, or in some way to control and modify its operations so as to produce a result which it would not have produced itself.[10]

Because social welfare policies entail benefit allocations outside the market system, some analysts interpret these policies as providing for unilateral exchange (from society to the individual) rather than reciprocal exchange.[11] Pruger, however, has shown that this is not always the case.[12] Social welfare policy involves reciprocal exchange, but the form of reciprocity is different from that which operates in the market system. Reciprocity in the market system may be characterized as a relatively direct, voluntary, face-to-face exchange between buyer and seller; the substance of the exchange is concrete, usually cash for goods and services; the conditions governing the exchange are unambiguous in that both buyer and seller know when payments begin, how much interest is being charged, when they have completely discharged their obligations, and the like. In the social welfare system, exchange is relatively indirect because it takes place between recipient and society via welfare agencies, and it is often involuntary in the sense that recipients, usually in distress, do not have much leeway to choose among competing vendors of social welfare. The coin of exchange is nebulous. Benefits are often given with the expectation that the recipient will repay society by behaving in "socially acceptable" ways—getting a job, being a good mother, and generally practicing moral discipline. In addition, the conditions governing the exchange are unclear. Must the recipient take *any* job that is made available? Is he obliged to practice exceptionally *high* moral discipline? How long is the obligation in force?

Pruger suggests one reason recipients of social welfare benefits frequently fall into disrepute is that the conditions of exchange are so open-ended on the return side of the ledger that some recipient groups are virtually unable to discharge their obligations to society. While we will analyze social welfare policies as designs for allocating benefits that are usually free or well subsidized and, therefore, may be interpreted as a unilateral exchange according to market criteria, it should be recognized that those on the receiving end of social welfare often incur stringent obligations. As Zald points out, "Although many welfare recipients may not pay money for the service that they receive, they may pay much more: gratitude, political acquiescence, and the like. Thus, the lack of reciprocity depends on specification of coin."[13]

Within the benefit-allocation framework, social welfare policies are seen as choices among principles or guidelines to determine what benefits are to be offered to whom, how these benefits are to be delivered, and how they are to be financed. The elements of this framework, of course, are not physical structures which a microscope might reveal but social constructs involving intellectual processes of choice. The four major dimensions of choice in this framework may be expressed in the form of the following questions:

1. What are the bases of social allocations?
2. What are the types of social provisions to be allocated?
3. What are the strategies for the delivery of these provisions?
4. What are the methods of financing these provisions?

A few words are in order about the genesis of this approach. Eveline Burns was one of the first analysts to utilize this general framework in her seminal study, *Social Security and Public Policy.* Burns' organizational focus was on four types of decisions that inform the design of programs in the realm of social security: (1) those related to the nature and amount of benefits; (2) those concerned with eligibility and the types of risks to be covered; (3) those regarding the means of financing social security; and (4) those relevant to the structure and character of administration. Our analytic approach in this book seeks to extend the pathways of policy analysis charted by Burns and others.[14] We emphasize clarification of the dimensions of choice that cut across the entire field of social welfare policy rather than delineation of the specific choices that obtain in a sector or realm of this field, such as social security.

Dimensions of Choice

We treat the bases of social allocations, types of social provisions, strategies of delivery, and modes of finance as "dimensions" of choice because each will be examined along three axes: (1) the range of alternatives within each dimension; (2) the social values that lend support to these alternatives; and (3) the theories or assumptions implicit in these alternatives. This framework of choice is illustrated in Figure 2–1, a graphic presentation of the dimensions we will discuss in the following chapters.

Allocations and Provisions

The first two dimensions of choice are expressed forthrightly in the query, "Who gets what?" The bases of *social allocations* addresses the "who" of social welfare policy.

Social welfare policies always include some designation of beneficiaries, those whose welfare is to be enhanced through policy implementation. And even though these policies are supposed to serve the abstract interests of society as a whole—the elusive "public interest"—the direct and immediate benefits (i.e., social provisions) are usually distributed differentially

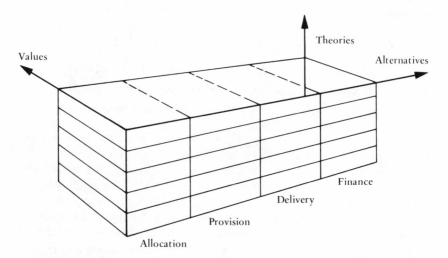

FIGURE 2–1
Dimensions of Choice.

among segments of the public. We will have more to say about notions of the public interest later on. Suffice it to note for now that few social welfare policies benefit everybody equally. Thus, choices are required and they are continually made as trade-offs occur among what policy planners think is desirable, what circumstances warrant as necessary, and what the public will countenance.

Numerous criteria are used to determine who is eligible for social provisions, such as marital status, employment status, residence, family size, I.Q., health, age, education, length of military service, ethnicity, religion, and income, to name a few. Our concern in examining the bases of social allocations, however, is not to catalog the many possibilities that may be employed to define eligibility. Rather the issues of choice that we will address in Chap·er 3 are focused around a set of general principles which inform the design of eligibility criteria. Thus the *bases of social allocations refers to the choices among the various principles upon which social provisions are made accessible to people and groups in society.*

The bases of social allocations are the guidelines for the operational definition of eligibility criteria. *What* it is that people become eligible to receive involves policy choices about the nature of the social provision. In policy analysis the traditional choice has been whether social welfare benefits should be offered in cash or in kind via goods and services. There are, however, other types of benefits that are commonly distributed through social welfare policy, such as power, vouchers, and opportunities, which permit different degrees of consumer sovereignty than the cash/in-kind choice dichotomy. In Chapter 4 we analyze the range of alternatives in this dimension of choice. Our objective is to distinguish the various forms of social provision and their implications for the consumer of policy benefits. Thus, *questions about the nature of social provisions refer to the forms in which benefits are delivered.*

Delivery and Finance

The third dimension of choice is addressed to the alternative strategies for delivering social provisions. Here the choices are not of the "who" and "what," pronominal quality, but rather encompass issues pertaining to the adverb "how," a qualifier of action. That is, after decisions about the "who" and "what" of social welfare policy are resolved, arrangements must be made for getting the selected social provision to the eligible consumer. The ways delivery systems are designed to achieve this objective are closely related and are of crucial significance to the first two dimensions of choice because it is through the delivery mechanism that policy guidelines regarding eligibility and the nature of the social provision are operationally expressed. Consider, for example, a proposal for an employment counseling service. Should it be centrally located in a downtown facility or dispersed in small units to neighborhood centers throughout the city? Should counselors be highly trained professionals or local residents with little formal training? Should the service be offered if it duplicates one that exists? Should it be incorporated under a unified administrative umbrella that includes health and legal aid services? These choices are suggestive of how elements in the design of delivery systems can exert influence on who gets served and the type of benefits they receive, policy guidelines concerning the nature of social provisions and bases of social allocations notwithstanding. Included among these elements are overall composition, linkages, location of facilities, and caliber and adequacy of personnel.

When we examine this dimension of choice in Chapter 5 we consider questions about how to structure relationships, connections, and exchanges among distributors of social provisions and between distributors and consumers. *Delivery strategies refer to the alternative organizational arrangements among distributors and consumers of social welfare benefits in the context of local community systems (neighborhood, city, and county), the level at which the overwhelming majority of distributors and consumers come together.*

Finally, if social welfare policies are viewed as benefit allocation mechanisms functioning outside the marketplace, somewhere along the line choices must be made concerning the sources and types of financing. It is important to recognize the distinction we make between funding benefits and delivering benefits. To clarify where funding ends and delivery begins, it will help to think in terms of a simple flow chart. *Funding choices involve the various sources through which social provisions flow, usually in the form of cash, and the conditions placed upon this movement up to the point that it reaches distributors.* As indicated before, distributors are those agencies, units of agencies, and individuals that make direct contact with the consumer, usually at the local level. Delivery choices involve the organizational arrangements that are made in the local system to move social provisions, either in cash or other forms, from the point that they reach these distributors.

Some of the major alternatives in financing social welfare policies concern whether the funding source is public, private, or mixed; the level of government utilized, and types of tax levied for public financing. It also includes the conditions that govern funding arrangements such as grant-in-aid formulas, specification of purpose, and timing. This dimension of choice will be examined in Chapters 6 and 7.

While the dimensions of allocation, provision, delivery, and finance will be analyzed in the following five chapters as separate entities, each containing its own range of alternatives, it should be emphasized that in the design of social welfare policies many of these alternatives are interdependent. For instance, a decentralized delivery system results when the social provision is in the form of power, as in certain policies for community control of local institutions that propose transfers of decision-making authority from middle-class and professionally oriented bureaucracies to consumers of service who are poor and generally without influence. Similarly, the basis of social allocations and methods of finance are closely interwoven when eligibility for benefits involves some form of payments as in subsidized user charges and contributory social insurance schemes.

An Example:
Public Assistance Policy

At this point we will tie the dimensions of choice to a concrete case so the reader can see how the framework is applied in the *first step* of social welfare policy analysis. The case selected involves the nationwide public assistance programs, with particular emphasis on policy choices in the Aid to Families with Dependent Children (AFDC) program. First, we will describe the core public assistance programs and some of the major reforms which shaped AFDC through 1967.

The federal-state public assistance program was established under the Social Security Act of 1935 wherein federal grants were provided to states to set up and administer programs for financial assistance to the needy. Initially, three categories of needy people were covered by this Act: the elderly under Title I, Old-Age Assistance (OAA); dependent children, under Title IV, Aid to Dependent Children (ADC); and the blind, under Title X, Aid to the Blind (AB). A fourth category was added in 1950 under Title XIV, Aid to the Permanently and Totally Disabled (APTD, which by 1970 was adopted by every state except Nevada).

In 1961 Aid to Dependent Children was changed to Aid to Families with Dependent Children (AFDC), reflecting an emphasis on maintenance of the family unit. And temporary legislation, later made permanent, allowed for an extension of this category at the states' option, to provide financial aid to children of unemployed parents (AFDC–UP). Without this UP option, federal aid to poor families of dependent children could be obtained only if one parent was incapacitated, dead or absent from the home (the latter providing somewhat of an incentive for desertion by unemployed fathers). About one-half of the states had exercised the UP option in their programs by 1970.

These public assistance programs are financed by federal and state contributions, the ratio of which is established by formulas for each category. In meeting their share, states may require local government contributions. The federal grants, appropriated from general revenues, are open-ended. This means that the sum paid by the federal government is a function of the reimbursement formulas applied to the amount of money states spend in a given year, rather than a maximum figure set by Congress. The federal share of public assistance payments was based on equal matching grant formulas whereby each state was reimbursed equally in proportion to their assistance costs until 1958 when a sliding scale was introduced into the reimbursement formulas, giving states with limited resources a proportionately higher matching grant than wealthy states. Federal financing for the administrative and service costs of these programs was handled somewhat differently, with state expenditures being reimbursed at a flat rate of 50 percent.[15]

Needy individuals and families who do not qualify for aid under the four federal categories of support may apply to a fifth category, a nonfederal program called General Assistance (GA). General Assistance is funded entirely by the state or locality and is usually more parsimonious than the other categories with regard to the duration and amount of assistance furnished.

In 1965 a broad program of medical assistance (MA) was enacted, wherein the various arrangements for meeting the medical costs of recipients under the four categorical programs were unified in a separate program. This program, popularly known as Medicaid, also allows the states an option to offer payments to the "medically indigent," people whose economic resources are insufficient to pay all their medical costs but who may not otherwise qualify as needy for cash assistance under the categorical programs.

Medicaid and the five categorical programs, OAA, APTD, AFDC (–UP), AB, and GA, form the generic core of public assistance in this country. Within this categorical framework established by federal legislation, the states have considerable latitude to design their own programs according to local norms and preferences, one reflection of which is the twenty different titles found among the fifty state agencies designated to administer public assistance programs.[16] These titles include: Departments of Public Welfare; Social Services; Family and Children Services; Institutions and Agencies; Human Resources; and Economic Security, to name but a few. More profound variations emerge with regard to standards of eligibility and levels of assistance provided. For example, in 1968 the top five states each paid an average grant of over $50 a month per AFDC recipient compared to average grants of $20 or less paid by the bottom five states. And in more than one-half of the states, AFDC grant payments equalled less than the minimum amount of income required to meet basic needs according to cost standards which these states themselves had set.[17]

Between 1960 and 1967 two major shifts have taken place in the orientation of the AFDC program: the move to service and the move to work. The

1962 amendments to the Social Security Act held great promise that the poor could be serviced out of poverty through an intensive effort by trained and skilled caseworkers. In retrospect this may seem a rather quaint notion, but at the time it was supported with much faith, enthusiasm, and money. Under these so-called "service" amendments, substantial funds were made available to the states for the purpose of training skilled caseworkers and providing intensive social services designed to prevent and reduce dependency. Funding for these provisions was on a matching grant basis of three federal dollars to every state dollar, rather than the usual 50 percent federal reimbursement for administrative and service costs.[18] It was envisioned that the costs of these special services would pay long-range dividends in restraining the growth of public assistance rolls. However, beyond prescribing that in order for agencies to qualify for these funds caseworkers must carry no more than sixty cases, the precise nature of the intensive service and how social workers' activities were to reduce dependency were never clarified.[19] Thus, a report of the President's Commission on Income Maintenance Programs makes the observation:

> A cynical, but not inaccurate, definition of social services provided in public assistance would be: A social service is anything done for, with, or about the client by the social worker. If a social worker discusses a child's progress in school with an AFDC mother a check is made under "Services related to education." . . . When the discussion turns to the absent father and possible reconciliation a check is made under "Maintaining family and improving family functioning."[20]

Despite efforts to increase the quantity and quality of social services, AFDC rolls experienced persistent growth of between 150,000 to 290,000 people each year from 1962 to 1966.[21] Between 1966 and 1967 the rate of growth accelerated to 600,000 a year and continued climbing (See Table 2-1). The total payments made under this program from 1962 to 1967 increased 75 percent, from 1.29 to 2.25 billion dollars. As relief rolls continued to swell and costs increased, by 1967 the move to service labored under darkening shadows of doubt.

The thrust of legislation enacted in 1967 was to swing AFDC away from the service orientation toward a work-oriented approach. As Steiner notes, "When the 1967 Social Security Amendments made their way through Congress, the old slogans—service instead of support, rehabilitation instead of relief—were abandoned and work incentives became the new thing in the continuing search for relief from relief costs."[22] The 1967 amendments to AFDC established a work incentive program to provide training and employment to "all appropriate individuals," which included welfare mothers with young children. (Work programs previously were

TABLE 2-1

Number of Public Assistance Recipients (In Categorical Programs for Selected Years, 1940 to 1970).*

Number of Recipients (In thousands)

Period	Old-age Assistance[1]	Aid to the Blind[1][2]	Aid to the Permanently and Totally Disabled[1]	Aid to Families with Dependent Children			General Assistance[4]	
				Families	Total Recipients[3]	Children	Cases	Recipients
December:								
1940	2,070	73.4		372	1,222	895	1,239	3,618
1945	2,056	71.5		274	943	701	257	507
1950	2,786	97.5		651	2,233	1,661	413	866
1955	2,538	104.1	69	602	2,192	1,661	314	743
1960	2,305	106.9	241	803	3,073	2,370	431	1,244
1961	2,229	102.7	369	916	3,566	2,753	411	1,069
1962	2,183	98.7	389	932	3,789	2,844	354	900
1963	2,152	96.9	428	954	3,930	2,951	352	872
1964	2,120	95.5	464	1,012	4,219	3,170	346	779
1965	2,087	85.1	509	1,054	4,396	3,316	310	677
1966	2,073	83.7	557	1,127	4,666	3,526	298	663
1967	2,073	82.7	588	1,297	5,309	3,986	352	782
1968	2,027	80.7	646	1,522	6,086	4,555	391	826
1969	2,074	80.6	702	1,875	7,313	5,413	422	860
1970	2,082	81.0	803	2,552	9,659	7,033	547	1,056

[1] Represents data for payments to recipients of the specified type of assistance under separate programs and under the combined state adult assistance programs.
[2] Beginning September 1965, excludes state blind pension program in Pennsylvania administered under state law without federal participation.
[3] Includes as recipients the children and 1 or both parents or 1 caretaker relative other than a parent in families in which the requirements of such adults were considered in determining the amount of assistance.
[4] Data incomplete

* From *Social Security Bulletin*, April 1972.

available on a much smaller scale mainly to fathers of families receiving aid under AFDC-UP.) In addition, the provision of necessary day-care services was authorized so that mothers would be free to work and, for an incentive, the first $30 of monthly earnings plus one-third of the remainder were exempted from determination of continued eligibility for assistance. The amendments also extended the 1962 provisions for social services with two specific objectives: (1) assuring to the maximum extent possible that the appropriate individuals enter the labor force and accept employment; and (2) reducing the incidence of births out of wedlock and otherwise strengthening family life. And there was a significant reorganization in the Department of Health, Education and Welfare leading to the administrative separation of social services and financial aid; through fiscal policies states were encouraged to have eligibility and income maintenance functions detached from service functions and performed by different workers instead of being the combined duties of the client's caseworker, as in the past.

Finally, the whole business was given some teeth with the provision that public assistance could be terminated for the individual who refused to accept work or training without "good cause." And there was a provision for a "freeze" to be placed on the number of recipients that would be covered by federal grants for AFDC, closing the open-ended grant arrangement that had existed for the program. This meant that once a state's AFDC rolls grew beyond the stipulated size, the costs of assistance to the additional families would not be shared by the federal government. The provision for a "freeze" on federal funding was postponed and later repealed.[23]

WIP the perversely accurate acronym for the Work Incentive Program, creates the image of an instrument used to drive beasts of burden. Through some creative bureaucratese it was quickly transformed to WIN (Work INcentive). While WIN is a more positive program symbol than WIP, it is a thin disguise for the stick of assistance termination and the threatened freeze on federal grants poised behind the carrot of work training, day-care services, family planning, and earnings exemptions. With welfare rolls rising, assistance payments below minimum standards of adequacy in half the states, and with the inequitable patchwork of local eligibility requirements and payments, and the introduction of punitive and coercive measures, by the end of 1967 AFDC was in the unenviable position of being viewed with disenchantment by liberals and conservatives, givers and receivers, government agencies and the general public alike. It was a program that Mitchell Ginsberg, then head of New York City's Welfare Department, lamented, "is designed to save money instead of people and tragically ends up doing neither."[24]

Application of the Framework

Now let us superimpose the dimensions of choice on the AFDC programs. For those unfamiliar with public assistance, this program is a complex operation, difficult to grasp and to understand. The analytic approach to policy analysis provides a way of thinking about this program that extracts and organizes its major elements, making the whole more readily comprehensible. Using the framework we have outlined, all of the information regarding the substance of AFDC policy may be divided into the four choice categories and conveniently summarized as follows:

A. *Bases of social allocations*
   1. Needy families with dependent children are eligible for assistance where one parent is incapacitated, dead, or absent from the home, with "need" defined locally. Eligibility was extended in 1962 at the state's option to include needy families where parents are unemployed (AFDC–UP). By 1967, to qualify for assistance, eligible persons, including mothers with young children, must be not only needy but also willing to accept work training and employment under the work incentive program.

B. *Nature of social provision*
   1. Those eligible for this program receive cash assistance payments, the amounts of which are determined by each state and which frequently average less than the state's own estimates of minimum standards of adequacy. Earnings of AFDC recipients were taxed at the rate of 100 percent (with a discount for working expenses introduced in 1962) until 1967, when exemptions on earned income were authorized.
   2. Social services are also provided, but were limited up to 1962, at which time financial support was made available to increase professional casework services oriented toward the improvement of family functioning. What these services were to entail, beyond some form of psychiatric counseling, was only vaguely defined. More tangible forms of service were established in 1967, emphasizing work training and employment placement, day-care, and family planning.

C. *Delivery system*
   1. Up to 1967, social services and income maintenance functions were combined and performed under the same administrative unit. Caseworkers distributed both financial aid and social services. After 1967 these functions were administratively divorced and performed by different workers, with an emphasis placed upon hiring AFDC recipients to perform certain delivery roles related to day-care and eligibility determination. Also, in 1967 more emphasis was placed upon making connections with other distributors; for example, service delivery involved linking up AFDC recipients with programs for work training under the Department of Labor.

D. *Finance*

    1. AFDC costs are shared by federal, state, and, in some cases, local governments. Federal contributions for assistance payments were initially open-ended and equal matching grants based on a formula using the state's average monthly payments. Administrative and service costs were reimbursed at a fixed rate of 50 percent. In 1958 the equal matching grant formula was changed to a variable matching grant, which increased the proportion of the federal contribution to states with limited resources. In 1962 the fixed rate of reimbursement for service costs was increased to 75 percent, under specified conditions. In 1967 an amendment was passed imposing a limitation on federal participation in AFDC payments based on the number of families receiving aid in each state at that time, thereby changing from an open-ended to a closed-ended grant. (This last amendment was later repealed.)

Specification of the dimensions of choice is the first step of a two step process in social welfare policy analysis. Here we have asked: What benefits are to be allocated, and to whom? and, How are these benefits to be delivered and financed? These questions may be answered without reference to purpose. Now we turn to the "Why?" question of purpose, a question addressed to the values, theories, and assumptions that inform social choices.

Social Values and Social Choice

Some answers to the "why" of social choice can be found through the explication of underlying values. The importance of illuminating the values embedded in policy designs is emphasized by Alva Myrdal:

> An established tendency to drive values underground, to make analysis appear scientific by omitting certain basic assumptions from the discussion, has too often emasculated the social sciences as agencies for rationality in social and political life. To be truly rational, it is necessary to accept the obvious principle that a social program, like a practical judgement, is a conclusion based upon premises of values as well as upon facts.[25]

The analyses of values and social welfare policy may be approached from at least two levels. At the upper level the analytic focus is upon policy in the generic sense. Rather than examining each of its dimensions of choice and the values expressed therein, at this level the question is addressed to the general purpose of this "mechanism." Specifically, to what extent does it achieve distributive justice? At this level of generality there are basically three core values that shape the design of policy: equality, equity, and adequacy. As we will see, however, these values are not always in harmony.

Equality

Though it is one of the bedrock values of distributive justice, equality is a value somewhat open to interpretation. There are at least two salient notions of equality, differentiated by Aristotle: numerical equality and proportional equality.[26] They represent the equalitarian and meritarian elements of distributive justice. Numerical equality implies the same treatment of everyone—to all an equal share. Proportional equality implies the same treatment of *similar persons*—to each according to his merit or virtue. These interpretations of equality offer conflicting prescriptions for the treatment of dissimilar persons in the name of distributive justice. In the concept of "proportional equality," Vlastos points out, "the meritarian view of justice paid reluctant homage to the equalitarian one by using the vocabulary of equality to assert the justice of inequality."[27] To clarify this distinction and to reduce the definitional awkwardness, we will use the term "equality" in its numerical sense and will subsume the meaning of proportional equality under the value of "equity."

Social welfare policy is influenced by the value of equality with regard to the outcome of benefit allocations. Specifically, this value prescribes that benefits should be allocated in such a way as to equalize the distribution of resources and opportunities available in society. In some policies this value is predominant; as for instance, the development of a quota hiring plan for the equal allocation of work roles among different groups of people. In a modified version there are opportunity-oriented policies where the objective of an equal share to all is recast in terms of an equal opportunity to obtain an equal share; for example, fair housing legislation demands that people with dissimilar racial and ethnic characteristics receive exactly the same treatment in their quest to obtain shelter. It does not, however, insure equal *results* for everybody.

The influence of this value in shaping the design of AFDC is evident to the extent that money is taken from wealthy states and individuals and given to those that are poor. While such redistribution takes place through AFDC, it falls considerably short of producing the ideal of an equal share for all because distributive justice is also responsive to other values.

Equity

This value denotes a conventional sense of "fair treatment." There is a proportional quality to notions of fair treatment—if you do half the work you deserve half the reward. This value prescribes that people receive that which they deserve based upon their contributions to society, modified only by considerations for those whose inability to contribute is clearly not of their own making. Accordingly, there are many "equitable inequalities" that are normatively sanctioned, as in policies that offer preferential treatment for veterans and in unemployment benefits that vary in proportion to prior earnings.

In the AFDC program, equity is stressed through the doctrine of "less eligibility," announced by the English Poor Law Commissioners in 1834. In the Commissioners' words:

> It may be assumed, that in the administration of relief, the public is warranted in imposing such conditions on the individual relieved, as are conducive to the benefit either of the individual himself, or of the country at large, at whose expense he is to be relieved.
>
> The first and most essential of all conditions, a principle which we find universally admitted, even by those whose practice is at variance with it, is, that *his situation on the whole shall not be made really or apparently so eligible as the situation of the independent laborer of the lowest class.* [Emphasis added.][28]

One reason for the extremely low level of public assistance in most states is the ingrained belief that such aid should not elevate the conditions of recipients above or to the same level as those of the poorest worker. Here, the emphasis on equity supports the maintenance of incentives to work. It is perhaps interesting to note that some proponents for increasing AFDC levels of support argue their case in the name of equity. They do not ask that dissimilar people, those who work and those who do not work, be treated equally and awarded similar standards of living. Rather, the argument is made that "motherhood" should be considered an occupation, one more trying than most. This view was expressed by a ten-member panel (nine of whom were men) commissioned by the Department of Health, Education and Welfare to study the problems of American workers. The panel recommended, among other things, that welfare mothers be provided government subsidies to stay home and care for their children.[29] This case gains momentum when we calculate the per capita costs of day-care services (between $2,000 and $3,000) that are required to allow AFDC mothers the freedom to go out and work.[30]

Adequacy

Adequacy refers to the belief that it is desirable to provide a decent standard of physical and spiritual well-being, quite apart from concerns for whether benefit allocations are equal or differentiated according to merit. Thus, as Frankena explains, the quest for distributive justice involves:

> a somewhat vaguely defined but still limited concern for the *goodness of people's lives,* as well as for their equality. The double concern is often referred to as respect for the intrinsic dignity or value of the human individual. This is not the position of the extreme equalitarian but it is essentially equalitarian in spirit; in any case it is not the position of the meritarian, although it does seek to accommodate his principles.[31]

Standards of adequacy vary according to time and circumstances. In medieval times, serfs were usually provided with the necessities to keep them healthy and productive. At the turn of the twentieth century, $624 a year was estimated as a "living wage" for a family of five in New York City.[32] Sixty-five years later, in the same locality, an intermediate budget for a family of four was $11,236.[33] In addition to the economic aspects of material existence, standards of spiritual well-being also vary. In the Middle Ages these standards had a basically religious connotation; the vicissitudes of life on earth were suffered for spiritual salvation in the hereafter. Today, spiritual well-being is more of a secular concern; it involves, for instance, the sense of being able to control one's destiny, freedom of expression, self-realization, security, and happiness.

The value of adequacy is expressed rather faintly in AFDC and honored more in violation than execution. Nevertheless, its presence is reflected in the fact that grant levels are not set arbitrarily, but are based on state estimates of the costs of basic needs.

Overall, as a benefit allocation mechanism the AFDC program is more responsive to concerns for equity than for adequacy and equality. This emphasis stems, at least in part, from the broader societal context in which the program operates. In capitalist society the value of equity is generally accentuated—those who work hard deserve to be rewarded. The capitalist is a man reaping the just fruits of his labor, according to normative standards. Socialist societies theoretically place greater stress on the value of equality. As Marx wrote, "The secret expression of value, namely that all kinds of labour are equal and equivalent, because, and so far as they are human, labour in general cannot be deciphered, until the notion of human equality has already acquired the fixity of a popular prejudice."[34] Once the notion of human equality has achieved the status of a "popular prejudice," differential treatment of dissimilar people is significantly reduced if not completely abolished because, judged by the most important of characteristics—their humanness—everybody is the same.

From this somewhat lofty perspective on the generic form of social welfare policy, the "why" of policy design may be analyzed in terms of the quest for distributive justice as manifest in the differential realization of adequacy, equity, and equality.[35] Although a policy may emphasize any one of these values, the emphasis is often tempered by the demands of the other two as efforts are made to approximate distributive justice.

Value Preferences

Moving down a rung to view policy more specifically with regard to the dimensions of choice, we also analyze the value preferences expressed at this level. Here a much larger range of social values enters into the consideration of choice. For instance, the values of privacy, dignity, work, and independence may influence the criteria of eligibility, the forms of social provision, and the design of delivery and finance arrangements. To illustrate, Table 2–2 lists the four types of policy choice and some of the competing values that are likely to influence these choices. These four value dichotomies suggest but do not exhaust the range of possibilities. They were selected because the stretch of values represents variations on central issues of policy choice whose common theme is exemplified in the polarity of individualism versus collectivism. These issues concern the ways and extent to which expressions of individual (or micro-unit) interests are given free rein or are harnessed in service of the common good. As Marshall explains:

> The claim of the individual to welfare is sacred and irrefutable and partakes of the character of a natural right ... but the citizen of the Welfare State does not merely have the right to pursue welfare; he has the right to receive it, even if the pursuit has not been particularly hot ... But if we put individualism first, we must put collectivism second. The Welfare State is the responsible promoter and guardian of the welfare of the whole community, which is something more complex than the sum total of the welfare of its individual members arrived at by simple addition. The claims of the individual must always be defined and limited so as to fit into the complex and balanced pattern of the welfare of the community, and that is why the right to welfare can never have the full stature of a natural right. The harmonizing of individual rights with the common good is a problem which faces all human societies.[36]

TABLE 2–2

Dimensions of Choices and Competing Value Orientations.

Individualist Orientation	Dimension of Choice	Collectivist Orientation
Cost effectiveness ◄———	Allocation ———►	Social effectiveness
Freedom of choice ◄———	Provision ———►	Social control
Freedom of dissent ◄———	Delivery ———►	Efficiency
Local autonomy ◄———	Finance ———►	Centralization

Cost effectiveness   may be applied to each dimension of choice. When applied to the basis of social allocations it is measured by the extent to which each dollar of benefit is allocated to those who are most in need and could not otherwise command the benefit on the open marketplace; the guiding thought is that there be no waste of resources. With the cost effectiveness criteria, individual treatment varies according to individual circumstances. To implement this value requires that a high degree of selectivity be employed in determining those who are eligible for benefits. Applied in the extreme, this value can produce invidious distinctions among people, dividing the community into groups of the dependent and the independent, the incompetent and the self-sufficient.

Social effectiveness   may take different forms. One way it is measured in allocative decisions is by the extent to which all individuals are treated as equal members of the social body. Here the notion of effectiveness is related to the fact that nobody who is potentially eligible will feel inhibited about applying for benefits because of shame, stigma, or the organizational rigamarole that is often required to implement selective procedures. Allocations are universal in the sense that no special need or defect of the individual must be exposed for scrutiny in order to become eligible for benefits; the "badge of citizenship" is sufficient basis for entitlement. In the AFDC program, the basis of social allocations—a thorough and probing means test of every applicant—is clearly influenced more by concerns for cost effectiveness than social effectiveness.[37]

Richard Titmuss has observed that the apparent strain between realization of cost effectiveness and social effectiveness may be a function of the short-range view that is generally taken on cost effectiveness, especially in cases such as the provision of medical benefits where policy objectives include prevention as well as treatment. For example, if access to medical provision entails a means-test investigation that is demeaning, time-consuming, or otherwise inconvenient, clients may procrastinate about seeking medical aid until the symptoms of disease are so painful that they can no longer be ignored. At this advanced stage the cost of treatment is usually more expensive. In the calculus of the long-run, cost effectiveness and social effectiveness can be brought into harmony when universal allocation of medical provisions saves more in prevention than selective allocation saves by limiting treatment only to those in dire need.[38]

Freedom of choice   is reflected in the extent to which provisions are offered in forms that allow recipients to exercise their individual preferences. Thus, for example, when social provisions are in the form of cash, a high degree of consumer sovereignty is preserved. *Social control,* on the other hand, is reflected in the extent to which the form of the social provision limits individual choice. With provisions in the form of service, recipients are limited to consuming whatever specific items (e.g., housing, medical care, counseling, therapy, advice, information) the program offers. Of course, they have the freedom to take it or leave it, but that is where the choice ends. In some social welfare programs, such as AFDC, social provisions are linked so that freedom of choice in one area of provision is bought at the price of social control in another. In AFDC, recipients are given cash grants and may exercise a degree of choice in how they meet their daily requirements for material existence. However, this provision is frequently linked to service provisions. That is, in some communities AFDC clients must accept services in order to receive the cash grants. This requirement limits their freedom of choice; for example, it requires that they be at a certain place for a certain period of time to meet with a caseworker or that they engage in employment training.

Freedom of dissent and efficiency   are values that enter the design of the delivery system and influence whether it is structured primarily along democratic or bureaucratic lines. Blau succinctly states the choice.

> Bureaucratic and democratic structures can be distinguished . . . on the basis of the dominant organizing principle: efficiency or freedom of dissent. Each of these principles is suited for one purpose and not for another. When people set themselves the task of determining the social objectives that represent the interests of most of them, the crucial problem is to provide an opportunity for all conflicting viewpoints to be heard. In contrast, when the task is the achievement of given social objectives, the essential problem to be solved is to discover the efficient, not the popular, means for doing so.[39]

In the example we have been using, the AFDC program, the delivery system is organized primarily along bureaucratic lines. However, the choice is not always this clear-cut. In other social welfare programs the social provision is so loosely formulated that the local delivery system is charged with the dual purpose of deciding on specific objectives and then carrying out their decisions. For instance, the War on Poverty and Model Cities Program required delivery systems that incorporate substantial democratic as well as bureaucratic elements in their structure. The problem in these systems, it often turns out, is that neither value is served very well or one value is emphasized at the expense of the other.[40]

Local autonomy and centralization   are values that find expression in financing and administration of programs. Strains between these values are most likely to emerge when program costs are shared by the federal government or, in the private sector, by a nationwide voluntary organization. Cost-sharing arrangements are implemented through federal grants-in-aid that vary along a continuum from general purpose/block grants to special purpose/categorical grants. The block grant is a lump sum contribution for local social welfare programs. This type of grant carries few specifications or requirements on how the money should be spent beyond indications that it is intended for a general realm of program such as health, community development, or income maintenance. This arrangement preserves a high degree of local autonomy. At the other end of the continuum is the special purpose grant with detailed standards that must be met to qualify for funding. Here, local discretion regarding the use of funds is restricted according to precise criteria established by the grant-making government. In most cost-sharing arrangements the methods of finance fall somewhere short of either end of the continuum, reflecting the mutual desirability of local autonomy and central planning.

The AFDC program, for example, while based on categorical grants, contains elements of both values. The federal grants-in-aid for this program define quite specifically the category of persons in whom the central government is interested. And various conditions are attached to these grants concerning citizenship, residence requirements, and the provision of social services. Yet, in at least two crucial aspects of a program of this type local autonomy prevails. States are free to exercise broad discretion in defining the criteria of need and the amount of financial assistance that is provided to recipients. The centralist thrust of this method of finance is thus mitigated in part because, as Burns explains, "to prescribe in the federal act both the standards of need which determine eligibility and the minimum level of living to be assured all eligible applicants raises major issues regarding federal interference in an area which traditionally has been thought of as peculiarly a matter for local determination."[41]

Theory and Social Choice

The comprehension of the subtle and complex relationships between value preferences and social welfare policies offers one level of insight into the "why" of social choice. Another dimension of analysis that has a bearing on this question involves theories and assumptions about how clients, delivery systems, methods of finance, and types of social provisions function, independently and in concert. Much of this kind of theory-derived knowledge is fragmented and only partially verified. This is not to deny the influence of social science knowledge on choice, but rather than overestimate what is known, we use the term "theory" to cover the influence and support that social science insights render to policy choices. We classify as *assumptions* those suppositions for which there have been little systematic effort to obtain and codify evidence. In the general sense the term "assumptions" is used to designate theories "writ small."

To illustrate, let us turn for a final look at the ADFC program. At least three assumptions that informed major policy choices in this program may be identified and seriously challenged by empirical evidence later uncovered.

First, the 1962 "service" amendments were supported by the belief that the psychiatric model of casework service would bring about change in the economic dependency of individuals in poverty level populations. Implicit here is the theory that poverty is mainly a function of individual deficiencies that can be transformed and alleviated through the casework process. This theory was not always applied on an extensive basis to public assistance recipients. Until the 1950s assistance recipients were just as likely to be considered "victims of external circumstances such as unemployment, disability, or the death of the family's breadwinner," who "needed to be 'relieved'—not treated or changed."[42]

After reviewing studies of casework efforts to treat and rehabilitate those on public assistance, Carter concludes:

> It becomes clear that it is time to reassess the purposes of casework services offered welfare recipients and other low income groups for whom problems identified for alleviation are complex and interrelated with other personal, family, and community or societal problems . . . there are serious questions as to what behavioral changes can be set in motion without provision first being made for a decent level of living and access being provided to a range of social resources within the agency and the community.[43]

Second, the separation of income maintenance from the administration of social services is predicated on the assumption that services will thereby be improved because: the caseworker-client relationship would no longer be tinged by the coercive undertones emanating from the worker's discretionary authority over the client's budget; clients would be free to accept or reject services as needed; and caseworkers, released from the task of administering grants, would have more time to engage in the service enterprise. It is a plausible line of reasoning. But it is one open to critical examination. Neither the strength of the caseworker's coercive powers and its substantive effects on relationships with clients, nor the extent of client initiative to seek services when routine house visits by the caseworker are terminated is clearly discernable. It is quite possible, as Handler and Hollingsworth suggest, that the coercion argument is exaggerated and, more importantly, that in the absence of routine home visits many welfare clients would be reluctant to seek help from an unknown official downtown. Thus, "requiring welfare clients to take the initiative may have the effect of cutting off a reasonably valuable service that most clients, in their own words, seem to like."[44]

As a final example, the shift in emphasis from welfare to "workfare" for AFDC recipients reflects the fairly common assumption that jobs are available for anyone who really wants to work. The problem is seen again primarily as individual deficiency—the lack of skills and adverse attitudes toward work—though of a different nature than those amenable to psychiatric casework. The solution is to equip people for jobs and motivate them to seek employment via the Work Incentive Program (WIN). And the availability of jobs in the external system is almost axiomatic. (As we will see in Chapter 4, a class of assumptions concerning the availability of external resources frequently enters in the choice of social provisions.) While facts about WIN are in short supply, what is known suggests that the assumptions implicit in this policy choice need serious rethinking. Levitan and Taggart's study indicates that of the 167,000 people who had enrolled in WIN through March, 1970, more than one-third had dropped out of the program and, all told, only 25,000 had gotten jobs. Those who moved on to work were "creamed" from the pool of early applicants. That is, the movement into jobs was highly selective of applicants who were better prepared for jobs. The group that got jobs included a high percentage of unemployed fathers receiving AFDC–UP who probably would have found employment sooner or later without WIN. In light of the program's "conspicuously unspectacular performance," the study observes, "the wisdom of expanding WIN is questionable, and the theoretical arguments for such a move are even more dubious."[45]

We should point out that in the examples presented the influences of value and theory on policy have been treated separately as a matter of analytic convenience. In reality, theory and value do not separate out quite so neatly. Social facts do not organize themselves into a coherent framework simply by being observed. A theoretical viewpoint is required. But if theory informs the ordering of social facts, what is it that informs theory? On this issue Gunnar Myrdal's insight is worth noting.

> Prior to answers there must be questions, and the questions we raise stem from our interests in the matter, from our valuations. Indeed, our theories and all our scientific knowledge are necessarily pervaded by valuations . . . Value premises are required not only in order to enable us to draw practical and political inferences from observations and economic analysis, but . . . in order to formulate a theory, to direct our observations, and to carry out our analysis.[46]

Summary

In this chapter we have outlined an analytic approach to the study of social welfare policy. The essence of this approach may be summarized as follows:

1. To view social welfare policy as a benefit allocation mechanism, the design of which requires that four types of choices must be made: choices pertaining to allocations, provisions, delivery, and finance

2. To seek a clear and precise understanding of the basic alternatives within each of these four dimensions of choice

3. To obtain insights into why any one of these alternative policy choices may be preferred over others by explicating the values, theories, and assumptions implicit in the policy design

The implication here is not that certain choices are inherently preferable to others. Different choice preferences will be registered by different policy planners, depending upon the values, theories, and assumptions given the most worth and credence. Our objective in the following five chapters is to take each dimension of choice, delineate the basic policy alternatives, and examine the interplay of values, theories, and assumptions therein. The focus of social welfare policy analysis involves not only the substance of a plan or program, but also the planning process. "Who plans?" is a question of policy choice that we will address in the last chapter.

Notes

[1]Eveline M. Burns, *Social Security and Public Policy* (New York: McGraw-Hill, 1956), p. ix.

[2]Daniel Moynihan, "Toward a National Urban Policy," *Public Interest,* No. 17 (Fall 1969), 5.

[3]H. Wentworth Eldredge, "Toward a National Policy for Planning the Environment," in *Urban Planning in Transition,* ed. Ernest Erber (New York: Grossman Publishers, 1970), p. 8.

[4]Louis B. Wetmore, "Preparing the Profession for Its Changing Role," in *Urban Planning in Transition,* ed. Ernest Erber (New York: Grossman Publishers, 1970), p. 235.

[5]Charles E. Lindblom, "The Science of 'Muddling Through,'" *Public Administration Review,* Vol. 19 (Spring 1959), 79–88.

[6]Richard Titmuss, *Essays on 'the Welfare State'* (2nd ed.) (London: Unwin University Books, 1958), pp. 34–55.

[7]Harold Wilensky and Charles Lebeaux, *Industrial Society and Social Welfare* (New York: Russell Sage, 1958), p. 143.

[8]For example, see Alfred Kahn, *Theory and Practice of Social Planning* (New York: Russell Sage, 1969), pp. 18–20.

[9]Alfred Skolnik and Sophie Dales, " Social Welfare Expenditures, 1970–1971," *Social Security Bulletin,* Vol. 34, No. 12 (December 1971), 3–16. There are various other schemes for classifying the realms of social welfare policy. For example, Romanyshyn divides welfare programs into three functional types which he describes as offering social provisions, social service, and social action. John Romanyshyn, *Social Welfare: Charity to Justice* (New York: Random House, 1971), pp. 153–54.

[10]T. H. Marshall, "Value Problems of Welfare Capitalism," *Journal of Social Policy,* Vol. 1, No. 1 (January 1972), 19–20.

[11]For example, see Richard Titmuss, *Commitment to Welfare* (New York: Pantheon Books, 1970), p. 124; and Martin Wolins, "The Societal Function of Social Welfare," *New Perspectives,* Vol. 1, No. 1 (Spring 1967), 5.

[12]Robert Pruger, "Social Policy: Unilateral Transfer or Reciprocal Exchange," *Journal of Social Policy* (Oct. 1973), pp. 289–302.

[13]Mayer Zald ed., *Social Welfare Institutions* (New York: John Wiley & Sons, 1965), p. 4.

[14]The analytic questions we will deal with have been explored, for example, by Martin Rein, *Social Policy* (New York: Random House, 1970); Richard Titmuss, *Commitment to Welfare* (New York: Pantheon Books, 1968), pp. 130–36; Kahn, *Theory and Practice of Social Planning,* pp. 192–213; and Gilbert Steiner, *The State of Welfare* (Washington, D.C.: Brookings Institution, 1971), pp. 1–30.

[15]For more complete details of these funding arrangements, see, President's Commission on Income Maintenance, *Background Papers* (Washington, D.C.: Government Printing Office, 1970), pp. 254–60.

[16]Since this was written, the Social Security Act Amendments of 1972 were passed leading to an administrative rearrangement of the public assistance system. State administration of Old-Age Assistance, Aid to the Blind, and Aid to the Permanently and Totally Disabled will be discontinued. In the place of these programs, a nationally financed and nationally administered program "Supplementary Security Income for the Aged, Blind, and Disabled," will be created. This new program is administered by the Social Security Administration and supported by funds from the general treasury. The program of Aid to Families with Dependent Children, however, continues to be administered by the States.

[17]President's Commission on Income Maintenance, *Background Papers,* pp. 235–49.

[18]Until 1972, this funding arrangement for social services was open-ended. That is, there were no appropriations limits on the amount of funds the federal government had to match. The total federal contribution was a function of the amount that states could raise for their share. Under the Revenue Sharing Act of 1972 this

arrangement was altered, with a ceiling placed on the amount of federal matching funds that would be made available to the states.

[19]A prominent example of the extreme faith upon which the movement for intensive services by trained caseworkers relied is expressed in the design of a study which compared special intensive services by professional caseworkers with fifty multiproblem families over two and one-half years to a control group receiving routine services by staff without professional training. The primary assumption upon which the study is based is that some degree of variation in social casework skills can have a significant impact upon the severe problems created by economic deprivation. The results of this study showed no significant differences between the two client groups and was deemed inconclusive due to methodological flaws. But it is in the methodological design that faith is revealed. The goals of the service and how workers' activities related to these goals were defined in such general terms as to be unmeasurable. See, Gordon E. Brown, ed., *The Multi-problem Dilemma: A Social Research Demonstration with Multi-Problem Families* (Metuchen, N.J.: Scarecrow Press, 1968).

[20]President's Commission on Income Maintenance, *Background Papers*, p. 307.

[21]While efforts were made to upgrade services, the results were seriously limited by the dearth of trained social workers available for these jobs and turnover difficulties in departments of public assistance. A study of turnover in public assistance agencies in New York City during 1964 indicates that 30 percent of the workers resigned within nine months of their appointment. Lawrence Podell, "Attrition of First-Line Social Service Staff," *Welfare in Review*, Vol. 5, No. 1 (January 1967), 9–14. In 1966 the national turnover rate for public assistance agencies was 22.8 percent. This figure is almost double the national turnover rate of all professionals in civil service positions on a federal, state, and local level at that time. Further comparisons along these lines are reported by Irving Kermish and Frank Kushin in "Why High Turnover? Social Work Staff Losses in a County Welfare Department," *Public Welfare*, April 1969, p. 138. And a survey of 766 AFDC recipients in the summer and autumn of 1967 gives evidence of a very low level of social service activity in the field. "For the majority of AFDC families, social services means a visit of a caseworker a little more than once every three months for a little more than thirty minutes per visit, with an occasional client's call to her caseworker." Joel F. Handler and Ellen J. Hollingsworth, "The Administration of Social Services and the Structure of Dependency: The Views of AFDC Recipients," *Social Service Review*, Vol. 43, No. 4 (December 1969), 412. For some observations on the lack of trained personnel, See Chapter 4, p. 100.

[22]Steiner, *The State of Welfare*, p. 25.

[23]For a detailed description of these 1967 amendments, see, Charles E. Hawkins, "The Welfare and Child Health Provisions of the Social Security Amendments of 1967," *Welfare in Review*, Vol. 6, No. 3 (May/June 1968), 1–34.

[24]Cited in the *Report of the National Advisory Commission on Civil Disorders* (New York: Bantam Books, 1968), p. 457.

[25]Alva Myrdal, *Nation and Family*, (MIT Paperback Edition) (Cambridge: MIT Press, 1968), p. 1.

[26]Aristotle, *The Politics* (Modern Library Edition) (New York: Random House, 1943), pp. 260–63.

[27]Gregory Vlastos, "Justice and Equality," in *Social Justice,* ed. Richard Brandt (Englewood Cliffs, N.J.: Prentice-Hall, 1962), p. 32.

[28]Cited in Karl de Schweinitz, *England's Road to Social Security* (Perpetua Edition) (New York: A. S. Barnes and Co., 1961), p. 123.

[29]Dept. of Health, Education and Welfare, *Work in America* (Washington, D.C.: Government Printing Office, 1972).

[30]See, for example, William Shannon, "A Radical, Direct, Simple, Utopian Alternative to Day-Care Centers," *New York Times Magazine,* April 30, 1972; and Sheila M. Rothman, "Other People's Children: The Day Care Experience in America," *Public Interest,* No. 30 (Winter 1973), 11–27.

[31]William Frankena, "The Concept of Social Justice," in *Social Justice,* ed. Richard Brandt, (Englewood Cliffs. N.J.: Prentice-Hall, 1962), p. 23.

[32]See, Robert Hunter, *Poverty,* ed. Peter d'A Jones (Torchbook edition) (New York: Harper & Row, 1965), pp. 51–52.

[33]United States Department of Labor, Bureau of Labor Statistics, *Three Budgets for an Urban Family of Four: Preliminary Spring 1969 Cost Estimates,* (Washington, D.C.: Government Printing Office, 1969), p. 3.

[34]Karl Marx, *Das Kapital,* ed. Friedrich Engels, Vol. 1 (Gateway Edition) (Chicago: Henry Regnery Co., 1959), pp. 33–34.

[35] For example, see, Richard Titmuss, "Equity, Adequacy and Innovation in Social Security," *International Social Security Review,* Vol. 2 (1970), 250–67.

[36]T. H. Marshall, *Class, Citizenship and Social Development* (Anchor Books Edition) (New York: Doubleday, 1965), pp. 258–59.

[37]An analysis of cost effectiveness as it is expressed in different income maintenance strategies is provided by James Cutt, "Income Support Programmes for Families with Children: Alternatives for Canada," *International Social Security Review,* Vol. 23, No. 1 (1970), 100–112.

[38]Titmuss, *Commitment to Welfare,* pp. 69–71.

[39]Peter Blau, *Bureaucracy in Modern Society* (New York: Random House, 1956), p. 107.

[40]Various studies on the War on Poverty and Model Cities have documented this result. See, for example, Ralph Kramer, *Participation of the Poor* (Englewood Cliffs, N.J.: Prentice-Hall, 1969); Neil Gilbert, *Clients or Constituents* (San Francisco: Jossey-Bass, 1970); Neil Gilbert and Harry Specht, *Planning for Model Cities: Process, Product, Performance and Predictions* (Washington, D.C.: Dept. of Housing and Urban Development, Government Printing Office, forthcoming); Marshall Kaplan, Gans, and Kahn, *The Model Cities Program: A Comparative Analysis of the Planning Process in Eleven Cities* (Washington, D.C.: Dept. of Housing and Urban Development, Government Printing Office, 1970).

[41]Burns, *Social Security and Public Policy,* p. 231.

[42]Davis McEntire and Joanne Haworth, "Two Functions of Public Welfare: Income Maintenance and Social Services," *Social Work,* Vol. 12, No. 1 (January 1967), 24–25.

[43]Genevieve Carter, "Public Welfare," in *Research in the Social Services: A Five Year Review,* ed. Henry S. Maas (New York: National Association of Social Workers, 1971), p. 224.

[44]Handler and Hollingsworth, "The Administration of Social Services and the Structure of Dependency," p. 418. For a comprehensive historical review of the issues in "separation of services," see Winifred Bell, "Too Few Services to Separate," *Social Work,* Vol. 18, No. 2 (March 1973), 66–77.

[45]Sar Levitan and Robert Taggart, III, *Social Experimentation and Manpower Policy: The Rhetoric and the Reality* (Baltimore: Johns Hopkins, 1971), p. 53.

[46]Gunnar Myrdal, *Value in Social Theory,* ed. Paul Streeten (London: Routledge and Kegan Paul, 1958), pp. 254–55.

Basis of
Social Allocations

"I suppose you mean that you have no money to pay wages in," said I. *"But the credit given the worker at the government storehouse answers to his wages with us. How is the amount of the credit given respectively to the workers in different lines determined? By what title does the individual claim his particular share? What is the basis of allotment?"*

"His title," replied Doctor Leete, *"is his humanity. The basis of his claim is the fact that he is a man."*

EDWARD BELLAMY
Looking Backward

3 In his classic utopian novel, *Looking Backward,* Edward Bellamy views the "good society" as a place where every individual has a claim to an equal share of the goods and services produced by the nation. Entitlement does not depend upon being rich or poor, single or married, brilliant or dull, healthy or ill—man's title is his humanity.[1] In Bellamy's utopia, social allocations are arranged according to the principle that everyone deserves an equal share, with one exception. That is, Doctor Leete explains, "A man able to do duty [i.e., work] and persistently refusing, is sentenced to solitary imprisonment on bread and water till he consents."[2] Although this exception may seem rather harsh, in the context of the society that Bellamy designed, it is mitigated somewhat by the fact that work roles are structured to make every task dignified and to allow a wide choice of occupations to suit individual preferences. Nevertheless, as an introduction to the allocative dimension of choice in social welfare policy there is perhaps a small comfort in noting that even in utopian worlds where men are completely rational, live in harmony, and can achieve consensus on the hierarchy of social values they seek to realize, problems of social allocation are not entirely amenable to neat solutions of unqualified principle.

We began this chapter by describing the utopian predicament because in the real world few social welfare policy issues engender more vigorous debate than the choices of who shall benefit and the manner in which their entitlement is defined. At least we may take refuge in the thought that this debate does not reflect a pernicious strain that is found only in harsh reality.

The eligibility of those people chosen to receive the benefits of any social welfare policy may be predicated upon a variety of specific criteria from the esoteric (e.g., the percent of American Indian blood running through one's veins) to the mundane (e.g., the amount of money earned weekly). We refer to the general principles that underlie these criteria of choice as the bases of social allocations. In this chapter we will examine some of the fundamental alternatives among these general principles.

Attempts to develop general principles for placing eligibility criteria within an analytic framework usually begin with the distinction between universalism and selectivity. *Universalism* denotes the idea of benefits made available to an entire population as a social right. Examples are social security for the elderly and public education for the young. *Selectivity* denotes the idea of benefits made available on the basis of individual need, determined by a means test, for example public assistance and public housing for the poor. We are slightly fuzzy in these definitions, indicating that the terms denote ideas rather than firm meanings, partly because universalism and selectivity are sometimes used with different meanings. For instance, Hoshino observes that proposals for negative income tax programs in the United States are viewed by some as universal schemes because they apply "to all, or at least to all who would file an income tax return to qualify for benefits according to various formulas."[3] However, Hoshino would consider the negative income tax a selective program because allocations are based on a means test (and so would we). In addition, our equivocation of this point stems from an appreciation of the confounding variables that enter the universal-selective distinction, about which we will have more to say shortly. For the time being, though, let us stay with these terms as they have been defined.

The literature on social welfare policy contains an ongoing debate between those who favor universal or selective allocation principles.[4] Briefly, this debate is expressed along the following lines. In weighing the relative merits of these allocation principles, universalists emphasize the values of social effectiveness as manifest in the preservation of dignity and social unity that obtain when people are not divided into clear-cut groups of givers and receivers. In their view, all claims to benefits are equal. Selectivists tend to stress the value of cost effectiveness as manifest in the savings to the community that accrue when social provisions are free only to those who could otherwise not afford them.

But neither side is quite satisfied to let the debate rest there. Each also lays claim to at least a share in the values that support the other side. Universalists claim cost effectiveness as a by-product of their allocation principle, as indicated earlier (p. 44), because preventative treatment may obtain in certain cases when access to social provisions is not deterred by investigation of an individual's means and the stigma that may accompany eligibility so defined. It is in the long-run cost accounting of "an ounce of prevention to a pound of cure" that universalists infer an economic saving to the larger community. And as a bonus, they suggest that universal allocations are usually less expensive to administer than selective allocations which require constant screening, checkups, and benefit adjustments to insure that recipients are eligible and that they receive the proper level of assistance. The selectivists' rejoinder is to claim social effectiveness, if one measure of this value is the movement toward a more egalitarian society. This claim is made because selective allocations, by offering benefits only to the poor, tend to reduce inequalities more than universal allocations for which everyone in a designated population is eligible.

These are some of the general issues that provide a framework for the universal-selective debate. To place this debate in a substantive context, we will illustrate how the choice between universal and selective allocation principles translates to specific policy proposals and we will examine the values and assumptions that underlie these principles when they are applied in a concrete situation.

Universality and Selectivity in Income Maintenance

Over recent years there has been a continuing dialogue concerning the reform of federal income maintenance programs, largely in response to the widespread disaffection with public assistance programs (noted in Chapter 2). Numerous proposals outlining the potential virtues and abuses of various income maintenance schemes have been put forth by academicians and politicians.[5] These proposals can be analyzed from different perspectives. For example, they can be placed at different points along a continuum of generosity, depending upon where they define the poverty level and the proposed amount of financial aid to be offered. However, for the purposes of this discussion we are more concerned with the bases of social allocations in these schemes than with their proposed levels of support, the latter being a dimension of choice that is closely related to the nature of the social provision. From the perspective of allocative principles, the variety of proposed income maintenance programs can be divided into two broad categories: Negative Income Tax programs (sometimes referred to as guaranteed incomes) and Children's Allowances (sometimes referred to as Family Allowances).

The Negative Income Tax is the generic label for programs whose common feature is that they involve a modification of the federal income tax structure. Simply stated, the idea is that the personal income tax structure would become a two-way operation where money would flow to the government from people with incomes above a certain level as well as from the government to people with incomes below a certain level. In both cases the amount of money paid would be graduated according to the individual's income.

As it currently stands, the federal income tax structure allows for a deduction of $750 from taxable income for each dependent, in addition to other deductions. This deduction may be viewed as a form of government subsidy whose exact cash value is a function of the individual's tax bracket. That is, an individual in the 50 percent tax bracket can keep $375 for each dependent he can claim. The poor, those who earn too little to pay any taxes, cannot take advantage of the deduction and actually receive no benefit from this arrangement whereas the wealthy receive the greatest benefit. Accordingly, it may be argued that the Negative Income Tax is a mechanism to extend this federal subsidy to those who are too poor to benefit under the current system. Under this scheme, those below a certain income would receive a grant from the government. An essential characteristic of the Negative Income Tax is that the allocation of benefits is tied directly to an income test and thereby based on the principle of selectivity as previously defined.

In the Children's Allowance category, programs usually involve the provisions of a *demogrant,* described by Burns as "a uniform payment of certain categories of persons identified only by demographic (usually age) characteristics."[6] More than sixty nations throughout the world, including all of the industrialized West except the United States, offer some form of Children's Allowance as an integral part of their welfare system. In the United States the case is sometimes made that we have a children's allowance that operates through the dependents' exemptions in the federal income tax, which benefits only the wealthy. The development of these programs in other countries has achieved widespread support for various reasons, among which is the fact that children represent a substantial proportion of the poor and, wherever one places the blame, however one perceives the causes of poverty, children are always the innocent victims. An essential characteristic of the demogrant is that benefits are allocated to all families regardless of their economic circumstances and thereby reflect the principle of universality as previously defined.[7]

To illustrate the types of issues that are informed by an application of the universal-selective framework of choice, we will briefly describe the basic features of two specific proposals for income maintenance programs in these categories. The first proposal is for a selective program, the Family Assistance Plan (FAP), which was part of a package of welfare reform proposals that the President of the United States submitted to Congress in August 1969.[8] To avoid confusion we should explain that while this plan is called "family assistance," it falls into the category of selective programs because, appearances notwithstanding, the FAP employs a Negative Income Tax rather than the demogrant approach of Children's Allowances (or Family Allowances). The second proposal is for a universal program, a Children's Allowance scheme developed by Alvin Schorr, one of the foremost spokesmen for this type of program in the United States.[9] The basic features of these two plans are as follows:

Family Assistance Plan (FAP)

The original proposal covered family units of two or more individuals, at least one of whom had to be a child. The basic assistance payment that a family with zero income would receive is calculated on the basis of $500 a year for each of the first two family members, and $300 a year for each additional member. Thus, for a family of four with no income the basic payment or guaranteed minimum income equals $1600. There is no reduction in benefit for the first $720 earned during the year. After this $2320 ($1600 in assistance plus the $720 of exempt earned income), the assistance benefit is reduced by 50¢ for each additional dollar earned. This reduction of the basic benefit is sometimes referred to as the negative tax rate. For example, a family of four with an earned income of $1000 receives an assistance payment of $1460 for a total income of $2460; the assistance payment of $1460 is arrived at by taking the base payment of $1600 and subtracting one-half of the $280 that was earned beyond the first $720 of exempt earnings. With this negative tax rate applied to a family of four, an earned income of $3920 is the break even level, the point at which the assistance payment drops to zero.

In addition to this income test, determination of eligibility also involves a work requirement; to receive benefits under the FAP, those who would qualify according to income must register for manpower training programs and employment placement services with their local public employment agency, except for certain excluded persons such as the aged, disabled, and mothers of children under the age of six. Refusal to participate in manpower training programs or to accept suitable employment would, according to the proposed legislation, constitute grounds for denial of benefits to the individual involved (though the rest of that person's family would still be eligible). In support of this work requirement the plan also calls for the provision of day-care and related social services.

Children's Allowance (CA)

The Schorr proposal involves an allotment of $50 a month for each child under six and $10 a month for each older child. These payments would be made without regard to family income or other eligibility conditions such as the work requirement in the FAP. However, the proposal also calls for the elimination of present federal income tax exemptions for children and stipulates that the CA benefit itself would be considered taxable income. When translated into dollars and cents, these last two qualifications mean that families of equal size with children in the same age categories will receive exactly the same amount of benefits but, depending upon their personal income, these families will end up returning different amounts of the allowance to the government through the federal income tax. Thus, under the 1972 tax rates a family with one child under six and an income that places them in the 14 percent tax bracket, saves $105 by claiming the $750 deduction that may be taken for their child, while a family of equivalent size but in a higher tax bracket saves even more. Elimination of the dependent's exemption would mean a loss of a different amount of savings for these two families, the wealthier family suffering the heavier loss. While both families would receive $600 in CA benefits, this money would also be taxed according to their respective incomes.

The overall effect is that the higher the family's tax bracket, the lower the net gain received from the Children's Allowance, and those in the highest brackets actually would suffer a net loss. The significance of this effect is to make the Children's Allowance a benefit that is universal at the point of distribution, but selective at the point of consumption. We might add that this is not an attribute of only Children's Allowance. Rather, when we consider how the benefits are financed, some form of selectivity creeps into virtually all universal schemes. As Reddin has demonstrated, universal benefits are "those in which the universal gene is dominant but where there are also variant forms of 'recessive' selective genes incorporated in the structure."[10]

Considerations of Social Effectiveness and Cost Effectiveness

When the abstract principles of the universal-selective debate are applied to choices among concrete alternatives, such as the two income maintenance schemes described above, the ensuing discussion inevitably centers upon considerations of social effectiveness and cost effectiveness, how these values are defined, and assumptions regarding policy elements that facilitate and impede the realization of these values.

Measures of the relative cost effectiveness of such income maintenance proposals are usually arrived at by comparing (1) the total costs of the alternative schemes, (2) the extent to which funds allocated under each scheme fill the poverty gap, and (3) the amounts of "seepage" of funds to the nonpoor that each scheme allows. Implicit here is a definition of income maintenance that relates to improving the lot of the statistically defined poor, those with an income below $4200 for a nonfarm family of four, according to current federal guidelines. On the basis of the above criteria the selective Family Assistance Plan is clearly superior to the universal Children's Allowance. That is, the FAP tends to provide higher monetary benefits to the poorest families with virtually no seepage to the near-poor, working-class, or middle-class income groups. However, this advantage of the FAP quickly diminishes when we view the objectives of income maintenance as somewhat broader in scope, such as when the objective is to improve the lot of children. This objective is desirable because families in the working classes and middle classes, as well as the poor, can use additional income to improve the welfare of their children. From this viewpoint, cost effectiveness is defined quite differently and the Children's Allowance schemes may come closer to satisfying this value. As Cutt points out:

> Universal schemes may be considered to be redistributive in a horizontal sense—from the childless to those with children—and therefore may be seen as having a broader objective than a selective scheme, specifically the alleviation of need among children in any income group, rather than the more tightly focused alleviation of need in families defined as poor in a statistical sense.[11]

In addition, the universal scheme that we are considering contains an element of vertical income redistribution—from the wealthy to the poor —by way of the elimination of exemptions and the income tax that would be paid on the allowance. Cost effectiveness, then, is not an unequivocal attribute of either the universal or the selective bases of social allocations, although it tends to be identified more often with the selective approach.

On the other side of the value ledger, social effectiveness tends to be identified with the universal approach, though a definitive case is lacking here too. Estimates concerning the social effectiveness of income maintenance schemes are based on certain assumptions about the potential consequences of alternative approaches. These consequences include the effects on: (1) *incentives to work,* (2) *incentives to procreate,* (3) *stigmatization,* and (4) *social integration.* To illustrate some of the factors often weighed and analyzed when considering the bases of social allocations, let us examine some of the assumptions made in this context and the empirical evidence that exists which may influence our degree of confidence in predicting the consequences of alternative programs.

Work Incentives

The assumption here is that to the extent they eliminate some degree of economic stress, both the Family Assistance Plan and Children's Allowances would have a negative effect on the incentive to work. This is a variant of the conventional wisdom that a person who gets something for nothing will be prone to continue doing nothing. The disincentive to work would appear greater for the Family Assistance Plan because the basic payment in a zero work/zero income situation is higher. In this scheme an additional disincentive to work is introduced by the high tax rate (50 percent) on earnings above the first $720. That is, with regard to employment, persons who get nothing for doing something will be disinclined to seek work. According to these assumptions the FAP is seemingly less desirable than the CA schemes.

However, given the modest amounts of income offered by both proposals, neither alternative poses a serious threat to the spur of necessity as a factor in the decision to work. Under both schemes the benefits given to the poor would be insufficient to bring most of them substantially above the federally designated poverty level. In this case the "something for nothing" is simply not enough to undermine work incentives.

It would seem that a more trenchant case could be made that disincentives are generated by the high tax rate on the initial earned income under the FAP. Yet the issue is more complicated than it first appears because the lines of influence may flow in both directions. That is, the high tax rate may be an inducement to greater work effort as well as a deterrent. The popular belief is that the man who can keep only 50¢ of the dollar earned will be less inclined to work than the man who gets 90¢. However, assuming the desire for a certain standard of living, an individual who keeps only 50¢ may be moved to work harder and longer just to maintain his position; whereas the man who keeps 90¢ initially has more money to spend and may opt for more leisure time rather than to supplement his income by additional work. That is to say, except for extreme cases where the tax rate approaches 100 percent, the point at which a worker may decide that the additional income is not worth the effort is indeterminate. In fact, there is little empirical evidence to support the belief that a tax rate in the 50 percent range will necessarily have a deleterious influence on the work incentive. After reviewing a number of studies on the general relationships between income tax rates and work incentives Break concludes:

> Incomplete as the results still are, it is encouraging to note that neither
> in Great Britain nor in the United States is there any convincing evi-
> dence that current high levels of taxation are seriously interfering with
> work incentives. There are, in fact . . . a number of good reasons for
> believing that considerably higher taxes could be sustained without
> injury to worker motivation should the need arise.[12]

More recently, and in specific regard to the FAP, the evidence is mount-
ing that poor people do not revert to indolence at the first opportunity to
receive federal assistance. On the contrary, the initial findings of one
experimental Negative Income Tax program showed that "families receiving assistance worked just as hard as ever—and there were even some
indications that they had been stimulated to work harder." In this program
there were 1,359 families, the assistance benefits were higher than the
FAP's $1600 for a family of four, the tax rates on earned income ranged
from 30 to 70 percent, and no work requirements were imposed for eligibility. Earnings increased for 53 percent of the families in the experimental
group which received financial assistance, while over the same period 43
percent of the families in the control group which received no assistance
showed an increase in earnings. Further, the study suggests that psychological barriers or disincentives to work were not evident even for those
families whose earnings increased to the point where they were no longer
eligible for assistance.[13]

However, the question of whether income guarantees have an effect
upon work incentives cannot be put to rest on the basis of the findings of
a few studies. The economic variables dealt with in this experiment with
Negative Income Tax must be checked against studies of other programmatic arrangements, different population groups, and varying economic
conditions. Some of these variables are considered in a careful review of
research on the effects of improved welfare benefits and various work
incentive features in the Aid to Families with Dependent Children Program by Mildred Rein. She notes that improved benefits and work incentives appear to have the effect of *both* encouraging some people to work
and encouraging others to remain on, or to become eligible for, AFDC. She
concludes from her analysis:

> The continually increasing welfare-benefit levels (now inflated by the
> disregards [i.e., earned income which recipients do not report such
> as deductions from salary checks, child care expenses and carfare]) and
> the increasing income from mother's earning while on AFDC should
> also add to the incentive to work and to choose work and welfare over
> work alone.[14]

In any event, the safeguard against disincentives in the FAP proposal
considered in this discussion is the work requirement that is built into the

scheme. However, in light of the above evidence, it appears that the work requirement, which introduces a strong and distasteful element of coercion, may undercut the social effectiveness of this particular proposal more than it offsets any potential disincentives to work that the FAP benefit structure might generate.

Incentives to Procreate

While the FAP is faulted for presumably sapping the work effort, the Children's Allowance is sometimes considered problematic in another way. As Burns notes, a major objection "to the adoption of a children's allowance system—and to many people the most formidable—is the belief that it would stimulate procreation."[15] The assumption is that the Children's Allowance will act, in effect, as a baby bonus and will encourage population growth. On this issue the experiences of growth in countries that have Children's Allowance programs is informative, especially Western industrialized countries such as France and Canada.

In the mid-1930s the birth rate in France had fallen below the level necessary for replacement of the population. Because this situation was considered critical, an emphasis was placed upon the demographic potentialities of a number of social security measures. Among these measures was the Family Code of 1939 which extended coverage of the Family Allowance Act of 1931 to the entire population. Thus, in France the Children's Allowance programs developed, in part, as a policy instrument for the express purpose of increasing the birth rate (which gives us an idea of the strength of this assumption). To what extent were the desired results achieved? Five years prior to World War II France averaged 630,000 births a year. In the five years after World War II, this average increased to 856,000 births a year. Although there was a slight decline in 1953, since 1954 the birth rate per thousand has remained fairly constant, while the total population has been rising.

At first glance these data appear to support Friedlander's contention that the Family Allowance was successful in encouraging an increase in the birth rate.[16] However, as Schorr points out, during the same period the United States—with no Children's Allowance—also experienced a dramatic rise in the birth rate, while the birth rate in Sweden continued to decline throughout the 1950s despite its family allowance system.[17] And although families with three or more children gain the major benefits of the French allowance program, after World War II more families in France had one to three children, with a proportional decrease in the number of larger families. According to Schorr, French demographers are cautious in their interpretations of the influence of allowances upon population growth; they view the program as contributing "to a general natalist spirit which is now a force in itself."[18]

Turning to Canada, where a modest family allowance program was started in 1945, the birth rate has virtually paralleled that of the United States over the last quarter-century. While such a parallelism disposes of the argument that the Canadian allowance significantly affected the production of children, Moynihan has observed that in the program's first year of operation "the monthly production of children's shoes rose from 762,000 to 1,180,000 pairs."[19]

In light of existing evidence, the assumptions about the effects of the proposed Family Assistance Plan and Children's Allowances on work and family size must be viewed with a healthy skepticism. Undoubtedly for some people the FAP would provide disincentives to work and the CA would provide incentives to procreate. However, to generalize from these few to the many underestimates the complexity of human motivation. Decisions concerning work and family size address fundamental conditions of human existence. In these matters the influence of negative tax rates and allowance benefits must be weighed in the larger context where desires for self-betterment, pride of craft, the Protestant ethic, and a variety of social/psychological factors, not the least of which is the need to be well thought of by others, come to bear on decisions that people make.

Stigma and Social Integration

One of the most forceful claims for the social effectiveness of universal schemes such as Children's Allowances is that they avoid stigmatizing recipients while selective approaches such as the FAP engender a reverse effect. The assumption of the stigmatizing effects of the means test as a criterion of eligibility is held so firmly by so many that it has been almost compressed into fact. To achieve selectivity without stigma, Titmuss proposes the elimination of the means test and its "assault on human dignity" by employing, instead, a needs test applicable to specific categories, groups, and territorial areas.[20] To this suggestion, Kahn responds:

> It has yet to be demonstrated ... that a needs test to open special services to disadvantaged and perhaps socially unpopular groups will not carry some of the consequences of the means test. Nor, apparently, have even the most egalitarian of societies found it financially or politically possible to completely drop means test selectivity ...[21]

Precisely what is it about the means test that, presumably, results in an assault on human dignity? Perhaps this result is inferred because means tests are frequently applied to socially unpopular groups such as the poor who may feel stigmatized before they ever make an application for benefits. Certainly, college students, a privileged group, appear to carry the means-test burden lightly in making applications for financial aid. And in some cases they have been known to express a strong preference for means-tested selection over other bases of allocation.[22] Moreover, while his net worth usually suffers diminution, the average taxpayer experiences a form of means test once every year without apparent psychological damage to his sense of self-worth. Indeed, the social-psychological effects of the means test may be less inherently painful than is commonly assumed, even for the poor. At least there is provisional evidence presented by Handler and Hollingsworth that the means test *per se* is not a significant source of irritation to public assistance recipients.[23]

If the above evidence is at all persuasive, and we think it is, then why the dogged persistence of this assumption? Why is the means test so often the bugaboo of allocative choices? The answer is twofold. First, discussions of the means test tend to confuse the principle with the practice. Distinctions between the means test as an allocative principle and the actual administration of the means test are important considerations. As we have suggested, the principle may be quite innocuous where worth and self-esteem of individuals are concerned. It is in the application of this principle that the potential for denigration exists and is often realized for certain groups. For example, when the methods of determining eligibility include unscheduled home visits at all hours of the day and night, the message conveyed to the recipient is that he is untrustworthy and no longer entitled to a private life. Such administration of selective allocations is clearly damaging to a person's sense of competence and self-respect.[24] Practices of this nature support the belief in the stigmatizing effects of the means test and create much of the disapproval. However, what is actually at issue in these cases is not so much the principle as the manner in which it is translated into operational procedures. This should not obscure the fact that the principle can be operationally defined according to a simple and dignified procedure whereby the applicant declares his needs and resources without all the fuss and prying that characterize the means test at its worst. The means test need not be mean-spirited.[25]

The second reason that means-tested schemes frequently are maligned as a basis of social allocations relates to their societal effects on a more general level. By their very nature, programs based on this selective principle divide society into distinct groups of givers and receivers. The argument against selectivity contains an implicit blending of this divisive outcome with the notion that receivers are stigmatized. However, these effects can be weighted independently. That is, whether or not stigma necessarily attaches to recipient status, it still remains that selective programs do not have a binding influence on the social fabric. Rather, they tend to fracture and polarize society along sharp lines defined according to those below and those above an arbitrary level of income. The poor are identified as a distinct social class with recipient status, while the near-poor, working classes and middle classes are lumped together on the donor's side of the transaction. It is an arrangement ill suited to create social harmony. In contrast, universal schemes such as the Children's Allowance facilitate social integration by screening these potential divisions and emphasizing instead the common needs of families in a variety of economic circumstances. Of the various issues we have discussed, this integrative function poses one of the most potent arguments for the social effectiveness of the universal approach to social allocations.

Another Perspective on Allocative Principles: A Continuum of Choice

At the beginning of this chapter we suggested that the universal-selective dichotomy represents an initial effort to develop an analytic framework for understanding choices related to social allocations. For the remainder of this chapter we will examine the bases of social allocations from another perspective. Our purpose here is to expand and refine the analytic concepts that may be brought to bear on this dimension of choice.

While the universal-selective dichotomy serves as a useful starting point in the conceptualization of eligibility principles, the bases of social allocations are more intricate than these ideas imply. Abstract dichotomies of social phenomena in reality often translate to continua of choice. Thus, there are many instances of policies wherein benefits are made accessible to people in *selected* categories, groups, or geographic regions without recourse to an individual means test. Up until now we have used "selectivity" in the narrow sense to designate only means-tested allocations. Yet, as Titmuss points out, selectivity may be based on differential needs without the requirement of a means test.[26] The dilemma, however, is that once the concept of selectivity is pried loose from strictly economic means-tested considerations, its definition may be expanded to cover innumerable conditions, even some generally interpreted as universalistic, in which case its meaning is dissolved. For example, some veteran's benefits, urban renewal relocation allowances, special classes for the handicapped, and cases of preferential treatment in the employment of disadvantaged minority group members involve the selective allocation of benefits based upon nonmeans-related criteria. In fact, once we yield to the broader definition of selectivity, even Children's Allowances are included under this heading in the sense that benefits are limited to families with at least one child. To conceive of these as examples of "selectivity," however, adds little to our understanding of the various conditions that may govern determinants of eligibility.

The problem, then, is to clarify a broader range of alternatives than are provided by "universalism" and "selectivity" (in the narrow means-tested sense) while still maintaining a degree of abstraction that permits generalizations which tell us something meaningful about the conditions of eligibility. Undoubtedly there are many ways to conceptualize allocative principles. Our view is to consider the different conditions under which social provisions are made accessible to individuals and groups in society. *From this perspective, the bases of social allocations may be classified according to four allocative principles: attributed need, compensation, diagnostic differentiation, and means-tested need.*

Attributed Need

Eligibility is conditioned upon belonging to a category or group of people having common needs that are not met by existing institutional arrangements in the market system. Under this principle, "need" is defined according to normative standards. Need may be attributed to as large a category of people as an entire population, such as in the case of health care in England, or to a delimited group such as working mothers, children, and residents of low-income neighborhoods. The two conditions that govern this principle are (a) *categorical allocations* that are (b) based upon *normative criteria of need.*

Compensation

Eligibility is conditioned upon belonging to certain categories or groups of people (a) who have made social and economic contributions, such as veterans, members of social insurance plans, and some farmers (who "contribute" by not producing); or (b) who have suffered unmerited disservices at the "hands of society" such as the victims of racial or religious prejudice, unemployment, and urban displacement. The two conditions that govern this principle are (a) *categorical allocations* that are (b) based upon *normative criteria for equity restoration.*

Diagnostic Differentiation

Eligibility is conditioned upon professional judgments of individual cases where special goods or services may be needed, as in the cases of the physically handicapped and emotionally disturbed. The two conditions that govern the principle are (a) *individual allocations* that are (b) based upon *technical diagnostic criteria of need.*

Means-Tested Need

Eligibility is conditioned upon evidence regarding an individual's inability to purchase goods and/or services. The individual's access to social provisions are limited primarily by his economic circumstances rather than by circumstances on which equity restoration, technical assessments, or normative definitions of need are based. The two conditions that govern this principle are (a) *individual allocations* that are (b) based upon *economic criteria of need.*

Allocative Principles and Institutional-Residual Conceptions of Social Welfare

Before further examination of these allocative principles, let us return briefly to an issue raised in Chapter 1 concerning the competing conceptions of the institutional status of social welfare. We reintroduce this issue because, the bases of social allocations are closely associated with the institutional and residual conceptions of social welfare. The purpose of this discussion is to help clarify how these conceptions are linked with policy design.

As noted earlier, with the institutional conception social welfare is perceived to be a normal ongoing first-line function of society, while with the residual view it is perceived to function as a temporary device when the normal channels for meeting needs fail to perform adequately or are insufficient for certain individuals. The fundamental distinctions concern the causes and incidence of unmet needs and problems in society. To what extent do these unmet needs represent failure of the system and to what extent do they represent a failure of the person or people afflicted? To what extent are these problems characterized as deviant or special cases rather than as normal occurrences? Answers to these questions are reflected in the choices regarding the bases of social allocations as suggested in Figure 3–1. Here the allocative principles are arranged along a continuum in terms of the degree to which they may be identified with institutional or residual conceptions of social welfare.

When allocations are made on the basis of attributed need, the problem of unmet need is considered a normal occurrence attributable to systematic inadequacies. Under these conditions eligibility is determined according to an organic status such as citizen, child, working mother, resident, and the like, rather than on the basis of a condition determined by a detailed exami-

ALLOCATIVE PRINCIPLES

Attributed Need	Compensation	Diagnostic Differentiation	Means-tested Need

Institutional Conception of Social Welfare ◄————————————————► Residual Conception of Social Welfare

FIGURE 3–1
Allocative Principles and Conceptions of Social Welfare.

nation of individual characteristics or evidence of the applicants' special circumstances. Policies designed along these lines exemplify the institutional conception of social welfare as they seek to create stable, ongoing arrangements for meeting normal needs.

At the other end of the continuum, where means-tested need is used as the allocative principle, the problem being addressed is usually considered more a special circumstance arising out of a deficiency of the individual, who is for one reason or another unable to earn an income adequate to satisfy his needs. To be poor or have a low income is not an organic status in the sense that it may be defined in terms of an inherent set of rights and obligations such as those of the working mother, but rather a relative condition that is determined mechanically by calculating all of the income and resources available to an individual against an arbitrary level of economic well-being. Policies designed along these lines exemplify the residual conception of social welfare as a safety net that affords temporary support until the individual is rehabilitated, educated, retrained, or whatever is necessary to make him self-sufficient.

The allocative principles of compensation and diagnostic differentiation fall midway somewhere between institutional and residual conceptions of social welfare. The principle of compensation is closer to the institutional view because it implies a systemic failure or "debt." Here eligibility is determined according to organic status. Diagnostic differentiation is closer to the residual view because it implies individual deficiencies and requires a more or less mechanical assessment of the applicant's special characteristics for eligibility.

This paradigm suggests that the residual conception of social welfare will persist as long as diagnostic differentiation and means-tested need (i.e., allocative principles which seek to differentiate among individuals) are incorporated in the design of social welfare policies. Under these principles, no matter how benign the operational mechanism for eligibility determination, it is probable that the condition of unmet need will be attributed more to either chance or individual deficiency than to recurring institutional strains or failures.

It appears that there will always be cases in which it will be both necessary and desirable to differentiate among individuals for the allocation of social welfare benefits. While the balance is shifting towards a larger institutional role for social welfare, it is unlikely that the residual functions will completely disappear. However, this does not mean that the negative connotations associated with residual functions must endure. If attributed need and compensation are expanded as bases of social allocation, an adequate institutional core of social welfare may emerge. Then, as Shlakman suggests, the residual function becomes smaller and more manageable, and "it has a potential for emerging as the most flexible, most professionally oriented service, providing for the peculiarity of need and exceptional circumstances that cannot be met effectively by programs based on presumed average need."[27]

Problems in
Operationalizing the Allocative Principles

The fourfold classification of allocative principles we have outlined simplifies the structure of choice in the interest of order. To compensate for the inherent distortion requires at least a brief glimpse at some of the problematic facets of eligibility determination according to these principles. Differences among the conditions that govern the principles are not always self-evident. For instance, distinctions between normative definitions and technical assessments of need are often clouded. Is the allocation of special classes for ethnic minority students with low I.Q. scores based upon valid technical measurements of the individual's academic potential, or is it based upon the cultural norms of a white, middle-class group that may be inapplicable to other groups? The technical assessment of social-psychological needs is a sensitive business in which science, art, and prevailing norms intermingle. The allocative principle of diagnostic differentiation encounters a serious dilemma when supposedly technical assessments of individuals result in patterns of benefit allocation that differentiate among groups to the disadvantage of minorities or underprivileged people.[28]

The principle of compensation is invoked to redress group inequities imposed by vagaries of the social structure or to reward contributions made by individuals and groups. But the restoration of equity to those who are "victims of society" may be deferred because these cases are controversial or undiscernible to the public which is responsible for the normative definition of inequity. Is the ghetto dweller entitled to a special travel allowance if public transportation is not available to his area of employment, since the middle-class man drives to work on publicly subsidized highways? To what extent are the inequities of past generations a legitimate debt to charge against present generations? Is it equitable to compensate past inequities through the creation of present inequities? These questions merely suggest the complex interplay among values and social choice that attach to the design of social welfare policies employing the allocative principle of compensation.[29]

Even the relatively straightforward principle of means-tested need becomes entangled in a web of value-laden choices at the point of application. First, of course, a standard of need must be operationally defined. Here it is interesting to note how the "iron law of specificity" operates in matters of social policy. The "iron law of specificity" holds that (a) policy makers experience discomfort with the uncertainty that attaches to socially meaningful problems, such as racism, unemployment, and poverty with which they must deal; (b) to ease the discomfort they are quick to latch on to an arbitrary but plausible specification of such problems that is concrete and readily comprehensible; (c) once the specification has been made it is treated as a literal substitute for the problem in subsequent policy decisions; and (d) continued usage reinforces the substitution, and in time the meaning of the problem and alternative operational definitions are ignored.[30] Consider, for example, the notion of poverty and how closely it has become associated with the Social Security Administration's poverty index of $4200 (as of 1973) for an urban family of four, based on a standard of nutritional adequacy.[31] This definition is plausible and convenient to use, but it overlooks the existential quality of poverty as a condition of life.[32] Compare the poverty index to Robert Hunter's observation, "To live miserable we know not why, to have the dread of hunger, to work more and yet gain nothing—this is the essence of poverty."[33]

Here we need a major caveat lest the "iron law of specificity" be taken too literally. That is, specificity operates in the way outlined above only if the issue of choice is one on which it is possible to achieve fundamental agreement among the parties to whom the specification is offered. (It might be Congress, a presidential commission, a citizens' organization, or a local welfare agency board of directors.) More precisely, it must be a question of choice about which these parties do not hold strong preconceived notions that are in disagreement but around which there is floundering and uncertainty. (We would suggest that this situation is more likely to obtain around the definition of a problem such as poverty, crime, and unemployment than around the details of its solution, even though different problem definitions influence the types of policies that will be put forth as solutions.) If the situation is marked not so much by uncertainty as by the existence of strong opposing views among those to be convinced, then specification is likely to have the reverse effect, making agreement more difficult to achieve. In these cases, particularly when controversial solutions are being offered, there is a certain expedience to abstration, which we will discuss in the next chapter.

Once the standard of need has been settled in means-tested allocations, there still remains the problem of determining how individuals measure up to this level. The scope of economic resources weighed in formulas for eligibility determination is open to question. Should it include valuables of sentimental as well as economic worth (e.g., wedding rings), insurance premiums (e.g., burial insurance), and the tools of one's trade? What about the income of relatives (distant or close)? When eligibility determination includes relatives' income as a resource and the relatives are held liable for support, then in effect they too must be subjected to a means test. From a societal viewpoint the justification of relatives' liability laws is based in part on the claim that such laws encourage mutual support within the kinship system, thereby strengthening family bonds. This is a shallow assumption that quickly bottoms out when put into practice. In order to qualify for public aid in many states, public assistance applicants may be required to sue their legally liable relatives who do not contribute voluntarily or they may be required to allow the assistance agency to sue their relatives as a condition of eligibility. In either case, it has been observed that these sanctions against uncooperative or irresponsible relatives are "strangely at odds with the stated purpose of increasing family cohesion."[34]

Having reviewed some of the problems associated with operationalizing the four principles that form the bases of social allocations, there is a final qualification concerning this dimension of choice to consider. That is, in practice these allocative principles are not mutually exclusive even though their underlying premises may seem somewhat incompatible as, for example, in the joint employment of attributed need and means-tested need. On the contrary, various combinations of allocative principles are found in the design of social welfare policies, or develop as policies are implemented, reflecting the tug, pull, and eventual compromise over competing values. We will illustrate this point with reference to two rather different types of social welfare programs: the national Old-Age, Survivors, Disability, and Health Insurance program under the Social Security Act and the Community Action Program under the Economic Opportunity Act.

In the social insurance program, eligibility for benefits is predicated upon the dual principles of attributed need and compensation. Here a persistent issue is the balance between adequacy and equity in the benefit allocation formula.[35]   The amount of benefit to which, for example, the retired worker is entitled under old-age insurance is designed, in part, to reflect his previous earnings and hence in most cases the amount of contribution that he and his employer made to the social insurance system. To the extent that eligibility for benefits bears some relationship to past contributions, a degree of equity is introduced into this system. However, eligibility is also based on the principle of attributed need. As Hohaus explains, social insurance "aims primarily at providing society with some protection against one or more major hazards which are sufficiently widespread throughout the population and far-reaching in effect to become 'social' in scope and complexion."[36] In the case of old-age insurance the attributed need is that of an adequate standard of living for the elderly who are no longer attached to the labor market. Thus, while the program seeks to some extent to compensate the retired worker for his contributions to the system, it also seeks to provide a level of adequacy for the low-income worker whose contributions were minimal. For the latter, a strict application of the principle of compensation would result in benefit levels far below even the meager living standard to which they were accustomed prior to retirement. In most social insurance programs the dual allocative principles of attributed need and compensation result in a system where the relationship between eligibility for benefits and contributions exists in an ordinal sense, but is limited in a proportional sense, as efforts to express equity are severely modified by concerns for adequacy.

In the development of the Community Action Program (CAP) the principle of attributed need was employed widely as the basis for social allocations. Initially, people became eligible for a variety of CAP-funded goods and services by virtue of their residence in designated low-income neighborhoods.[37] However, once the program began operating, these normative assessments of need were often modified. Levitan documents how CAP-funded neighborhood health centers which were to provide free health care services to all target area residents eventually incorporated a means test into allocation procedures, as did CAP-funded Neighborhood Legal Aid, Head Start, and employment opportunities programs.[38] In certain instances many neighborhood residents supported employment of the means test as an additional basis for allocations. These were cases where the services were relatively inelastic (e.g., a limited number of slots for Head Start students in a summer program), and applicants included large numbers of both poor and nonpoor residents of low-income neighborhoods. The poor were not convinced that attributed need was the most suitable allocative principle under such circumstances. For the Community Action Program, attributed need became a preliminary screening device, a necessary but not sufficient condition for eligibility determination.

In examining the bases of social allocations we have offered a view of some complicated and untidy features of this dimension of choice. Still we would suggest that the complexities of application notwithstanding, the four allocative principles—attributed need, compensation, diagnostic differentiation, and means-tested need—provide a useful framework for the systematic conceptualization of policy alternatives. Consider, for example, the provision of preschool day-care center services, a program demand that is gaining support from students, welfare mothers, and women's liberation activists, among others. To whom and on what basis should these services be made available? The four allocative principles offer an orderly framework of choice for conceptualizing the range of alternative answers that might be offered. Thus, as indicated in Table 3–1 at one extreme eligibility for this service might be extended to all families with young children, based upon a community-felt need for an institutional arrangement to allow mothers greater freedom during the early years of childrearing. However, such a diminution of maternal childrearing responsibilities for the sake of greater freedom is unlikely to receive normative sanction in a child-oriented and achievement-oriented society. A more plausible condition of eligibility might require casting attributed need, not into the mold of "untrammeled freedom," but rather in the image of freedom to achieve commonly valued objectives such as a career or an education. In this case, eligibility would be limited to working mothers and/or students. There are other options involving entitlement to day-care services on compensatory or diagnostic bases. Finally, there is the means test, which can be used independently or in combination with any of the above principles.

TABLE 3–1

Bases for Alternative Allocations of Day-Care Services.

Conditions of Eligibility	Examples of Alternative Allocations
Attributed need	All families
	Single parent families
	Families with working mothers
	Families with student mothers
Compensation	Minority families
	Families of servicemen
	Families of workers in specified occupational groups
Diagnostic differentiation	Families with physically or emotionally handicapped parents
	Families in short-term crisis situations
Means-tested need	Families whose earnings and resources fall beneath a designated standard of economic need

Who Wants to Benefit?

In this chapter we have focused upon a question that receives much attention in the design of social welfare policies: Who is to be *eligible* for benefits? But there is another side to this issue that is often ignored or misinterpreted by social welfare policy-makers. To conclude this chapter it seems fitting that we address the other side of this issue: Who *wants* to benefit?

In selecting the basis of social allocations there is a strong tendency to proceed on the assumption of receptivity. That is, those who will qualify as recipients are expected to come forth to claim their benefits or to readily accept social provisions that are offered. Eligible clients or consumers who do not fulfill these expectations are labeled "hard-to-reach" and attention is then directed to the development of more penetrating delivery structures. There is empirical evidence to show that many people in need of available social provisions can be reached only by special delivery methods.[39] It is important to remember that findings such as these highlight deficiences that occur in delivering needed services to clients in ways that take account of cultural differences. However, these are *not* problems of eligibility determination, but rather of service delivery, a subject dealt with in Chapter 5.

However, the assumption of receptivity, even with special delivery efforts, bears closer scrutiny than it is usually given. For a variety of reasons, those who are eligible for benefits are sometimes simply not interested in becoming recipients. They are hard-to-reach because they do not want to be reached. The costs of assuming recipient status may be perceived as outweighing the benefits. For instance, though it meant a considerable loss of federal funds, citizens in one city refused to have their neighborhood designated as part of a Community Action Program target area, in part because they believed it was a scheme for racial integration.[40] Religious or political convictions may inhibit receptivity to social provisions. As Harrington observed, there also exists a subculture of voluntary poverty, composed in the main of intellectuals rebelling against the "system," that does not respond to opportunities for advancement.[41] In addition, provisions designed for the hard-to-reach may have only minimal impact because of cultural preferences. A study by Eaton suggests this:

> Social planning for the abolition of marginality and poverty must proceed from the fact that many people are positively identified with the perpetuation of cultural differences ... even if this means the encouragement of values that handicap their capacity to compete equitably in school, youth organizations, or the job market.[42]

All this poses an unsettling dilemma for policy choices concerning the basis of social allocations. It is summed up in Bell's observation:

> ... While one may guarantee working-class families the same educational opportunities as middle-class families, what happens if they don't want to use this opportunity? Society may have an obligation to those who are kept down or cannot advance because it is not their fault. But if individuals—for cultural or psychological reasons—do not avail themselves of opportunities, is it the society's responsibility, as the prior obligation, to devote resources to them? But if not, how does one distinguish between the genuinely disadvantaged and those who are not? This is the inextricable difficulty of social policy.[43]

The issue of who wants to benefit cannot be carried much further in these general terms without some reference to what it is they would receive. In the next chapter we examine the nature of the social provision.

Notes

[1]Edward Bellamy, *Looking Backward* (Signet Classic Edition) (New York: New American Library, 1960), p. 75. Notice how this notion of entitlement parallels the quotation cited earlier (p. 42) concerning Marx's view on equality of human labor.

[2]Bellamy, *Looking Backward*, p. 95.

[3]George Hoshino, "Britain's Debate on Universal or Selective Social Services: Lessons for America," *Social Service Review*, Vol. 43, No. 3 (September 1969), 249.

[4]For example, see Peter Townsend, "Does Selectivity Mean a Nation Divided?" in *Social Services for All?* (London: Fabian Society, 1968), pp. 1–6; Richard Titmuss, *Commitment to Welfare* (New York: Pantheon, 1968), pp. 113–123; T. H. Marshall, *Class, Citizenship and Social Development* (Anchor Books Edition) (New York: Doubleday and Company, 1965), pp. 257–79; George Hoshino, "Britain's Debate on Universal or Selective Social Services,"; Mike Reddin, "Universality versus Selectivity," *The Political Quarterly*, January/March 1969.

[5]For a representative sample of the voluminous literature in this area, see James C. Vadakin, "A Critique of the Guaranteed Annual Income," *Public Interest*, Vol. 11 (Spring 1968), 53–66; Edward Schwartz, "A Way to End the Means Test," *Social Work*, Vol. 9, No. 3 (July 1964), 3–12; James Tobin, "The Case for an Income Guarantee," *Public Interest*, Vol. 4 (Summer 1966), 31–41; Alvin Schorr, "Against a Negative Income Tax," *Public Interest*, Vol. 5 (Fall 1966), 110–17; Michael Reagan, "Washington Should Pay Taxes to the Poor," *New York Times Magazine*, Feb. 16, 1966; Scott Briar, "Why Children's Allowances?" *Social Work*, Vol. 14, No. 1 (January 1969), 5–12; Irwin Garfinkel, "Negative Income Tax and Children's Allowance Programs: A Comparison," *Social Work*, Vol. 13, No. 4 (October 1968), 33–39; Helen O. Nicol, "Guaranteed Income Maintenance: Another Look at the Debate," *Welfare in Review*, Vol. 5, No. 6 (June/July 1967), 1–13.

[6]Eveline M. Burns, "Where Welfare Falls Short," *Public Interest,* No. 1 (Fall 1965), 88.

[7]Actually, not all Children's Allowance programs are universal in the sense that they cover all families in the country. In some countries, such as France, eligibility for the children's allowance is employment-related. In France the program is financed through payroll taxes imposed on the employer, rather than out of general funds. Eligibility is extended to employees, though some provisions are made for coverage of the unemployed. For a more detailed description of the French scheme, see Wallace Peterson, *The Welfare State in France* (Omaha: University of Nebraska Press, 1960), pp. 19–39.

[8]For this illustration we are using the original proposal described in "Toward a Full Opportunity for Every American: The President's Proposals for Welfare Reform," *Welfare in Review,* Vol. 7, No. 5 (September/October 1969). A slightly revised version of this proposal (with base benefits increased to $2400 for a family of four) competing with three similar but more generous FAP proposals introduced to Congress by Senators George McGovern, Fred Harris, and Abraham Ribicoff, encountered a stormy reception in Congress. These various proposals are described by Nancy Duff Levy and Michael Trister, "Status of Welfare Reform: Enactment Likely by Early 1972," *Clearinghouse Review,* Vol. 5, No. 9 (January 1972). Despite the optimism of the Levy and Trister analysis, the FAP did not pass Congress and, as of this writing, it is in a state of limbo, awaiting the results of additional experimentation over the next few years.

[9]Schorr, "Against a Negative Income Tax." For alternative proposals and a more detailed discussion of costs, see Alvin Schorr, *Poor Kids* (New York: Basic Books, 1966).

[10]Reddin, "Universality versus Selectivity," p. 14.

[11]James Cutt, "Income Support Programmes for Families with Children—Alternatives for Canada," *International Social Security Review,* Vol. 23, No. 1 (1970), 104–5.

[12]George Break, "The Effects of Taxation on Work Incentives," in *Private Wants and Public Needs,* ed. Edmund Phelps (New York: W. W. Norton, 1965), p. 65.

[13]Fred Cook, "When You Just Give Money to the Poor," *New York Times Magazine,* May 3, 1970, pp. 23 and 109–12. A more detailed breakdown of these findings is presented by David N. Kershaw, "A Negative-Income-Tax Experiment," *Scientific American,* Vol. 227, No. 4 (October 1972), 19–25. For a description of the research design used in this study, see Harold W. Watts, "Graduated Work Incentives: An Experiment in Negative Taxation," *The American Economic Review,* Vol. 59, No. 2 (May 1969). And for a general survey of the literature, see David Macarov, *Incentives to Work* (San Francisco: Jossey-Bass, 1970).

[14]Mildred Rein, "Determinants of the Work-Welfare Choice in AFDC," *Social Service Review,* Vol. 46, No. 4 (December 1972), 563–64. For a more detailed analysis, see Leonard Hausman, "The Impact of Welfare on the Work Effort of AFDC Mothers," *Technical Studies* (Washington, D.C.: Government Printing Office, 1970), pp. 83–100.

[15]Eveline M. Burns, "Childhood Poverty and the Children's Allowance," in *Children's Allowances and the Economic Welfare of Children,* ed. Eveline M. Burns (New York: Citizen's Committee for Children of New York, 1968), p. 12.

[16]Walter Freidlander, *Individualism and Social Welfare* (New York: The Free Press, 1962), p. 161. Peterson, *The Welfare State in France,* notes that the rise in population is in part accounted for by a decline in the death rate from 15.3 per thousand in 1939 to 12.2 per thousand in 1955.

[17]Alvin Schorr, "Income Maintenance and the Birth Rate," *Social Security Bulletin,* Vol. 28, No. 12 (December 1965), 2–10.

[18]Schorr, "Income Maintenance and the Birth Rate," p. 4. Additional evidence on this issue is presented by Vincent Whitney, "Fertility Trends and Children's Allowance Programs," in *Children's Allowances and the Economic Welfare of Children,* ed. Burns, pp. 123–39.

[19]"The Case for a Family Allowance," *New York Times Magazine,* February 5, 1967, p. 71.

[20]Titmuss, *Commitment to Welfare,* p. 122.

[21]Alfred Kahn, *Theory and Practice of Social Planning* (New York: Russell Sage, 1969), p. 203.

[22]For example, in 1970 students at the School of Social Welfare, University of California, Berkeley, strongly requested that the means test be the *main criterion* for determining the award of fellowships and other financial aid.

[23]Joel Handler and Ellen Hollingsworth, "How Obnoxious is the 'Obnoxious Means Test'? The View of AFDC Recipients" (Madison: Institute for Research on Poverty Discussion Paper, University of Wisconsin), January 1969. Also see, Richard Pomeroy and Harold Yahr, in collaboration with Lawrence Podell, *Studies in Public Welfare: Effects of Eligibility Investigation on Welfare Clients* (New York: Center for the Study of Urban Problems, City University of New York, 1968).

[24]A penetrating description of the ways administrative practices are used to intimidate and deter public assistance applicants is presented by Frances Fox Piven and Richard Cloward, *Regulating the Poor: The Functions of Public Welfare* (New York: Pantheon Books, 1971), pp. 147–82. Also see Betty Mandell, "Welfare and Totalitarianism: Part I. Theoretical Issues," *Social Work,* Vol. 16, No. 1 (January 1971), 17–25.

[25]For example, see George Hoshino, "Can the Means Test Be Simplified?" *Social Work,* Vol. 10, No. 3 (July 1965), 98–104.

[26]Titmuss, *Commitment to Welfare,* pp. 114–15.

[27]Vera Shlakman, "The Safety-Net Function in Public Assistance: A Cross-National Exploration," *Social Service Review,* Vol. 46, No. 2 (June 1972), 207.

[28]For further discussion of some of the complexities in the application of this principle, see Joseph Eaton and Neil Gilbert, "Racial Discrimination and Diagnostic Differentiation," in *Race, Research and Reason,* ed. Roger Miller (New York: National Association of Social Workers, 1970), pp. 79–88.

[29]Different strategies and implications of compensation are examined in Neil Gilbert and Joseph Eaton, "Favoritism as a Strategy in Race Relations," *Social Problems,* Vol. 18 No. 1 (Summer 1970), 38–51.

[30]The "iron law of specificity" is based on our experiences participating in and observing the behavior of numerous planning and policy-making bodies. To see it operate in a microcosm (for those who doubt its power), we would suggest that at the next meeting in which you participate where a policy decision is pending on a fairly abstract issue around which there is some floundering, deliberately make a proposal that is simply plausible and contains some specification of the issue in concrete units, such as amount of dollars, units of service, numbers of people to be served, and the like. Then mark the time it takes for the discussion to shift from philosophy to considerations of whether the decision should involve a little more or a little less of the concrete units in your proposal.

[31]Martin Rein observes, "The SSA procedure for defining and measuring poverty is especially vulnerable to the criticism that when a choice among alternative estimating procedures was necessary the rationale for selection was arbitrary, but not necessarily unreasoned," in *Social Policy* (New York: Random House, 1970), p. 452.

[32]For an approach to the measurement and policy implications of poverty defined in existential terms see Morton S. Baratz and William G. Grigsby, "Thoughts on Poverty and Its Elimination," *Journal of Social Policy,* Vol. 1, No. 2 (April 1972), 119–34.

[33]Robert Hunter, *Poverty,* Peter d'A. Jones ed. (New York: Harper & Row, 1965, originally published 1904), p. 2.

[34]Winifred Bell, "Relatives' Responsibility: A Problem in Social Policy," *Social Work,* Vol. 12, No. 1 (January 1967), 38.

[35]See, for example, Richard Titmuss, "Equity, Adequacy, and Innovation in Social Security," *International Social Security Review,* Vol. 23, No. 2 (1970), 259–68.

[36]Richard Hohaus, "Equity, Adequacy, and Related Factors in Old Age Security," in *Social Security: Programs, Problems and Policies,* William Haber and Wilbur Cohen eds. (Homewood, Ill.: Richard Irwin, 1960), p. 61.

[37]Drawing boundaries is a recurrent problem with this method of allocation. Exactly where any given central city low-income neighborhood begins and ends is a matter that even carefully designed empirical research rarely settles to everyone's satisfaction. For a technical analysis of this issue, see Avery Guest and James Zuiches, "Another Look at Residential Turnover in Urban Neighborhoods: A Note on 'Racial Change in a Stable Community' by Harvey Molotch," *American Journal of Sociology,* Vol. 77, No. 3 (November 1971), 457–471. We should add that methodological efforts at boundary definition in most Community Action Programs were superficial.

[38]Sar Levitan, *The Great Society's Poor Law* (Baltimore: Johns Hopkins, 1970).

[39]For example, see Oliver Moles, Robert Hess, and Daniel Fascione, "Who

Knows Where to Get Public Assistance?" *Welfare in Review,* Vol. 6, No. 5 (September/October 1968).

[40]Neil Gilbert, *Clients or Constituents* (San Francisco: Jossey-Bass, 1970), p. 75.

[41]Michael Harrington, *The Other America* (New York: Macmillan, 1962), pp. 82–88.

[42]Joseph Eaton, "Reaching the Hard to Reach in Israel," *Social Work,* Vol. 15, No. 1 (January 1970), 96.

[43]Daniel Bell, "Meritocracy and Equality," *Public Interest,* Vol. 29 (Fall 1972), 29–68.

The Nature
of Social Provisions

*The only crucial question becomes one of waste or economy. The
two alternatives for redistributional reforms, in cash or in kind,
therefore have to be compared as to their effectiveness in relation
to financial outlays. Just because both systems are costly, they
must be scrutinized as choices. It would be an illusion to pretend
that both lines could be followed. No budget could expand widely
in two different directions.*

ALVA MYRDAL,
Nation and Family

4 The strain between collectivist and individualist tendencies is
nowhere more readily apparent than in the dimension of choice
that concerns the form of social provisions. Two forms of social
provision mark the traditional demarcation line of thought and
debate in this area of social welfare policy decision: *benefits in cash* versus
benefits in kind. For example, if they are eligible according to the allocative
principles employed, should those who qualify be provided with a subsidized unit of public housing or should they be provided with a sum of cash
equal to the subsidy with which to seek shelter on the private housing
market? While the issue is fairly simple to comprehend, the resolution is
quite another matter. Equally reasoned arguments have been made for the
primacy of both cash and in-kind provisions. As a point of entry to this
dimension of choice we will examine the opposing views concerning the
special advantages and failings of these two basic forms of social provision.

Basic Forms:
In Cash or in Kind

Alva Myrdal's lucid exposition of the case in favor of benefits in kind is developed within the context of child welfare provisions, specifically in opposition to cash children's allowances and in support of child welfare benefits in kind.[1] The gist of this position, however, may be applied more generally to a variety of programmatic contexts.

In-kind benefits, according to Myrdal, are less expensive than cash payments. They are cheaper because of the economies of large-scale enterprise that accrue to the production of certain items of consumption. Standardization of the product and the consequent decrease in advertising costs also contribute to the overall reduction of expense for in-kind benefits. For a simplified illustration, take the objective of providing a pair of shoes for every child in the nation. The in-kind argument holds that it is less costly to arrange for the government to own or control a few large factories across the country that use exactly the same materials purchased in massive quantities and that produce only one style of shoe of durable quality which is distributed free through a central government store in each city. The in-cash alternative would give each family a money grant to select among the dozens of shoe styles of varying degrees of durability produced by numerous smaller factories (using diverse materials) and distributed through dozens of stores, each of which must advertise their wares to compete on the private market. In sum, a standard benefit, mass produced and centrally distributed by government, is seen as eliminating many of the supposed wasteful attributes of competition in the open marketplace.[2]

Continuing this line of argument, Myrdal suggests that assistance in kind is also more effective than cash subsidies. The effectiveness of social provisions can be measured according to different criteria, and here the major criterion of effectiveness is the degree to which benefits impact squarely upon the targets for which they are intended. If the purpose of policy is, for example, to enhance child welfare, then the question of effectiveness translates to how much of the benefit is consumed in a manner that directly serves this objective.[3] Under this criterion, the drawback of cash subsidies is that they cannot be controlled at the point of consumption. There is no way to guarantee that a children's allowance (or for that matter a cash subsidy for any designated purpose, short of increasing happiness) will not be incorporated into the general family budget and used to purchase a variety of items only a portion of which apply *directly* to the socially defined purpose of the grant which in this case is to increase the welfare of the child.

One reason "liberal" economists usually favor cash provisions is that they tend to define welfare maximization as the highest plane of satisfaction or "happiness" an individual can achieve for a given outlay of public funds. Theoretically it can be demonstrated, for example, that the rational man, given $20 to spend as he pleases will invariably achieve a higher level of satisfaction than the one given $20 worth of goods and services determined by federal planners. However, this position assumes that our consumer is indeed rational and capable of judging precisely what is in his best self-interest. More important, this position assumes that policy is motivated primarily for the good of the designated beneficiary as he defines it rather than according to the preferences of the larger collectivity.[4] Finally, it assumes that the choices made by the consumer to maximize his happiness also will enhance the "common welfare" so that the larger collectivity does not suffer for the satisfaction of its members.[5]

The case for the superior effectiveness of in-kind benefits hinges on the fact that this form of social provision allows for the control of consumption patterns. Thus, benefits such as free clothing, medical care, and school lunch programs can be designed and distributed so that the full impact of the provision is centered upon the socially defined needs of the target populations. On this point Myrdal observes:

> What is needed in social policy is less interest in philosophizing about power over production, which is a complicated problem, and more interest in increasing control from the consumption side, which is a comparatively easy task for competent social engineering ... Cooperation, finally, may be the key word for this social policy in a deeper sense because it rests fundamentally on social solidarity, on pooling of resources for common aims, wider in their loyalty than just insurance of individual interests.[6]

Hence, we arrive at the core of the argument supporting benefits in kind, and find it recommends the imposition of social controls whereby individual interests are harnessed for the collective good. As Holden puts it:

> Indeed, the decisive and overriding concern of those who favor benefits in kind as opposed to cash grants appears to be that only through in-kind assistance is society able to exercise a measure of control over the final utilization of the tax dollar ...[7]

The term "social control" has a distinctly negative connotation in social welfare settings. Critics of social welfare charge that the institution is essentially a device for the social control of the poor and underprivileged, a repressive mechanism that keeps people in their place and that maintains

conformity to an unjust order. But the frequency with which this indict-
ment is made does not constitute proof of guilt. Yet, to be sure, the charge
is not without substance, nor is it of recent origin. As Briggs notes:

> Many of Bismarck's critics accused him, not without justification, of
> seeking through his legislation to make German workers "depend"
> upon the state. The same charges have been made against the initiators
> of all "welfare" (and earlier, of poor law) policy often without justifi-
> cation, yet it was Bismarck himself who drew a revealing distinction
> between the degrees of obedience (or subservience) of private servants
> and servants at court. The latter would "put up with much more" than
> the former because they had pensions to look forward to. "Welfare"
> soothed the spirit, or perhaps tamed it.[8]

In general, social welfare professionals find social control a disagreeable
element of policy. We mention this point because the objectionable functions associated with, and the resistive feelings aroused by, the term social
control should not paralyze our facility to weigh the case for provisions in
kind. Social controls are required to regulate a complex and highly interdependent society. Regulation that replaces the power of the individual by
the power of the community, Freud observed, "constitutes the decisive
step of civilization."[9] The issue is not whether we will have controls but
whether they will be deliberately designed to realize our ideals of human
dignity and justice or to serve pernicious ends—to sooth or to tame the
spirit.

Clearly, Alva Myrdal's proposals endeavor to use social control for
estimable purposes. Yet the dilemma of social control exercised through
the provision of in-kind benefits is that while it may facilitate the realization of collective aims, even with the best of intentions, it also operates to
inhibit individual freedom of the consumer, rich or poor. Myrdal is cognizant of the objections raised by this problem. However, she suggests that,
at least in regard to provisions for child welfare, in-kind benefits really
should pose no constraints on consumer sovereignty because, "beneficiaries
of the communal goods, the children, have rarely had much voice in
decisions about the use of the family income."[10] This defense is not
completely persuasive, even when applied only to children's benefits. For
as Friedman points out:

> The belief in freedom is for "responsible" units, among whom we
> include neither children nor insane people. In general, this problem is
> avoided by regarding the family unit as the basic unit and therefore
> parents as responsible for their children.[11]

While forcibly advocating benefits in kind, Myrdal's position is decid-
edly less than doctrinaire. And even she is not completely persuaded by

her own argument that in-kind benefits for children do not limit freedom of choice. Hence the counsel to exercise caution when applying the principle of in-kind allocations, especially for benefits that are inexpensive and involve items around which family choices frequently are made and often are imbued with personal meaning:

> Clothing falls in that category, and it thus seems to be difficult to subsidize in kind. Here personal taste is delicate and social prestige has become involved. Even if some class equalization in clothing, especially for children, is judged desirable, it would probably be extremely unwise to force any uniformity on families ... It would be cheaper, perhaps extremely rational but still a bit inhuman, to provide layettes, bedding, and baby carriages for all newborn children. All these cost items, invested with so much tender care, are certainly not appropriate for communalization.[12]

As a final qualification, Myrdal advises that a serious preference for benefits in kind rather than cash subsidies can only be entertained when an adequate family income exists. In circumstances where an adequate family income does not exist, cash assistance for children is considered an "appropriate deviation" from the in-kind principle.

Turning now to the other position, there are two pervasive themes that find expression among those who advance the case for benefits in cash as the preferred form of social provision. First, the alleged savings of benefits in kind do not go unchallenged. While economies of scale may apply to certain forms of technology, we may question to what extent in-kind personal services such as social casework and vocational counseling can achieve cost reduction from large-scale organization.[13] The reason for this is that social services tend to draw upon what Thompson describes as "intensive technology," whereby a variety of techniques are employed to change and aid the client, with the precise treatment configuration based upon constant feedback concerning the state of the client.[14] This type of technology is customed to individual cases, which hinders the prospects of standardization. And it appears that the types of social provisions that are more amenable to standardization, such as clothing, involve items of consumption where the sacrifice of freedom of choice is somewhat discomforting even among staunch advocates of in-kind benefits. Moreover, though these benefits in kind may eliminate some of the wasteful attributes of competition, it can also be argued that the increased competition associated with cash benefits is more likely to generate innovations resulting in significant cost reductions over the long haul.

Where economies of scale are not clearly operative the question pivots on whether cash subsidies that stimulate competition in the private marketplace and oil the palm of the "invisible hand" are really less expensive than provisions in kind that foster cooperation and the growth of publicly-run or publicly-controlled bureaucracy. Examining this choice in the context of education, Friedman opts for grant subsidies rather than the in-kind provision because

> [Grants] would bring a healthy increase in the variety of educational institutions available and in competition among them. Private initiative and enterprise would quicken the pace of progress in this area as it has in so many others. Government would serve its proper function of improving the operation of the invisible hand without substituting the dead hand of bureaucracy.[15]

The more potent theme supporting the argument for benefits in cash is its appeal to the maximization of consumer sovereignty and freedom of choice. Though claims are made that each form of social provision allows for more economical utilization of resources, there is considerable assertion and little empirical evidence on either side. In many cases arguments concerning the apparent costs of cash versus in-kind benefits are employed as "neutral" or surface justifications for the underlying currents of individualistic and collectivist thought. There is a compelling quality to the argument for consumer sovereignty. In essence it posits the right to individual self-determination: the right of one man to squander his resources on luxurious or frivolous items for whatever psychological or material benefits he may so derive, and the right of another to husband his resources toward whatever future he envisions. It is, among other things, the right of individuals to exercise self-indulgence as well as self-denial.

But this viewpoint also relies heavily on faith that the market mechanism works according to principle and is in fact responsive to consumer demands. On this point, those who favor collective interventions are not convinced. Thus, Galbraith argues that the consumer "is subject to forces of advertising and emulation by which production creates its own demand." According to this proposition, which he labels the "dependence effect," consumer wants are not independently determined. Rather, it is the producers who not only create goods and services, but also manufacture the desires for them among consumers.[16] The counterargument to this proposition is that producers really cannot determine consumer wants; they merely provide information about what is available and endeavor to convince the consumer of the worth and value of their product.[17] Whether or not the "dependence effect" is as consequential as Galbraith would have us believe, his proposition discloses one of the hidden perils of unqualified acceptance of the market mechanism: namely, consumer ignorance must be taken into account when considering voluntary exchange in pursuit of rational self-interest. Rational choices require objective information about the items to be consumed. Such knowledge is expensive and difficult to obtain. The predicament is more intense if one is poor and ill-educated to begin with. As Rivlin explains:

> Unless he knows what he is buying, a consumer cannot choose rationally. Yet, in the social action [i.e., welfare] area, it is very difficult for him to find out anything about the quality of service before he uses it. Moreover, the costs of shopping around or sampling the merchandise of a hospital or a school may be prohibitive.[18]

At the very least, then, social control of consumption offers a degree of protection to the unwary or the ignorant consumer. From this perspective it might be said that it is not so much freedom to choose that is reduced as freedom to err or to choose poorly on the basis of limited knowledge. The response to this perspective might be that without freedom to err self-determination is a hollow construct. Where the collectivist sees the desirability for social protection, the individualist is prone to interpret this coverage as paternalistic infringement upon individual responsibility.

The issue of provisions in cash versus in kind has been pitched at a fairly high level of generality. From this level we can observe the thrusts and counterthrusts of contending sides, but no general solution is visible. To draw a general conclusion about the primacy of either cash or in kind benefits would involve imposing an absolute standard in a realm of policy choice where relativity is the more appropriate stance. Much depends upon the esteem in which individual freedom and consumer choice are held compared to social control and the collective good. But even the most ardent supporters of consumer choice bow to the necessity of collective interventions under certain circumstances, such as when the mentally incompetent are concerned and where government intervention is justified because the market mechanism is inoperative due to technical conditions.[19] And those who prescribe benefits in kind are sensitive to both the need for an adequate cash income and the social and psychological benefits of self-expression and autonomy derived from consumer choice. For them, as Mencher suggests, "the problem is not the potential conflict between individual rights and social controls but the maintenance of maximum opportunity for individual choice as an integral part of the supporting system of governmental responsibility."[20] To achieve this balanced state, a mixture of different forms of social provision that offer varying degrees of consumer sovereignty and social control must be considered.

Alternative Forms:
An Extension of Choice

We have discussed the nature of social provisions in terms of two basic forms that benefits can take, cash or in kind. There is a certain forensic utility to this classification of the choices in that it affords reasonably firm lines for debate. Yet to think of social provisions in these terms alone oversimplifies the reality that policy-makers face in practice. Finer distinctions which identify benefits that do not fit neatly into these categories are possible and desirable for analytic precision.

Social provisions may come in a variety of forms from vague sets of circumstances to concrete goods. Embedded in these varied forms is a dimension of transferability—the extent to which the provision allows for consumer choice. For example, public housing units, home repair services, cash supplements for housing, and rent vouchers offer varying degrees of freedom of choice to the consumer. Conversely, they insure to varying degrees that the provision will not be used for other than its intended purposes. In terms of form and transferability, social provisions may be classified broadly into six categories: opportunities, services, goods, credits, cash, and power.

Opportunities   are sets of circumstances in which incentives and sanctions are employed to achieve desired ends. The broadness of the description indicates that this is the vaguest type of direct social provision. Yet the indefinite quality does not diminish its importance; much of social welfare policy is concerned with the creation and distribution of opportunities. Unlike goods or services, benefits in this category involve the provision of civil rights or an "extra chance." Sometimes the extra chance is built into the basis of social allocations as in the additional points on civil service exams awarded to veterans or the special efforts that some schools make to recruit minority students. In these cases there is considerable overlap between the nature of the provision and the basis of social allocations. Opportunities ultimately may lead to the acquisition of other benefits. However, opportunities have no immediate transfer value inasmuch as they must be utilized within the context that they are offered. A recipient of opportunity "X" cannot trade it for opportunity "Y," or for goods, services, or other social provisions.

Services   involve the performance of certain functions in the client's behalf such as teaching, counseling, planning, healing, and training. These provisions are nontransferable in terms of their immediate market value to recipients.

Goods   are concrete commodities such as food, clothing, and housing. These benefits have limited transfer value, generally confined to marginal channels of exchange such as pawn shops, "flea markets," and informal barter.

Credits   are benefits in the form of tax credits or vouchers for goods and services. They have a structured exchange value and may be transferred for a choice among resources within a delineated sector: tax credits can be used to offset medical expenses; food stamps can be exchanged for a variety of edible goods; and educational vouchers can be used to purchase teaching services in the institution of one's choice. But none are of value outside their respective sectors. Provisions in this form generally are considered to offer greater degrees of freedom of choice than those in the form of goods or services. As a form of social provision, vouchers have special appeal because they preserve a modicum of consumer sovereignty (within a sector) while allowing for the exercise of social control (between sectors). Thus, they attract a range of proponents with collectivist and individualist predilections.[21]

Cash   benefits are provided through public assistance, children's allowances, and social insurance, among other programs. This form of social provision, of course, has universal exchange value, offering the most latitude for consumer choice.

Power   benefits involve the redistribution of influence over the control of goods and resources. Often the redistribution of influence is sought through policies that require representation of the poor, clients, or other disadvantaged people on the boards of agencies that dispense social welfare benefits, such as Community Action Agencies and Model Cities organizations. In these cases the social provision is incorporated into policy decisions about the structure of the delivery system (which we will examine in Chapter 5). While power cannot be "spent" in the same way as cash or credits, it offers a higher degree of latitude to command social and economic choices than provisions in the form of goods, services, or opportunities. In this sense, power has a fluid exchange value.[22]

In addition to these six types of social provisions, there is another qualitatively different type of social provision that is considerably more indirect in its benefit to individuals and groups. A good deal of important social welfare policy in itself does not result in an easily identifiable benefit to specific individuals in need. Rather these policies establish programs which are *instrumental* in the development and implementation of other programs that provide direct benefits. *Instrumental provisions* are those which encourage more efficient and effective arrangements among agencies which supply direct social welfare benefits.

To illustrate, let us consider the proposed Allied Services Bill of 1972. The major objective of this legislation was to create integrated systems of local social services that would move clients along the continuum from dependence to independence and self-support. The bill provides funds for states to develop an Allied Services Plan that would indicate the steps to be taken in linking and coordinating local efforts. States that produce acceptable Allied Services plans would become eligible for two types of benefits. First, under certain circumstances they would be allowed to transfer 20 percent of currently available federal categorial funds among the different programs included in the plan. Second, various federally imposed technical and administrative requirements that might inhibit implementation of the plan would be waived, such as reporting procedures and requirements for state-wide organization of federally financed programs. The proposed legislation, however, does not include additional funds for services. In essence this policy would provide for the transfer of administrative discretion from the federal to the state level. Such a provision is instrumental inasmuch as the benefit to individuals or groups of service recipients is neither immediate nor direct.

Instrumental provisions play an important part in molding the process through which policy choices concerning tangible social welfare benefits are made. Because they are most pertinent to the process of social welfare planning, we will engage in a more detailed discussion of instrumental provisions in Chapter 8, where policy choices concerning the question "who plans" are examined and an example of policy with an instrumental provision is analyzed. For the remainder of this chapter our major concern will be the nature of social provisions that offer the direct forms of aid to individuals and groups.

Substance of the Social Provision

Our elementary categorization of six types of benefits in terms of their form and transferability is useful, to a point, in permitting insights into the nature of social provisions, particularly for cash, credits, and goods, which are fairly concrete forms of benefit. A tremendous variety is possible within each of these categories. For example, the provision of goods may include numerous commodities in food, clothing, and shelter; cash may be provided in amounts ranging from small sums to thousands of dollars; and credits may be designed to cover part or all of the costs of different goods and services. Despite the many alternatives, there is a palpable quality to these types of provisions that makes them readily comprehensible. The substance of these social provisions is virtually self-evident; most of the relevant qualities of the benefit become known as soon as the amount of cash, type of goods, and credit sector are specified. Consider a policy to provide credits for educational services. The educational voucher is worth a designated sum of money and can be exchanged to pay for designated educational programs. Different programs might be housed in a single local public school, spread out among a few local public and private schools, or encompass all accredited schools in the country. The point is that once the value of the voucher and the sector in which it can be exchanged are decided upon and plugged into the policy, the nature of the social provision is substantially clear.[23]

For the other categories of benefits—opportunities, services, and power —the substance of the social provision is more abstruse. To gain a clear understanding of what is being provided requires probing beyond a first level specification of the type of service, the area of opportunity, and the resources over which a redistribution of power is sought. For instance, take a simple proposal to provide family counseling services. The type of service has been designated as counseling rather than teaching, training, or planning. Yet the substance of the social provision remains virtually unknown, although proposals for service provisions frequently are framed at about this level of specificity. Among other things, a counseling service may emphasize distribution of information, psychoanalysis, behavior modification, or alteration of environmental contingencies. It may center upon individuals, family units, or groups. It may be short-term or long-range. And it may be conducted by personnel with a variety of backgrounds and training who base their practice on alternative theories of change.[24]

Likewise a day-care service may actually provide for custodial care or comprehensive child development depending upon the staff-child ratio, staff qualifications, program content, equipment, and related characteristics of the service.[25] Opportunity benefits in the area of employment may range from equal access to preferential treatment, to discrimination-in-reverse through the use of federal subsidies, legal sanctions, and political pressure. In the area of education there is considerable debate regarding what constitutes the substance of opportunity provisions of "affirmative action" policies running the gamut from special recruitment efforts to modifying admission standards.[26] The redistribution of power in various settings may cover a broad range of influence patterns from that exercised by members of a citizens' advisory committee to community control of local institutions.[27] Without clarification of these substantive aspects of service, opportunity, and power benefits, we are severely limited in our assessments of precisely what it is that social programs seek to provide.

Expediency of Abstraction

To prescribe that policy analysts should strive for precision and specificity in defining the nature of social provisions is not to deny the political functions of taking refuge in abstraction. Our major concern here is with how one goes about comprehending social welfare policy by dissecting the various dimensions of choice. We allow ourselves a momentary lapse in this mission because in the real world of policy choice there is something to be said for ambiguity in the design of social provisions. And we think it appropriate to say it at this point, if for no other reason than to balance with a little wisdom that comes from practical experience the wanton analytic impulse to dissect social choices endlessly. The advantage of leaving the nature of the social provision vague when strong contending views prevail concerning the specifics of solutions to social problems is not a terribly well-kept secret. The advantage is that it allows those who formulate policies to obtain a wider base of support for their plan. If the social provision is defined at a high enough level of abstraction so that different parties may read into it what they please, it is easier to reach agreement to implement a plan. And upon implementation there is greater flexibility and potential for experimentation. Of course, once the abstract provision of the plan is operationally transformed, its supporters may shudder in disbelief at what they helped to create and seek its undoing with a vengeance. Hence, there is a fragile quality to the political expedience of abstraction; it can smooth the way for passage of social welfare legislation without necessarily developing the commitments required to support a program over the long haul.

To illustrate, let us examine the Community Action Program (Title II-A) of the Economic Opportunity Act of 1964, a dramatic case in point. It took approximately six months for this program to move from the drawing board to enactment. John Donovan indicates that no single piece of domestic welfare legislation of comparable importance had moved through Congress with such ease and rapidity in a quarter of a century. He also observes: "Actually, there were only a few people in Washington early in 1964 who had any very clear notion of what community action in fact was."[28]

According to the bill presented to Congress, the Community Action Program was defined as a program:

> 1. Which mobilizes and utilizes, in an attack on poverty, public and private resources of any urban or rural, or combined urban and rural geographical area (referred to in this title as a "community"), including but not limited to a state, metropolitan area, county, city, town, multicity unit, or multicounty unit;
>
> 2. Which provides services, assistance, and other activities of variety, scope, and size to give promise of progress toward elimination of poverty through developing employment opportunities, improving human performance, motivation, and productivity, and bettering the conditions under which people live, learn, and work;

3. Which is developed, conducted, and administered with the maximum feasible participation of residents of the areas and members of the groups [served] referred to in section 204(a); and

4. Which is conducted, administered, or coordinated by a public or private nonprofit agency (referred to in this title as a "community action organization") which is broadly representative of the community.[29]

This statement is seemingly innocuous, in part because of the legal syntax, but also because the deft phrasing is general enough to allow different minds to draw different conclusions about the major emphasis of the social provision being offered. The task force of professionals responsible for drafting the antipoverty bill viewed community action as a mechanism for increasing the participation and power of poor in the political life of the community. Moynihan notes that "the occasionally-to-be-encountered observation that Community Action Programs are a federal effort to recreate the urban ethnic political machines that federal welfare legislation helped dismantle, would not misrepresent the attitudes of the task force."[30]

With a few exceptions, during the congressional hearings on the antipoverty bill, there was little explication of the idea that a major provision of community action was to be the transfer of power to the poor. One notable exception was the attorney general, Robert Kennedy, who made the point that the poor were powerless to affect the institutions that served them. He suggested that the aim of the Community Action Program be to change this pattern of powerlessness.[31] Also, Robert F. Wagner, mayor of New York, recognized and was rather unenthusiastic about the provision of decision-making power to the poor. He stated: "I feel very strongly that the sovereign government of each locality in which a community action program is proposed should have the power of approval over the makeup of the planning group, the structure of the planning group, and over the plan."[32]

However, what emerged from the hearings was a number of interpretations, many of which implied that the major provision of community action would involve instrumental, opportunity, or service benefits.[33] Stressing the instrumental provision, Marion Crank, speaker of the Arkansas House of Representatives, told the subcommittee: "The important new feature of Title II is that it will encourage a coordinated effort toward solving some of the serious problems in our area."[34] And emphasizing the provision of service, Robert C. Weaver noted: "The community action programs would focus upon the needs of low income families and persons.

They would provide expanded and improved services and facilities where necessary in such fields as education, job training and counselling, health, and housing and home improvement."[35] But the nebulous quality of the social provision of community action was perhaps most typified in the comments of Representative Perkins who continually referred to Title II as the "community facilities provision."[36] Under the circumstances, it is not surprising that the requirement for "maximum feasible participation" in Section 202 (a) (3), which was to become for politicians the *bete noir* of community action, slipped through the congressional hearings virtually unquestioned.

Thus, depending largely upon the different viewpoints and preferences of those assessing the policy, it was assumed that the major social provision of community action would take one of three forms: (1) an instrument to coordinate the planning and delivery of services; (2) an increase in the level of services made available to the poor; or (3) an increase in the decision-making powers of the poor to formulate and administer their own local programs.

In the legislation the Community Action Program was defined broadly enough to encompass all of these provisions. But two things were left unclear. First was the order of importance and priority to be given these provisions. The possibility that the various provisions were not consonant with one another was largely overlooked; for example, that the transfer of power to the poor might require tactics that would militate against simultaneously increasing the flow of goods and services and impede efforts at coordination. No guidelines were offered for trade-offs among different objectives. Second, and more significantly, there was little probing of the substance of these various social provisions. What types of services did the poor need and want? How much power and influence was enshrouded in the phrase "maximum feasible participation"? Did "participation" mean that the poor were to be advisors or to have a controlling vote? Serious consideration of these choices undoubtedly would have delayed passage of the legislation. Instead it sailed through Congress on the ethereal plane of abstraction.

However, when it finally came down to implementation and efforts were made to specify and operationalize "maximum feasible participation," the program provoked a sense of betrayal and encountered heavy resistance. By 1965, as the first guidelines for involvement of the poor in local decision-making were issued, the mayors were already expressing considerable displeasure over what had been wrought and were demanding that local governments be given greater control over the program.[37] The Bureau of the Budget also reacted by suggesting that the poor should be involved less as policy makers and more as workers for Community Action Agencies.

In 1966, Congress began to impose its own restrictions on the uses of community action funds. And by 1967 the legislation was amended to clarify the substance of the social provision of "maximum feasible participation." The amendments of 1967 gave state, county, and city governments the power to incorporate local Community Action Agencies within their governmental structure or officially to designate other groups to fill this role. Although very few local governments chose to exercise this option, the amendments served to symbolize and reaffirm their fundamental authority and control over local programs. In addition, these amendments designated that Community Action Agency boards must consist of no more than one-third poor people, with the remaining membership divided equally between public officials and representatives from the private sector. When the dust had settled the definition of "maximum feasible participation" as power allocated to the poor through the social provision of community action was being carefully measured on the scale of political feasibility.[38]

Social Provisions as Reflections of Policy Objectives

Earlier we suggested that the choice of one form of social provision over another could be understood in reference to certain underlying values, mainly informed by individualist and collectivist orientations towards social control and consumer sovereignty. While this may afford a general level of explanation and insight, choices concerning social provisions obviously are more complicated than the blunt registration of individualist and collectivist preferences.

Social provisions also directly reflect policy objectives. To comprehend fully why a policy design contains specific provisions requires insight into the assumptions that underlie policy objectives. To achieve such insight we must analyze policy objectives so that we perceive them not simply as ends, but as constructs of means–ends relationships. That is, objectives are the articulation of what are believed to be the important cause and effect relationships of social problems, a statement of the theoretical outlook of those involved in the formulation of policy.

In practice, of course, social welfare policy objectives are rarely stated in theoretical terms since that would tend to make decision-makers sound too tentative and unsure. The notion that "objectives are only theories" does find its way into many research and demonstration programs. But, on the whole, program objectives are put forth with a remarkable degree of assurance that the social provision offers a valid solution to a clearly understood problem.

Policy-makers invariably possess insufficient knowledge. For those in the public sector a condition of political life is that they regularly adopt a higher degree of confidence than may be justified in the efficacy of social welfare programs they must sell to their constituents. If their confidence is misplaced, they lose credibility and may suffer at the polls. Assessing what is at stake in the candid interpretation of policy is a predicament for elected officials engaged in making public decisions. However much planners, administrators, and policy analysts may sympathize with this plight, it is not their own. To be effective in what they do requires a clear grasp of the theoretical and tentative quality of policy objectives. Moynihan's charge that the failure of professionals in the development of the War on Poverty "lay in not accepting—not insisting upon—the theoretical nature of their propositions," may be somewhat inflated but it underscores the point at issue.[39] That is, professional obligation entails the critical examination of the theories and assumptions that support the choice of different social provisions. As Suchman explains:

> The process of seeking to understand the underlying assumptions of an objective is akin to that of questioning the validity of one's hypothesis. Involved is a concern with the theoretical basis of one's belief that "activity A will produce effect B." Such concerns are the earmark of professional growth. So long as one proceeds on faith in accepted procedures without questioning the basis for this faith, one is functioning as a technician rather than a professional. The future development of the various fields of public service as science as well as art will depend to a large extent upon their willingness to challenge the underlying assumptions of their program objectives.[40]

With this in mind let us take another look at the Community Action Program (CAP) and direct our efforts toward understanding why various interpretations were given to the social provision of this vaguely formulated policy. We have already noted that the major thrust of CAP was presumed to be in the form of instrumental, service, or power provisions, depending upon the different viewpoints and preferences of those assessing the policy. By and large these different viewpoints and preferences are not derivatives of whim; rather, in most cases they reflect certain underlying theories and assumptions about the causes and remedies of poverty.

There are many intricate theories of poverty, but the purpose of this discussion is to illustrate generally how theory applies to the analysis of social provisions. Rather than present the details of these theories, we will consider three independent variables around which many poverty theories tend to be organized: *resource deficiency, individual deficiency,* and *institutional deficiency.*[41]

From the viewpoint of *resource deficiency,* lack of resources such as health care and adequate housing is conceived not only as a characteristic of poverty but also as a factor that contributes to its development and perpetuation.[42] More plainly, this is a formal expression of the conventional assumption that, "to get you must first have." To the extent that social provisions of CAP are concentrated upon special kinds of services, such as neighborhood health center and home improvment services, it can be said that program objectives are based on the proposition that poverty can be reduced by changing the circumstances under which people live, especially the availability of health and housing resources.

The perspective of *individual deficiency* is based, in its most primitive form, on Social Darwinism; here poverty is attributed to inherent personal defects which make certain people less fit to survive than others. A less invidious version of the individual deficiency theme focuses upon the "culture of poverty" as the independent variable; here poverty is explained in terms of a cultural and environmental milieu, rather than inherited attributes, that incapacitates the poor. The defect is not in the biology, but in the values, norms, and behaviors of the poor. In either case, the poor people somehow must be changed.[43] To the extent that social provisions of CAP are concentrated upon counseling, training, and educational types of services, program objectives are based on the proposition that to reduce poverty we must change the skills, values, and behaviors of people living under these circumstances.

Poverty may also be explained in terms of *institutional deficiency.* The basic assumption here is that social welfare institutions are malfunctioning and that they operate in such a way as to sustain the conditions of poverty. This perspective is addressed through two social provisions of the Community Action Program. The objective of the instrumental provision, wherein CAP is interpreted mainly as coordinating and planning services, is to improve institutional performance by making it more rational, efficient, and comprehensive. The institutional deficiency here is seen primarily as a technical problem amenable to solution through administrative channels. The provision of power, on the other hand, involves the perception of institutional deficiency as a political problem. The objective is to make social welfare more responsive to the needs of the poor, not through technical rationality, but by increasing the political capacity of the poor to influence the institutions that serve them. To the extent that CAP is interpreted in terms of these social provisions, program objectives are based on the proposition that to reduce poverty we must change institutional structures that contribute to the maintenance of this condition.

Which are the best or the preferred interpretations of the Community Action Program? On this question the analysis sheds little light. An explication of the theories and assumptions that underlie the choice of different social provisions does not create the rules for choosing. It does help to clarify what we are choosing, which is useful in two respects. First, it offers a basis for making judgments about the coherence of policy design in terms of the complementarity of social provisions. Many social welfare policies are designed with multiple objectives, requiring the delivery of more than one type of social provision. In some cases, these objectives may be incompatible because of their underlying assumptions. For instance, it has been suggested that the objectives of service and power provisions of CAP were ill-suited for simultaneous pursuit under one program. The reasons for this can be explained by the different assumptions underlying the objectives. To put it bluntly, if the poor suffer mainly from individual deficiencies (i.e., need services), then increasing their power vis-à-vis service-giving agencies is to place the healer in the arms of the lame. Whereas if institutional deficiency as a political problem is the major thrust of change efforts, then offering increased services only buffers and protects the status quo.

The second function of this analysis is to specify the major independent variables on which we are putting our money, so to speak. Clarification on this point provides guidelines to assemble available empirical data that bear on the validity of the assumptions and also furnishes referents for policy evaluation once it is implemented. On issues of social welfare rarely is the evidence so clear and overwhelmingly weighted in one direction as to be determinate. Nevertheless it is pertinent to inquire about whether evidence exists that a social provision will produce the anticipated outcome. Faith may be a potent sedative for uncertainty, but in the design of social provisions it is an insufficient basis for choice.

Yet the influence of sheer faith in underlying theories and assumptions cannot be ignored; while, ideally, we emphasize the requirement of an empirical grounding, choices regarding social provisions are often as not, in the balance, light on evidence and heavy on faith. We could draw on a dismally large number of illustrations.[44] A prominent example is cited by Connery, *et al.,* in discussing the major assumptions supporting the social provisions of community mental health programs:

> In 1963, when the basic legislation was being considered, Dr. Cummings noted: "There are at the moment, as far as I know, no American studies that demonstrate that, when the quality of care is held constant, community-based treatment facilities function any better than those located in large hospitals." If this remarkable statement is valid, it would appear that the nature of mental health services and the investment of hundreds of millions of dollars throughout the country

was substantially shaped for decades to come on the basis of firmly held and persuasively argued beliefs that lacked a substantial empirical base.[45]

We introduced this section by suggesting that to understand why specific choices are made concerning the social provisions of policy entails an elaboration of theories and assumptions underlying policy objectives. Theories and assumptions have since been discussed in the same breath. At this point we would advise that a distinction be drawn (along the lines noted in Chapter 2) between theories and assumptions, with the former considered to be derived largely from empirical insights and the latter based upon articles of faith and ideology. Obviously, this distinction will often be difficult to make and it will always be relative. Yet heightened sensitivity to the "why" of social choice is engendered by considering not only the proposed cause and effect relationships that underlie policy objectives, but also the degree to which these relationships are informed by theory or assumption—by the tenets of evidence or faith.

What Is Not Provided?

In analyzing the nature of social provisions, we have placed attention upon delineating the alternatives in terms of the form and substance of social welfare benefits. We have also sought to understand the reasons for social choices among these alternatives with reference to broad value orientations as well as theories and assumptions underlying specific policy objectives. Overall, the focus of concern has been upon what is provided. It may then seem somewhat odd to conclude this chapter with the question, "What is not provided?" However, there is another class of latent assumptions often built into the design of social provisions, which we must recognize and examine in a thorough analysis of this dimension of choice. These assumptions do not bear directly upon the cause and effect relationships relating to specific policy objectives, but rather are integral to the design of social provisions in general. They have to do with assumptions about what exists in the external system and can be counted on to accompany the provision of social welfare benefits.

The availability of human resources and supportive services are assumptions concerning what exists in the external system, typically built into the design of social provisions. One need not look very hard to find that the social provisions of welfare policies frequently require human resources that are nonexistent and unlikely to develop within a reasonable period of time. Indeed, it is almost embarrassingly simple to uncover examples.

Consider, for instance, these brief observations on the following four programs.

Public Assistance

In 1965 it was estimated that to obtain the full advantage of services under the 1962 amendments, 31,000 graduate social workers would be needed by 1970. At the time of this estimate, public assistance agencies employed less than 2,500 graduate social workers, and fewer than 3,000 graduate social workers were being produced annually for all public and private programs, most of whom were predisposed to work for private agencies.[46] While the legislation did contain provisions to increase the supply of qualified workers, they were severely inadequate for the task. Examining this record, Steiner notes:

> In some ways the services emphasis did not have a real test, but the disturbing factor is that is was always obvious that personnel to do the job were not available . . . No one had ever claimed that just anybody could provide services. That is the way it worked out, however, and what the House Ways and Means Committee saw in 1967 was the big picture: five years of service, no results. Of course, there was no point in offering as an explanation the absence of trained personnel because there was no more likelihood that trained personnel could be provided in subsequent years than had been the case in previous years.[47]

Community Mental Health

Conservative estimates of the manpower requirements for staffing the nationwide network of centers proposed in the 1965 amendments to the Community Mental Health Centers Act showed a need for 30,000 professionals from the four basic mental health disciplines of psychiatry, psychology, psychiatric social work, and mental health nursing. As reported during the congressional hearings, this figure equalled almost half the total supply of such professional personnel available at that time. Though federal training grants were made available to train additional mental health professionals, the expansion of human resources in these areas are clearly subject to the strictures of prolonged training, especially for the upper echelon of this group, the psychiatrists. This fact led one team of investigators to conclude that, "Even with money available to pay them, it seems highly questionable whether these professionals will be available in sufficient numbers to make the program a reality."[48]

Model Cities

In the 1960s one of the major efforts to combine social and physical planning for the rehabilitation of urban areas was framed in the enabling legislation of the Demonstration Cities Act of 1966 and implemented through what has come to be known as the Model Cities Program. Between 1966 and 1967, 148 localities throughout the nation received funds from the Department of Housing and Urban Development (HUD) to hire staff and to prepare Comprehensive Development Plans (CDP's) within the first program year. The HUD guidelines stipulated that cities follow a predefined, rational, orderly, step-by-step approach in developing their CDP's. The technical requirements for these CDP'S was an ambitious challenge to local community planning. However, as it turned out, this was a challenge that most cities simply could not meet. Even with the extensive assistance of outside consulting firms, few cities were able to do more than approximate the technical planning model prescribed by HUD. By 1969 it became apparent that most cities lacked the staff expertise and resources to do comprehensive planning according to HUD's rigorous model, and in light of products already submitted, the planning model was simplified.[49]

Manpower Training

An expanded role for manpower programs (such as WIN discussed in Chapter 2) is envisioned in the 1970 Manpower Report. Commenting upon this trend, Levitan and Taggart observe that there are major obstacles to large-scale increases in the manpower effort that are often overlooked, not the least of which is the availability of human resources.

> One constraint is the lack of trained manpower to administer projects, a problem which will become more intense as administration is decentralized even if the programs are not expanded. Too often it is assumed that demand will create supply. As proof, many point to the fact that while there were only a handful of manpower "experts" ten years ago there are now many thousands. No doubt there has been an increase in competent personnel, but the administrative difficulties of the programs suggest that many of the instant experts are lacking adequate preparation. If the programs are continuously expanded, it is doubtful that personnel can be supplied to take care of needs.[50]

In addition to human resources, the availability of supportive services also warrants consideration in the analysis of social provisions. For example, a remedial manpower training service, no matter how competent its staff, may be a provision of limited utility if recipients are unable to obtain basic education, medical aid, day-care for children, and other supportive services, not to mention eventual job placement and, perhaps, relocation assistance. Dubinsky decribes one such training program forged in a cauldron of heated rhetoric and arduous negotiations between indigenous black groups from Pittsburgh's poverty neighborhoods and local construction unions. Out of a hard-won struggle, the basic provision of on-the-job training slots was finally secured. But when the program was implemented the trainees often did not show up for work. At the point of success, major difficulties were encountered because a supportive service that received casual attention in the policy design failed to materialize. Many job sites were out of reach of public transportation and few trainees owned automobiles. Only as an afterthought, following a period of confusion and hardship for trainees and program officials, was this necessary supportive service created through a special contract for transportation with the city bus company.[51]

Social provisions are often dependent for implementation upon a complex system of interrelated services and human resources. In examining the design of social provisions we must be attentive to what exists in this larger context, the field or system in which the benefit is being offered. Thus, through the analytic lens applied to this dimension of choice, we view the form and substance of social provisions not only in terms of values, theories, and assumptions regarding what is explicitly proposed, but also with an eye toward what is taken for granted as available from the external system in the way of supportive services and human resources. Accordingly, we may begin to discern both what is intended and what is possible in the choice of policy benefits.

Once these benefits have been decided upon, it is necessary that some organizational structure be created to connect the social provision with relevant supportive services and the recipient population, which leads us to the next chapter and an analysis of the systematic arrangements for the delivery of social provisions.

Notes

[1]Alva Myrdal, *Nation and Family* (MIT Paperback Edition) (Cambridge: MIT Press, 1968), pp. 133–53. A similar position is offered in Charlotte Whitton, *Dawn of Ampler Life* (Toronto: MacMillan of Canada, 1943). And for an utopian proposal where benefits in kind are employed more generally as the foundation of a guaranteed standard of living, see Paul Goodman and Percival Goodman, *Communitas* (2nd ed. rev.) (New York: Vintage Books, 1960), pp. 188–217.

[2]Myrdal, *Nation and Family,* pp. 141–42.

[3]The question of how *directly* the objective is served, can be asked quite apart from the issue of how *well* the objective is served. The former involves effectiveness in terms of impact, the latter in terms of performance or ultimate outcome.

[4]For further discussion of this assumption see James Buchanan, "What Kind of Redistribution Do We Want?" *Economica,* Vol. 35 (May 1968); and Martin Rein, "Social Policy Analysis as the Interpretation of Beliefs," *Journal of the American Institute of Planners,* Vol. 37, No. 5 (September 1971).

[5]This assumption, drawing upon the interrelated notions of the "common welfare" and the "harmony of human interests," is examined by Gunnar Myrdal, who observes, "We want to believe that what we hold to be desirable for society is desirable for all its members." See Gunnar Myrdal, *Value in Social Theory,* ed. Paul Streeten (London: Routledge and Kegan Paul, 1958), p. 137

[6]Alva Myrdal, *Nation and Family,* p. 151.

[7]Gerald M. Holden, "A Consideration of Benefits-in-Kind for Children," in *Children's Allowances and the Economic Welfare of Children,* ed. Eveline M. Burns (New York: Citizen's Committee for Children of New York, 1968), p. 151.

[8]Asa Briggs, "The Welfare State in Historical Perspective," in *Social Welfare Institutions,* ed. Mayer Zald (New York: John Wiley & Sons, 1965), p. 62.

[9]Sigmund Freud, *Civilization and Its Discontents,* trans. and ed. James Strachey (New York: W. W. Norton, 1962), p. 42.

[10]Myrdal, *Nation and Family,* p. 150.

[11]Milton Friedman, "The Role of Government in Education," in *Economics and The Public Interest,* ed. Robert Solo (New Brunswick: Rutgers University Press, 1955), p. 124.

[12]Myrdal, *Nation and Family,* p. 150.

[13]See, for example, Shirley Buttrick, "On Choice and Services," *Social Service Review,* Vol. 44, No. 4 (December 1970), 427–33; Anthony Pascal, "New Departures in Social Services," *Social Welfare Forum* (New York: Columbia University Press, 1969), pp. 75–85.

[14]James Thompson, *Organizations in Action* (New York: McGraw-Hill, 1967), pp. 17–18.

[15]Friedman, "The Role of Government in Education," p. 144.

[16]John K. Galbraith, *The Affluent Society* (New York: Mentor Books, 1958), p. 205.

[17]For example, see Friedrick Hayek, "The *Non Sequitor* of the 'Dependence Effect,'" in *Private Wants and Public Needs,* ed. Edmund S. Phelps (New York: W. W. Norton, 1962), pp. 37–42.

[18]Alice M. Rivlin, *Systematic Thinking for Social Action* (Washington, D.C.: Brookings Institution, 1971), pp. 137–38.

[19]A more detailed discussion of these conditions is presented by Milton Friedman, "The Role of Government in a Free Society," in *Private Wants and Public Needs,* ed. Edmund Phelps (New York: W. W. Norton, 1962), pp. 104–17.

[20]Samuel Mencher, *Poor Law to Poverty Program* (Pittsburgh: University of Pittsburgh Press, 1967), p. 336.

[21]For example, see Friedman, "The Role of Government in Education"; Buttrick, "On Choice and Services"; and Christopher Jencks, "Private Schools for Black Children," *New York Times Magazine,* November 3, 1968.

[22]At some point in the utopian future, status/prestige as a distinct category may be appended to this list of social provisions. In Bellamy's society in *Looking Backward* (see Chapter 3) the distribution of opportunities as well as goods and resources was more or less equal among the population. But here the link between status/prestige and wealth/power was broken. Status positions and symbols that conferred honor and esteem with neither direct nor indirect material benefits (i.e. had no market value) became the major form of social provision to compensate those who made special contributions to society.

[23]It should be noted that with both cash and vouchers, our analysis of the substance of *social* provisions ends at the point that recipients obtain either of these benefits. These benefits are allocated outside the marketplace. The subsequent choices that are made concerning how these benefits are to be spent involve individual market transactions. What is purchased becomes a matter of individual choice on the open marketplace much like any other, whether it is how to spend the weekly paycheck, the tax refund from the government, or the credit at a local department store.

[24]For a review of the various perspectives that might be included under this type of provision, see Scott Briar and Henry Miller, *Problems and Issues in Social Casework* (New York: Columbia University Press, 1972).

[25]See, for example, Pamela Roby, "How to Look at Day-Care Programs," *Social Policy,* Vol. 3 No. 2 (July/August 1972), pp. 220–26.

[26]Neil Gilbert and Harry Specht, "Institutional Racism and Educational Policy," *Journal of Social Policy* (Winter 1973), pp. 27–39.

[27]Further discussion of these alternatives is presented in the next chapter.

[28]John C. Donovan, *The Politics of Poverty* (New York: Pegasus, 1967), p. 40.

[29]U.S. House of Representatives, *A Bill to Mobilize the Human and Financial Resources of the Nation to Combat Poverty in the United States,* 88th Cong., 2d sess., March 1964, H. R. 10443, pp. 17–18.

[30]Daniel P. Moynihan, "What Is 'Community Action'?" *The Public Interest,* No. 5 (Fall 1966), 7.

[31]U.S. House of Representatives, Economic Opportunity Act of 1964. *Hearing before the Subcommittee on the War on Poverty Program* (Washington, D.C.: Government Printing Office, 1964), Part I, p. 305.

[32]Statement of Robert F. Wagner before the Ad Hoc Subcommittee on the Poverty Program of the House Education and Labor Committee, April 16, 1964, pp. 3–4 (mimeographed).

[33]For a more thorough discussion of these various interpretations, see Moynihan, "What Is 'Community Action'?"

[34]Statement by the Honorable Marion H. Crank, Speaker of the Arkansas House of Representatives, before the Ad Hoc Subcommittee on the Poverty Program of the House Education and Labor Committee, April 10, 1964, p. 3 (mimeographed).

[35]Statement of Robert C. Weaver before the Ad Hoc Subcommittee on the Poverty Program of the House Education and Labor Committee, April 16, 1964, p. 12 (mimeographed).

[36]Quoted in Elinor Graham, "Poverty and the Legislative Process," *Poverty as a Public Issue,* ed. Ben B. Seligman (New York: Free Press, 1965), pp. 251–71.

[37]For example, see Advisory Commission on Intergovernmental Relations, *Intergovernmental Relations in the Poverty Program* (Washington, D. C.: Government Printing Office, 1966); and William F. Haddad, "Mr. Shriver and the Savage Politics of Poverty," *Harpers,* December 1965, pp. 43–50.

[38]In 1973 the scale tipped and the Office of Economic Opportunity (OEO) was being dismantled. Some of its programs were to be transferred to other agencies such as the Department of Health, Education, and Welfare. However, federal support for the Community Action Program, the keystone of OEO, was to be totally eliminated.

[39]Daniel P. Moynihan, *Maximum Feasible Misunderstanding* (New York: Free Press, 1969), pp. 188–89.

[40]Edward A. Suchman, *Evaluative Research* (New York: Russell Sage, 1967), p. 41.

[41]For a concise review of the literature and an elaboration of these perspectives on poverty, see Martin Rein, *Social Policy* (New York: Random House, 1970), pp. 417–45.

[42]For an excellent example along this line of study, see Alvin Schorr, *Slums and Social Insecurity* (Washington, D. C.: Government Printing Office, 1963).

[43]A thorough exposition and critique of the culture-of-poverty perspective is presented by Charles A. Valentine, *Culture and Poverty* (Chicago: University of Chicago Press, 1968).

[44]See Chapter 2, footnote 19.

[45]Robert H. Connery, *et al., The Politics of Mental Health* (New York: Columbia University Press, 1968), p. 478.

[46]Advisory Council on Public Welfare, *Having the Power We Have the Duty,* Report to the Secretary of Health, Education, and Welfare (Washington, D.C.: Government Printing Office, 1966), p. 79.

[47]Gilbert Steiner, *The State of Welfare* (Washington, D.C.: Brookings Institution, 1971), p. 39.

[48]Connery, *et al., The Politics of Mental Health,* p. 530.

[49]Marshall Kaplan, Gans, and Kahn, *The Model Cities Program: A Comparative Analysis of the Planning Process in Eleven Cities* (Washington, D.C.: Dept. of Housing and Urban Development, Government Printing Office, 1970); and Neil Gilbert and Harry Specht, *Planning for Model Cities: Process, Product, Performance, and Predictions* (Washington, D.C.: Government Printing Office, forthcoming).

[50]Sar A. Levitan and Robert Taggart, III, *Social Experimentation and Manpower Policy: The Rhetoric and the Reality* (Baltimore: Johns Hopkins, 1971), p. 85.

[51]Irwin Dubinsky, *Operation Dig: A Black Militant Program to Train Trade Union Craftsmen* (Ph.D. dissertation, Graduate School of Public and International Affairs, University of Pittsburgh, 1971).

The Structure of the Delivery System

*"You're very strict," said the Mayor, "but multiply your strict-
ness a thousand times and it would still be nothing compared
with the strictness that the Authority imposes on itself. Only a
total stranger could ask a question like yours. Is there a Control
Authority? There are only Control Authorities. Frankly, it isn't
their function to hunt out errors in the vulgar sense, for errors
don't happen, and even when once in a while an error does
happen, as in your case, who can say finally that it's an error?"*
FRANZ KAFKA,
The Castle

5 When Kafka's hero wanders through a bureaucratic maze continually confounded in his attempt to make sense of the system,
his fictional world is not far removed from the real life experiences encountered by many applicants for social welfare benefits. The system for delivering these benefits is arbitrarily closed to certain
applicants; others are able to enter the delivery system only to find themselves shuffled from one agency to another without receiving appropriate
assistance. And many will ask in despair for a "Control Authority"
through which to seek redress for their grievances. Often as not, the
answer they receive closely approximates the quote cited above.

This situation does not necessarily arise out of totalitarian mentalities or
bad intentions on the part of those who create the plans for the delivery
of social welfare benefits. From the viewpoint of planners and administrators the choices confronted in designing delivery systems are varied and
difficult to untangle. In this chapter we will examine these choices and

explore areas of uncertainty in the design of systems for delivering social welfare benefits. Though much of the analysis is applicable to the various forms of social provision discussed in the previous chapter, the specific emphasis here will be upon the delivery of provisions in the form of social services.

The delivery system, as noted in Chapter 2, refers to the organizational arrangements among distributors and between distributors and consumers of social welfare benefits in the context of the local community. We focus on "the local community" because this is the level at which the over-whelming majority of distributors and consumers come together. "Distributors" of service may be individual professionals, professional groups, public and private agencies, and voluntary associations acting separately or in concert to provide services in private offices, settlement houses, employment centers, welfare departments, multiservice centers and so forth.

The number of possible choices in designing delivery systems is quite large. Consider, for example, the following six choices (which by no means exhausts the possibilities):

Distributors may:

Be administratively centralized	or	Decentralized
Combine services (e.g. health, probation and welfare)	or	Offer single services
Physically locate under one roof	or	Maintain separate facilities
Coordinate their efforts	or	Never communicate
Rely on professional employees	or	Employ consumers to give services
Place decision-making authority in the hands of "experts"	or	Give major decision-making authority to the "community" (or service users)

If we were to consider only these six choices and treat them as though they were each dichotomous (which they are not), we would end up with sixty-four possible delivery system combinations. Obviously, then, we must find some means to make the selection manageable. However, before presenting the analytic concepts that can help to narrow and focus the discussion of this dimension of choice, it is useful to outline certain basic problems to which choices regarding the design of local delivery systems are addressed.

Problems of Service Delivery

In recent years, major changes have occurred in the size and scope of social welfare services. The great social upheavals of the 1960s were associated with an enormous increase in health, education, and welfare services, borne primarily by public funds. For example, between 1949 and 1959, public expenditures for these social services increased from only 13.7 to 27 billion dollars; but between 1959 and 1969, expenditures leaped from 27 to 83.8 billion dollars.[1] These increases were stimulated by national legislation to help communities deal with poverty, mental health, unemployment, delinquency, education, and the general quality of urban life. The development and growth of local services were accomplished, for the most part, with remarkable dispatch and no small amount of confusion.

Attendant upon this helter skelter expansion, increased attention has been directed toward issues concerning both the effectiveness of services and service delivery. Although the two sets of questions are interrelated, this chapter is addressed to the latter set—service delivery—which has to do with the relationships, connections, and exchanges among suppliers of social services and between suppliers and users of social services.

Broadly speaking, issues of the effectiveness of service delivery relate to three kinds of questions about arrangements in the delivery system: (1) Where shall authority and control for decision making be located? (2) Who will carry out the different tasks to be performed? (3) What will be the composition (i.e., number of types of units) of the delivery system?

Great social ferment and expansion of services are bound to induce heightened competition for resources. With increased competition, these service-delivery questions often emerge in environments that may be extremely turbulent, both politically and socially. In such environments the proposed answers to these questions are likely to reflect conflicting desires and social values. Thus, for example, in answer to questions about where authority and control should be vested, the value of participatory democracy may be emphasized regardless of its impact on the efficiency of service delivery. Issues having to do with the value of efficiency compete with other value questions that may be equally important to society but not equally relevant to service delivery—such as questions of providing jobs for low-income people in social agencies as reparation or compensation for past social injustices, and increasing participation in agency decision-making to spur community development for change-oriented social movements.

In the heat of controversy, the criticism of service delivery intensifies. Such criticism tends to focus upon the characteristic failings of local service-delivery systems which include *fragmentation, discontinuity, unaccountability,* and *inaccessibility.* These problematic facets of service delivery have been amply documented and analyzed in the literature.[2] Plans to reform the organization and delivery of social services usually concern one or more of these problems, though they rarely concern all.

For a brief operational description of these problems consider the following hypothetical circumstances: A man in an automobile accident is rushed by ambulance to ward "A" where he is examined; he is next taken to ward "B" for medical treatment, and then moved to ward "C" for rest and observation. If wards "A," "B" and "C" are in different parts of town, operate on different schedules, and provide overlapping services—that's *fragmentation*. If the ambulance disappears after dropping the patient at ward "A"—that's *discontinuity*. If the distance between the accident and ward "A" is too far or is there is no ambulance or if our patient is not admitted to the ward because of his social class, ethnic affiliation, and the like, or if he is taken to a ward for mental patients—that's *inaccessibility*. And when any or all of these circumstances obtain and our patient has no viable means of redressing his grievances—the delivery system suffers from *unaccountability*.

These problems have many facets, are interconnected at some points, and span a broader range of issues than we have just described. Problems of fragmentation concern organizational characteristics and relationships, especially coordination, location, specialization, and duplication of services. (For example, are services available in one place? Do agencies try to mesh their services?) Problems of inaccessibility concern obstacles to a person's entering the network of local social services. (For example, does bureaucratic ritualism and selectivity based on social class, race, success potential, or other characteristics exclude certain persons from service?) Problems of discontinuity concern obstacles to a person's movement through the network of services and the gaps that appear as an agency tries to match resources to needs. (For example, are channels of communication and referral lacking?) Problems of *unaccountability* concern relationships between persons served and the decision-makers in service organizations. (For example, is the person needing help able to influence decisions that affect his circumstances? Are the decision-makers in the service organizations to which he must turn insensitive or unresponsive to his needs and interests?)

Phrased as policy issues, these problems confront the policy planner and the administrator with a set of choices which, though conceptually distinct, become confounded with one another in practice. That is, the ideal service-delivery system is one in which services are *integrated, continuous, accessible* and *accountable*. However, taken separately each of these ideal elements strains against one or more of the others. Briefly, we may summarize some of the choices as follows:

1. *Reduce* fragmentation and discontinuity by increasing coordination, opening new channels of communication and referral, and eliminating duplication of services (possibly *increasing* unaccountability and inaccessibility).

2. *Reduce* inaccessibility by creating new means of access to services, and duplicating existing service efforts (possibly *increasing* fragmentation).

3. *Reduce* unaccountability by creating means for clients or consumers to have in-put into, and increased decision-making authority over, the system (possibly *increasing* fragmentation and discontinuity).

Problems in service delivery do not exist because there is a shortage of ideas about how to improve the situation. On the contrary, the technical repertoire of social planners and public administrators includes a wide range of strategies for effecting the delivery of local services. It is matters of choice and uncertainty that need to be resolved. We approach this task in the following sections by: identifying the choices among service-delivery strategies; analyzing the types of systemic changes related to different strategies; suggesting what else needs to be known empirically about the effects of these strategies; and explicating the alternative theoretical paradigms that influence the selection of different strategies.

Service-Delivery Strategies

Proposals for reform invariably accompany critical analyses of service delivery. While specific proposals for reform of service delivery contain considerable variation in detail, most correspond to one or another of six general types of strategies. Each of these strategies addresses one of the three service-delivery questions mentioned earlier:

A. Strategies to restructure authority for, and control of, policy making
  1. Coordination
  2. Citizen participation
B. Strategies to reorganize the allocation of tasks
  3. Role attachments
  4. Professional disengagement
C. Strategies to alter the composition (i.e., number and types of units) of the delivery system
  5. Specialized access structures
  6. Purposive duplication

Each of these strategies seeks to restructure local service systems in ways that presumably will enhance service delivery. That is, coordination and citizen participation each impinge in different ways upon the bureaucratic hierarchy of the system. Role attachments and professional disengagement alter the combination of roles and status characteristics of the system.[3] The development of specialized access structures and purposive duplication change the substantive composition of the elements in the system.

The following summaries describe the general thrust of each of the strategies and some of their potential consequences.

Strategies to Restructure Authority:
Coordination and Citizen Participation

Coordination. Social service workers, along with other professional groups, are quick to declare their faith in the generic, the whole man, and the comprehensive approach to serving clients. They recognize the complexity of social causation and the interdependencies among mental, physical, and environmental factors that influence clients' functioning and life chances. At the same time, the thrust among professionals is towards specialization, the development of high-powered technical skills within narrowly defined areas of expertise. In one sense coordination of services is advocated to mitigate the strains produced by the juxtaposition of specialization and the comprehensive approach in the professional value structure.

Coordination is a strategy aimed at the development of an integrated comprehensive social service system through either centralization or federation of service agencies.[4] These two processes are exemplified in recent approaches to the organization of local social services in England and the United States.

In 1970 the British Parliament passed the Local Authority and Social Services Act, prescribing a major reorganization of local service agencies. This reorganization entails the centralization of the staffs of, and the functions performed by, children's and welfare departments, community development services, home-help services, and other local agencies under the administrative auspices of newly created Local Authority Social Services Departments (LASSD). Prior attempts were made to integrate these services in the 1950s through the establishment of local agency coordinating committees. Titmuss notes that these attempts were not successful; local services continued to be characterized by "too much balkanized rivalry in the field of welfare," while demands for better coordination increased.[5] In turning to the LASSD as a mechanism for administrative centralization of decisions, the British have utilized what Simon recommends as among the most powerful of coordinative procedures.[6]

However, the implications of efforts to increase coordination through administrative unification go beyond merely posing a remedy for service fragmentation. For instance, administrative centralization of services tends to increase the organizational distance between clients and decision-making authorities. It is with this problem in mind that Townsend sounds a note of caution about LASSD's creating a monopoly over certain services and the possible adverse effects of such a development on social choice and accountability to service recipients.[7] Centralization may lead to an internalization and perhaps heightening of what were previously *inter*organizational strains. The potential for *intra*organizational conflict is sharpened, especially when a variety of heretofore autonomous agencies with different aims, technologies, and perceptions of clients and problems are cast into a unitary organizational mold, as in LASSD.[8]

In addition, the consolidation of services under one administrative structure limits service accessibility to one organizational door. The "single door" access to the service network is somewhat of a metaphor because the "door" may in fact be at a number of centers geographically dispersed throughout a community; it is a "single door" only in the sense that it functions according to the rules and regulations of one administrative authority; service network intake is concentrated in the hands of a relatively few gatekeepers bound by the same set of administrative policies. Operationally, the "single door" could prove to be a mechanism to rationalize service delivery from the standpoint of case referral and continuity, and/or an impervious barrier to the local service network for those individuals and groups that, inadvertently or by design, do not fit the administrative criteria of eligibility for service.

Another major approach to the coordination of services is through federation which occasionally involves the *geographic* centralization of different agency resources but not their administrative unification. Recent efforts along these lines have been made in the United States under the heading of "neighborhood service centers" sponsored by the Community Action Program of the Office of Economic Opportunity. Federative structures encompass a variety of more or less formal and binding arrangements. This variability is usually expressed by reference to the degree of time, resources, and organizational decision-making authority invested by member organizations in the joint enterprise.[9] Warren distinguishes between a federation and a coalition in this way: the former is an ongoing collaboration with a formal staff structure that has some decision-making authortiy generally subject to ratification by component agencies; the coalition is more informal and ad hoc with no sharing or modifications of component agency decision-making authority.[10]

Federative arrangements require that organizations pool their skills, resources, knowledge, and manpower in a cooperative venture. The costs to member agencies of such an undertaking frequently are incommensurate with the organizational benefits of coordination.[11] By and large the goals and policies of local service agencies are not like interlocking pieces of a big jigsaw puzzle that, given time, patience, and a constructive mentality, can be fit neatly into the frame of a common cause. The fit, of course, can be accomplished but with costs to organizational autonomy that many organizations are disinclined to pay. Thus, federative efforts often result in loosely knit coalitions that fall considerably short of the cooperative ideal of coordination. To illustrate, consider the following comparison of the ideal of coordination with the operational reality in a neighborhood service center:

> Take the hypothetical case of a welfare client entering the neighborhood service center and reporting to the receptionist that the ceiling in her apartment has collapsed, damaging some of the furniture and creating an unnecessary skylight. What should follow is something like this: the case is referred to a family service worker who gets all the details from the client. The neighborhood lawyer is asked by the family service worker to find out if the landlord is responsible for making repairs and paying the cost of damages. In the course of his investigation, the lawyer learns that the landlord owns a number of slum dwellings in the neighborhood; he reports this to the coordinator who, in turn, calls a meeting with the citizens' housing committee to discuss this problem. The committee decides to approach the landlord requesting that he upgrade his properties; the landlord refuses to do so and health aides are then sent to inspect the properties, the lawyer is asked to review the ramifications of a rent strike, and the citizens form a picket line around the landlord's home in suburbia. While the landlord is taking an impromptu vacation in Florida, the family service worker has not forgotten the client. The public assistance consultant is asked to obtain a relocation grant, the employment worker is called upon to place the client in a work-training program, the client's children are enrolled in the local day-care center, and other local resources —such as homemakers and Planned Parenthood—are utilized in an exhaustive effort to move the client out of poverty.
>
> This example suggests how component services might be integrated in a comprehensive attack on poverty—an ideal rarely achieved. In the actual situation, it would be discovered that the lawyer could provide service to the individual client and thereby advise on the landlord's responsibility for damages. But he could not counsel the citizens' committee on the legality of a rent strike, since providing service to a group is against agency policy; the rationale is that, by pooling resources, the group could afford to buy this service in a private market. The health aides would need organizational permission to leave the area they were currently inspecting in order to focus an intensive effort upon the landlord's properties which are dispersed throughout the neighborhood. Their moving would conflict with the Allegheny County Health Department's service strategy which involves saturating the neighborhood with inspections, section by section. The Planned Parenthood unit could provide immediate birth-control assistance only if the client

was graced by holy matrimony; otherwise, this agency's policy dictates that certain procedures, such as obtaining parental consent for girls under twenty-one or somehow establishing that they are "clearly emancipated," first be fulfilled. While the public assistance consultant could check on the availability of a relocation grant, like the others he has no power to transcend the rules and regulations of his agency; and grants of this nature are generally not provided by the Allegheny County Department of Public Assistance.

Each service unit is thus part of an autonomous organization, having its own goals, policies, and needs, which are at times different from those of the coordinator, the client, and the citizens. These service units "work together" in the sense of being situated, usually, under one roof in one neighborhood service center. While this proximity facilitates communication, it does not dictate cooperation.[12]

In comparing administrative centralization and federation as means to coordinate local social services, the crucial distinction resides in the different control mechanisms employed in each arrangement.[13] In other words, it hinges on the constraints and inducements used to insure commitment and to cement cooperation among the component service units. Federative structures involve voluntary collaboration of autonomous agencies wherein cooperation is based primarily upon reciprocity; units in these structures are not bound to a formal hierarchy of positions based upon rational-legal authority as under a centralized administration such as Britain's LASSD. Compared to bureaucratic authority, reciprocity is a tenuous mechanism of control. It is operative, as Dahl and Lindblom note, "provided that the people have the same norms and conceptions of reality."[14] The normative conceptions of local social service agencies, however, do not always fit this prescription.

Coordination is the strategy most widely employed in efforts to alter service delivery. It encompasses a variety of administrative decisions and organizational adjustments. In addition to large-scale efforts at syntonizing service-delivery units, this strategy also includes smaller-scale and less dramatic modifications of the delivery system. For example, if there is a bottleneck at the entry point to a service or series of services, an expanded intake unit which provides appropriate intervention may be developed; or, if some clients have difficulty reaching these service units a jitney transportation service might be introduced. These are examples of the types of service-delivery-related decisions that may enhance the consolidation of decision-making authority by coordination.

Citizen participation.   Unlike coordination strategies where redistribution of authority is geared to take place among agencies, the strategy of citizen participation is aimed at redistribution of decision-making authority and control between agencies and the client population. The rationale for citizen participation as applied to delivery systems is that clients will be guaranteed access and accountability if people like themselves are in positions to influence service-delivery decisions. Neither the good will of professionals (viewed at best as paternalistic and at worst as nonexistent by the most militant advocates of this strategy) nor bureaucratic rationality is considered sufficiently reliable to secure responsiveness to recipients' needs because both professionals and organizations have multiple objectives—their own survival in the system foremost.

Like coordination strategies, the redistribution of authority via citizen participation is distinguished according to different levels or types of participation wherein authority is shared to varying degrees. There are almost as many typologies of citizen participation as there are social scientists who write on this subject. For example, Arnstein identifies nine levels of participation ranging from manipulation to citizen control, in terms of the degrees of authority that are redistributed in different forms of citizen participation.[15] Spiegel discusses types of citizen participation from the point of view of the level of government involved, the functional area in which decisions are made, and the degree of technicism involved in the decision.[16] Kramer approaches the analysis of this strategy by focusing on the functions and purposes of different types of citizen participation which he describes as ranging along a continuum from receiving information, to advising, to planning jointly, to having complete control.[17]

But ignoring the various nuances, three modal types tend to emerge. First is *nonredistributive participation* or pseudo-participation; this may involve therapy, education, or plain deception; in any case, there is no perceptible change in the established pattern of authority. Second is *nominal participation* or tokenism; citizen influence on decision-making authority is clear and present though only to a degree that makes very little practical difference in final outcomes. Third is *redistributive participation* or "power to the people"; here the shift in authority is such that citizen participants are able to exert substantive influence on decisions affecting the delivery system.

Citizen participation is a strategy where the means represents a value in its own right, that value being democracy. The basic assumption is that a democratic delivery system will, indeed, be more responsive to client needs than a system where decision-making is the exclusive prerogative of professionals. However, it is possible that a system can be democratized and at the same time suffer a deterioration in the delivery of services, in which case the strategy might be valid for broader political reasons but not for the objectives being considered here.

Although participatory democracy connotes the idealized New England town meeting where everybody had a right to vote (except, of course,

women, slaves, and those too poor to own land), in practice citizen participation invariably requires the election or appointment of representatives.
People simply do not have the time or the inclination to participate in
every decision that affects them. The point is that, rhetoric notwithstanding, this strategy must come to grips with the notion of representativeness
and the concomitant issues of *which* citizens participate, on *whose behalf*,
and *how* they are chosen.

Recent experiences suggest some of the problematic facets of this strategy. For instance, neighborhood elections for city councilmen and other
representatives to the larger democratic order tend to differ from neighborhood elections for citizen representatives to local service-delivery systems
in at least one important respect—the voter turnout for election of citizen
representatives is, by comparison, usually negligible. In Pittsburgh less
than 2 percent and in Philadelphia less than 3 percent of eligible residents
participated in such elections.[18] Kramer reports that "the numerous neighborhood elections in San Francisco and Santa Clara can best be described
as psuedo-political processes."[19] In addition, it is not uncommon for
citizen representatives to be appointed by social service agencies or be
self-selected rather than chosen through some type of electoral process.[20]

What is lacking in many endeavors to select citizen representatives are
formal mechanisms of accountability to insure that the opinions and objectives of participants are valid expressions of local sentiment. In the absence
of such accountability, the strategy of citizen participation has the potential for reproducing, on a different plane, the very difficulties it seeks to
ameliorate. As Weissman observes, "Community control tends to become
control of the community by some elements to the exclusion of others and
does not necessarily lead to more effective services."[21] Under these circumstances, "welfare colonialism" may be replaced by an approach to local
planning and decision-making in which an elite group of citizen activists
monopolizes the roles of neighborhood spokesmen. And, in extreme cases,
citizen activists may even become a new generation of "political bosses"
who accumulate much of the power and many of the prerogatives they
opposed in the "welfare colonialists."[22]

Strategies to Reorganize
the Allocation of Tasks:
Role Attachments and Professional Disengagement

Role attachments.   Social services, in the main, are performed by professionals from the middle classes. Though services are offered to the entire
community, a disproportionate segment of the population in need of these
services comes from the lower socioeconomic classes. The class chasm
between servers and served is viewed, according to role attachment strat-

egy, as an impasse to movement into and through local delivery systems. The explanation for this impasse may be summarized as follows: The middle-class professional cannot understand the lower-class client's outlook on life, is ignorant about the behavioral patterns and values of the client's subculture, is inarticulate in the client's patois, and is perceived as officious and "uptight." This is so partly because professionals may be officious and partly because the norms of objectivity and impersonal treatment prescribe behavior that may be defined as unfriendly in the eyes of lower-class clients who are ignorant about the behavior and values of the professional subculture, inarticulate by middle-class standards, and who are perceived as recalcitrant or even threatening in the eyes of professionals. From this perspective, problems of access and discontinuity are cast more in terms of social stratification than organizational structure.[23] The case is put succinctly by Miller and Riessman:

> The agencies must take upon themselves the responsibility for seeing that the individual patient gets to the service, or gets from one service to another. Without the assumption of this responsibility, the concept of continuity of care or services will become a meaningless programmatic shibboleth. Nor can these problems be resolved through administrative improvements alone. *A human link is needed.*[24] (Italics added.)

This human link is the indigenous nonprofessional aide; a person who, by virtue of his style and special skills, can bridge the gap between professional agencies and lower-class clientele, serving what Brager describes as a social-class-mediating function.[25] Certainly, there are other general economic and political values that support the employment of indigenous nonprofessionals, but it is only as expediters of service that such employment is relevant to a discussion of delivery-system strategies.

At least three potential consequences of this strategy are counterproductive to the results envisioned. First, the employment of nonprofessionals may translate literally to mean that lower-class clients will receive services that are amateurish or of a lesser quality than is offered by professionals, the nonprofessional's style and indigenous savvy notwithstanding; i.e., the rich get professional service and the poor get participation. Second, even when nonprofessionals are competent to perform services, efforts to integrate them into the delivery structure normally engender stiff resistance from professionals. Pruger and Specht comment upon the inevitability and the source of this resistance.

> It is inevitable because it is rooted in the virtually irresistible structural forces that shape organizational behavior . . . In the case of the orga-

nizationally based professions, the forces that insure organizational discipline complement the pressures that induce professional reliability. And because much of the professional's self-image rests on this perception of his dearly bought competence, competitors arriving on the scene through nontraditional routes must almost certainly be considered impudent upstarts, if not conscious usurpers.[26]

Finally, even when nonprofessionals are effective in linkage roles and are integrated into the service-delivery structure, the latter will vitiate the former, and their effectiveness will wane under pressures to resolve the strains between bureaucratic conformity and the freewheeling style of the indigenous worker. After examining the integration of nonprofessionals into agency structures, Hardcastle concludes that "the diminution of the nonprofessional's indigenous qualities—the emphasis on primary role skills, extemporaneousness, and lower-class behavior and communication patterns—appears inevitable because of the essentially bureaucratic nature of the organization."[27] In addition, it is not surprising to find that once they are on the job, many nonprofessionals bend their efforts toward becoming professionals. They seek the financial and status rewards that accrue to those who achieve higher degrees of usable knowledge and skill.[28]

Professional disengagement. While the imperative of bureaucratic conformity may cramp the style of nonprofessionals, forcing them to adopt a professional or quasi-professional modus operandi, it has also been observed that the same imperative operates to inhibit professional functioning. For example, Levy describes a public welfare setting where the discrepancy between the needs of administration and those of clients poses an acute moral dilemma for many workers.[29] He suggests that the high turnover rate of workers in this setting was related to the irreconcilability of their inner feelings with the stringent logic of welfare administration. Piliavin states the case more generally:

> Social work has acquired many of the earmarks of a profession, including a professional association that has developed and promulgated standards, goals, and an ethical code for those providing social services. The members of this association and other social workers guided by its framework of values encounter a dilemma unknown to their early predecessors: they find agency policies and practices frequently in conflict with avowed professional norms.[30]

Given these circumstances, it seems that the way to enhance the delivery of social services is not to tinker with bureaucratic structure, but rather to disengage from it altogether. That is, professionals are advised to undertake private practice on a fee-for-service basis to circumvent the constraints to service delivery posed by agency policies; they are to change roles from bureaucrats to entrepreneurs. As many people who use social services could not afford to support a fee system, it is further proposed that the financial base for implementation of this strategy be furnished through government grants similar to those administered through programs of medical care to the aged.[31]

Allowing that government financing for private social services can somehow be accomplished through the use of vouchers, this strategy has certain limitations with regard to service delivery. The private practitioner may have expertise in public welfare, child guidance, corrections, marital counseling, family services, school social work, services to the aged, and the like, but he cannot possibly be a specialist in all of them. In this sense he is subject to the same professional myopia as the agency-based worker, except that agencies may incorporate a variety of specialists. Similar to the bureaucratic delivery of services, there is very little to prevent the private practitioner from imposing his particular brand of service upon the client, be it education, therapy, advocacy, or some other technology, rather than dealing with the recipient's special needs. And even for the least avaricious, the tendency to interpret client problems in terms of one's own expertise receives a dash of positive reinforcement in the fee-for-service proposition. As a means to improve the accessibility and coherence of the delivery system, the entrepreneurial model, therefore, may prove less effective in some ways than agency-based practice.

Moreover, the major assumption that recommends the use of this strategy is open to question. While some professionals may function poorly in organizational settings, it is not necessary to conclude that organizational demands produce inherent limitations on professional functioning. For example, reasoned arguments can be made that there is much greater latitude for individual discretion to negotiate the constraints and opportunities of organizational life than many professionals exercise, mainly because they lack the expertise required to be skillful and effective in their roles as bureaucrats. Most professionals prefer to identify themselves as helpers and service-givers; and training is consciously sought to prepare for these roles. They tend to ignore or reject the bureaucratic role that they must carry. Consequently, the demand for and supply of training for this role is minimal. In developing this line of thought, Pruger notes, "As virtually everything written or said about bureaucracy implies, achieving one's professional goals through a formal organization requires a competence as complex and demanding as any of those that professional helpers consciously seek to master."[32]

*Strategies to
Alter the Composition of the Delivery System:
Specialized Access Structures
and Purposive Duplication*

Specialized access structure.   According to this strategy, fragmentation, inaccessibility, and discontinuity of service are, to a degree, viewed as inherent to delivery systems characterized by the professional-specialized-bureaucratic gestalt. The objective of this strategy is neither to change the combination of roles in various elements of the system nor to change the authority relationships among these elements through centralization or federation. Its advocates recognize that specialized-professional-bureaucratic services perform important functions despite their drawbacks as delivery mechanisms. Instead of changing roles and the like, they want to change the composition of the delivery system by adding a new element —to function independently as a catalyst, to act upon other service agencies, to pry open their entry points, and to insure that the proper service connections are made by clients. In a word, *access* is to be provided as a social service.

Until recently, the provision of access was generally considered a marginal function of all agencies and professional staff in the delivery system rather than a core function around which to organize a distinct set of services. As a marginal function, access is unduly restricted by the narrow perspectives of agency specializations, relating primarily to the agency's core function instead of the particular problems brought by the client. This phenomenon is a by-product of neither incompetence nor malice. It is a normal structural reality of specialized service organizations. To facilitate client access to service while maintaining a relatively high degree of specialization, it is proposed that a new structure be added to the delivery system, one characterized as a "professionally unbiased doorway."[33] This doorway is to be created by developing special agencies that offer case-advocacy, advice, information, and referral services to assist clients in negotiating the bureaucratic maze.

Although it is in many respects a persuasive strategy, the consequences of access agencies may be more wished for than assured. To wit, from the client's perspective a possible effect of this strategy is to further fragment and complicate service delivery. Though access services are becoming increasingly important in complex urban societies, they are nonetheless among the least tangible of social services. Thus the access agency may be perceived by the client as merely another bureaucracy he must learn to negotiate, another base that he must touch before the proper resources are matched to his needs.

Access strategy is also likely to have a certain influence on the other service agencies in the delivery system. The addition of an access agency suggests that other service-providing agencies will diminish the access services they previously offered as a marginal function. For instance, there would be reduced pressures upon these service agencies to perform client referrals for those they are unable to serve, other than directing them to the access agency. The net impact of transferring the marginal access functions of many organizations to the core function of a single organization is presently unclear as to the extent to which it lessens traveling time, expense, or confusion in the client's search for service. Moreover, the separation of diagnosis and treatment engendered by this action, while theoretically possible, may prove rather clumsy in practice.

Purposive duplication.   Here the approach entails duplication of any or all of the services available in the existing system, whereas access strategy provides only for the development of agencies to service specialized access functions. Purposive duplication is advanced in two forms that have a surface resemblance but are dissimilar enough to warrant distinction—*competition* and *separatism.*

Competition involves creating duplicate agencies within the existing delivery system to compete with established agencies for clients and resources. This strategy increases choice. More important, competition is typically expected to have an invigorating effect upon agencies and professionals, sensitizing them to client needs and producing greater enterprise and creative efforts at service delivery. The consequences of this strategy, however, are not always fertile nor always compatible with its motives. Instead of a healthy competition for clients and resources, an internecine conflict may ensue between the powerfully entrenched agencies and those scraping for a foothold in the system, the outcome of which is reasonably predictable.[34]

The duplication of services to stimulate competition may be achieved through direct or indirect methods. The direct approach involves restructuring the delivery system so that funders actually create new agencies. In the Community Action Program, for example, funds were sometimes provided to develop new agencies that offered day-care, counseling, and community organization services rather than to expand the service offerings of traditional agencies functioning in these areas. The indirect approach involves changing the form of the social provision. In this method social provisions are distributed to consumers in the form of vouchers for services.[35]

Separatism differs from competition in both the systemic location of new structures and their purposes for being. In the separatist design, new agencies are created and organized *outside* the established delivery system, and they do not seek entry. Competition is likely to be an inadvertent—and unplanned—by-product of separatism, more so for resources than for clients. The intention is to form an alternative network that would serve certain disadvantaged groups who because of racial, ethnic, and socioeconomic characteristics are served poorly or not at all by the existing system due to organizational and professional proclivities already discussed. Proponents of separatism emphasize that this strategy contains social and political values for disadvantaged groups that transcend the enhancement of service delivery.[36]

Duplicatory strategies, in either form, are enormously expensive. The money may be well spent if the new agencies become a dynamic force for desired changes in the delivery system and reach those usually excluded from the service network. Weighing against these benefits are the risks of expending scarce resources to produce fruitless conflict and to create even greater fragmentation than currently exists.

Unsettled Questions

We have identified six major strategies for improving the delivery of social services by the properties of the delivery system they seek to alter: patterns of authority (*coordination* and *citizen participation*), roles and status (*role attachments* and *professional disengagement*), and substantive composition (*development of specialized access structures* and *purposive duplication*). We have analyzed them for their expected and unanticipated consequences. And some indication has been given of how one strategy proposed to cope with one problem of service delivery may exacerbate difficulties in other directions.

All of these strategies are plausible ways to develop more effective service delivery; they all contain different limitations and latent dysfunctions that might compromise or vitiate the advantages promised. And though some strategies may be complementary, there are obvious contradictions in using many of them simultaneously.

Currently, *coordination* appears to enjoy favor among federal policymakers, as reflected in the proposed Allied Services Bill of 1972 (described in Chapter 4). This can be a seductive idea. The idea of being able to exercise a degree of administrative control over groups of heretofore autonomous service agencies will have intrinsic appeal to almost everybody who has grappled with the problems of rationalizing service delivery. This attraction notwithstanding, even when coordination operates through administrative control, the integration of services may remain highly problematic.[37]

Before we can accurately judge the efficacy of coordination or any of the other reform strategies, certain empirical questions remain to be answered. We will not try to detail all of these questions, but we will attempt to distill some basic issues related to each strategy that are ripe for more intense empirical investigation.

Coordination

Within what range and mix of services does coordination operate most effectively to integrate service delivery? At issue here are the criteria for selecting the number and types of services incorporated within a coordinating structure that would produce a minimum strain and maximum cooperation and exchange among service units. There is substantial evidence, for instance, that certain service functions (such as social action and direct services) create disharmony and strain when joined.[38] We have little evidence, however, of what the optimal mix of services is and whether coordination is more likely to improve service integration when organized around a geographic base (e.g., all services in a designated neighborhood): a clientele with special demographic characteristics (e.g., the aged, young people, young married couples, and ethnic groups); functional areas (e.g., health and employment); or combinations thereof.

In addition, it is difficult to gauge what, if any, cost reductions are achieved through coordinated efforts. Again the evidence is sparse and tentative. The following conclusions drawn from a study of thirty service integration projects illustrate some of the variables that enter into measurements of efficiency.

> It may not be possible to justify services integration strictly in terms of total dollar savings. Centralized/consolidated operation of core services, record-keeping, joint programming, joint funding, joint training and/or central purchase of service arrangements on behalf of a number of service providers promote economies of scale and coordinated staff utilization, funding, planning and programming, and evaluation help reduce duplication.
>
> Although there are some cost savings resulting from economies of scale and reduction of duplication, they do not appear (at least in the short-run) to equal the input costs of administrative and core service staff required to support integrative efforts. However, if one includes protection of public investment in services as a measure of efficiency, then a stronger case can be made for service integration on grounds of efficiency. If the public investment in one service (job training, for example) is to have lasting benefit only if another service (a job placement service, for example) is also provided, the cost involved in assuring that the client gets the job placement services as well as job training may be justified in terms of protecting the investment in job training.[39]

Purposive Duplication

Under what circumstances do the savings that accrue to a large-scale organization make the duplication of services impractical? The research suggested by this question involves cost-benefit analyses of social service programs. One major argument against purposive duplication of services and in favor of coordination is the increased efficiency attributed to coordination. However, with different types of social services, the gain in efficiency may vary considerably.[40]   At the same time coordination or administrative unification is usually achieved at the expense of diversity. Ultimately, value judgments will be made concerning the relative desirability of efficiency and diversity in the delivery of social services. The more information available regarding the economic costs and social benefits of duplication, the better informed these value judgments will be.

Development of New Agencies

To what extent does the creation of an access agency facilitate entry into social services? One issue here has already been suggested—the addition of an access agency to the local service system might have the unanticipated effect of decreasing the net amount of information and referral services provided within that system (because other agencies might diminish the information and referral services they previously offered). This question remains open to direct empirical investigation. Another more complex line of study would involve a comparative analysis of the percentage of persons in need and searching for help that actually receive relevant services and how many bases these persons touch before such services are rendered by matched local service systems with and without access agencies.

Role Attachments

What types of local nonprofessional workers are best suited to withstand the strains inherent in the performance of linkage functions between professional workers and the community served? At issue here is the fact that "indigenous nonprofessional" is a designation for a variety of people with diverse values, commitments, aspirations, and reference groups. Workers in this category are likely to possess different capacities for coping with the pressure toward bureaucratic conformity and professionalism. Accordingly, a useful line of investigation suggested in a recent exploratory study develops a typology based on the differences among nonprofessional workers.[41]   In this study it was found that certain types of nonprofessional staff members appear to be better fitted than others to perform tasks such as bridge and outreach functions. Further investigation is needed to extend and substantiate these tentative findings.

Professional Disengagement

How does the move from agency-based practice to private practice affect access to and continuity of services offered? Though this strategy assumes that the delivery of social services will improve when the professional worker is freed from the restrictions imposed by bureaucratic organization, there is little evidence either to support or dispute this effect. A line of inquiry here might involve selecting a few cities for study in order to evaluate the effects of having similar services offered by private practitioners and agency-based practitioners with regard to the characteristics of the persons served, the percentage of referrals made, the percentage of follow-ups, and the like.

Citizen Participation

To what degree does substantive citizen participation in service agency decision-making processes increase accountability to the population being served? As indicated, election or selection procedures for citizen participants are frequently such that citizens who actually participate are not formally accountable to the groups of service users they ostensibly represent. We lack careful comparisons of the decision-making behavior of citizen participants and the expressed wishes and interests of the people they serve as well as delineation of selection procedures that produce participants with a high degree of accountability. One issue for further investigation involves, for instance, the extent to which elected representatives (on a block, neighborhood, and city-wide basis), appointed representatives, and volunteer (or self-selected) representatives differ in their accountability to the persons they serve.

Each of these unsettled questions contributes to the uncertainty that surrounds policy-makers concerned with selecting the right strategy to design the delivery of social services. To conclude that more research is needed (which it is) is the unblemished mark of academicians (which we are). To this advice the practititioner may nod abstractly in agreement while he continues to design and implement the policies that govern service delivery. This means that policy choices regarding service delivery may eventually benefit from future investigation, but they will not await the results; choices will be made based on the knowledge we possess, imperfect as it is.

Selecting Strategies

All of the strategies we have discussed are plausible approaches to improving the delivery of services. All contain different limitations; and there is considerable uncertainty surrounding the consequences of each approach. Given these circumstances, how do administrators and planners select a strategy or combination of strategies? From a policy-planning perspective, the answer to this question depends upon the operational context in which choices are made, the values to be maximized, empirical evidence about the consequences of different strategies and, in the absence of compelling evidence, theories and assumptions about how delivery systems function. It is the latter aspect of choice, theories and assumptions, to which the balance of this chapter is addressed.

Social service staff and organizations are the two major elements in the delivery system which may be manipulated to build coherent and effective connections between services and clients. Orientations that program planners bring to bear in considering service delivery, therefore, may be perceived as the result of the interplay of theories and assumptions regarding staff and organizations. Our purpose is to explain the ways in which these two major perspectives influence the selection of one or a combination of strategies for the delivery of social services.

Social Service Staff:
Perspectives on the Function of Professionalism

Broadly speaking, there are two perspectives a policy analyst may have regarding the function of professionalism in the behavior of social-service staff: *status enhancement* and *service.* From the perspective of status enhancement the policy planner views professionalism as a means to protect and enhance professional prerogatives and status. In contrast, with the service perspective the policy planner views professionalism as fulfilling a service function. This perspective corresponds to the ideal-typical model of a profession that Greenwood describes in terms of five distinguishing attributes: (1) *skills* based on a systematic body of theory; (2) *authority* derived from and functionally specific to professional expertise; (3) *sanction of the community* to perform special services over which the profession has a monopoly; (4) *a regulative code of ethics* that compels moral behavior and prevents the abuse of the powers and privileges granted by the community; and (5) *a professional culture* consisting of values, norms, and symbols.[42]   While self-regulative codes are also characteristic of many nonprofessional occupations, Greenwood suggests that the professional code "is perhaps more explicit, systematic, and binding; it certainly possesses more altruistic overtones and is more public service oriented."[43] From this perspective, the view of social-service staff functioning may be best summarized by reference to one of the central concepts of professional culture, the concept of career.

> A career is essentially a calling, a life devoted to "good works" . . . Self-seeking motives feature minimally in the choice of a profession; of maximal importance is affinity for the work. It is this devotion to the work itself which imparts to professional activity the service orientation and the element of disinterestedness. Furthermore the absorption in the work is not partial, but complete; it results in a total personal involvement.[44]

These virtues notwithstanding, from the service perspective, professionalization at its best is frequently perceived as incompatible with a spirit of social reform. An explanation for this is offered by Wilensky and Lebeaux as follows:

> The notion that professionalism is corrupting because it brings economic rewards and social recognition, making its adherents fat, comfortable, and lazy, is much too simple . . . more impressive is the argument that a professional absorbed in the technical side of his work aiming mainly at full use of his skills and training, preoccupied with that competent, efficient performance of which his professional colleagues would approve . . . does not have the time, energy or inclination necessary for social reform, for dedicated attention to the broader social purpose.[45]

Those who adopt the most extreme status-enhancement perspective would construe even this statement on professional functioning as the apologetics of those attendant to the service orientation. More in line with the dictum of status-enhancement is the notion that professionals are driven not so much by service ideals but, as Dumont suggests, by "personal dread of poverty, or the insatiable appetite for wealth, or the fascination with esoteric skills and complicated machinery, or the yearning for status and command of others."[46]

In a less polemic vein, from a status-enhancement perspective the ideal-typical attributes of a profession may still be viewed with a large measure of skepticism. Specifically, professional *skills* and expertise are challenged as inadequate, or cast in the mold of credentialism,[47] especially in the social services where results and achievements are difficult to evaluate and a professional credential is often presumed to be synonymous with evidence of ability.[48] Professional *authority* is perceived as a mechanism of client control flowing from the practitioner's service monopoly rather than his presumed technical competence.[49] *Community sanction* of the professional's service monopoly is viewed as bestowed by the established power structure to whom the professionals are accountable, not by client groups. The *self-regulative* code of ethics may be interpreted as a device to protect professionals from outside meddling and to reaffirm their claim to esoteric knowledge; that is, they prevent "outside interference" by asserting that only professional peers are competent to judge their work.[50] And finally, the good intentions and altruistic motives emphasized by the professional culture are also questioned.[51] It has been shown, for instance, that the difference between professionals and businessmen lies in the different paths to achievement and recognition afforded by their occupational situations rather than in the typical motives of these groups, which may be singularly characterized as success.[52]

These perspectives on professional functioning are rarely applied in their extreme forms. Most delivery systems planners recognize that the staff elements with which they deal exhibit attributes that are a mixture of both service and status-enhancement perspectives. However, it is not implausible to presume that to the extent to which this mixture is weighted in favor of one of the perspectives strategy choice is likely to be influenced accordingly. This suggests two broad propositions: (1) To the degree that staff functioning is perceived by policy planners *in terms of status-enhancement,* their efforts to improve or develop a service-delivery system will rely upon *strategies that constrain, modify, or otherwise limit the prerogatives of professional staff* by: (a) *redistributing authority from agencies to citizen-clients,* affording them some direct control over professionals (i.e., *citizen participation*); (b) *changing roles so that staff includes indigenous nonprofessionals* who are better equipped for certain functions (i.e., *role attachments*); and by (c) *adding elements to the system that create competition among professionals,* stimulating them to greater effort and eventually eliminating the less competent (i.e., *purposive duplication*). (2) Conversely, to the degree that *the service perspective* informs the policy planner's perceptions of reality, the choice of delivery strategies will be inclined towards *allowing professionals greater latitude* by: (a) *redistributing authority in ways that consolidate and strengthen the hierarchy of professional control* (i.e., *coordination*); (b) *changing the professional role from bureaucrat to entrepreneur,* thereby allowing professionals to ply their trade unencumbered by the prerequisites of organizational life (i.e., *professional disengagement*); and by (c) *introducing new access structures* that support specialization and produce further refinement in the division of labor among professionals (i.e., *specialized access structures*).

In the following table we summarize the propositions that are derived from the application of these perspectives to the three kinds of service-delivery questions we listed at the beginning of this chapter.

TABLE 5–1

Perspectives on Professionalism and Responses to Service-Delivery
Questions.

	Perspectives on Professionalism	
Service-Delivery Questions	Status-Enhancement	Service
Where shall authority and control rest?	Citizen participation	Coordination
Who carries out different tasks?	Role attachments	Professional disengagement
What will be the composition of the delivery system?	Purposive duplication	Specialized access structures

*Organizations: Perspectives on the Structure of
the Service Network*

Theoretical perspectives on the structure of the service network (which
is composed of the agencies in the delivery system) is another variable that
may inspire different strategy choices. Here the concern is with the impersonal forces of organizational behavior in a systemic context rather than
forces generated by professional behavior per se, though these phenomena
are separable only in the abstract.

There are two fundamental perspectives on organization that tend to
direct the policy analyst's perceptions and categorizations of reality: the
"rational" model and the "natural-system" model. These models are identified and explicated in a seminal paper on organizational analysis by
Gouldner as follows:

> In the rational model, the organization is conceived as an "instrument"
> —that is, as a rationally conceived means to the realization of expressly
> announced group goals . . . Fundamentally, the rational model implies
> a "mechanical" model, in that it views the organization as a structure
> of manipulable parts, each of which is separately modifiable with a
> view to enhancing the efficiency of the whole. Individual organiza-
> tional elements are seen as subject to successful and planned modifica-
> tion, enactable by deliberate decision.

The natural-system model regards the organization as a "natural whole," or system. The realization of the goals of the system as a whole is but one of several important needs to which the organization is oriented . . . The organization, according to this model, strives to survive, to maintain its equilibrium, and this striving may persist even after its explicitly held goals have been successfully attained. This strain towards survival may even on occasion lead to the neglect or distortion of the organization's goals.[53]

Thompson refines this formulation with the notion that the rational model involves a closed-system perception while the natural-system views organizations as open systems.[54] Each of these perspectives draws attention to certain aspects of organizational functioning and tends to neglect others. Needless to say, most planners and administrators are aware that organizations behave in accordance with both of these perspectives, though they are not always taken into account equally. There appears to be a strong susceptibility, reflected in the organizational literature, toward envisioning organizations in terms of *either* closed or open systems rather than as systems that are partially closed, half-rational, and that sustain otherwise contradictory tendencies. This susceptibility occurs, Thompson suggests, because there is no convenient conceptual means of thinking simultaneously of a system as half-open and half-closed.[55]

From an open-system perspective, explanations of organizational behavior emphasize the relevance of elements in the environment upon which the organizations are dependent or potentially dependent for survival and goal achievement, such as clients, suppliers of funds, staff, equipment, competitors, and regulatory groups.[56]   Taken together these elements constitute the "task environment."[57] Applying this perspective to the service network, the policy planner perceives the elements originating outside the subsystem of existing service agencies as the key leverage points for change. He seeks to manipulate these external elements, which are necessary for survival and goal achievement of organizations in the service network. Thus, we may speculate that to the extent that the policy analyst's thinking about the structure of service networks is characterized by an *open-system perspective,* his delivery-system strategies will be inclined to follow along lines that: (1) *organize the client element of the task environment to demand a share of authority and control over the service network* (i.e., *citizen participation*); (2) *move essential organizational resources* (e.g., *professional staff*) *outside of the service network hierarchy,* making them elements of the task environment (i.e., *professional disengagement*); and (3) *add new elements to the task environment* that will compete with the service network for clients and resources or that will operate independently as mediators between the service network and clients (i.e., *purposive duplication* and *specialized access structures*).

On the other hand, if the policy analyst views the service network more *in terms of a closed system,* attention, as Gouldner implies, is directed to *strategies which enhance the efficiency of this "instrument."* This may be done by *manipulating the parts of this instrument to place them in better balance* or *welding on an additional piece that will make the instrument more functional.* That is, the tendency will be to select strategies that: (1) *redistribute authority* either by centralization or federation but with authority always remaining within *the closed service network* (i.e., *coordination*); and (2) *incorporate new roles to improve network functioning over which service-network organizations exercise authority* (i.e., *role attachments*). In Table 5–2 we summarize the propositions that may be derived from the application of these perspectives to the three kinds of service-delivery questions.

Orientations to Service-Delivery

The interplay of theoretical perspectives regarding the structure of the service network and assumptions regarding the functions of professionalism generates four types of orientations that policy analysts may have toward service delivery, orientations which will predispose them to support particular strategies for service-delivery reform. These orientations are *professional/bureaucratic, egalitarian/bureaucratic, professional/activist,* and *egalitarian/activist.* The relationship between planner views on the struc-

TABLE 5–2

Perspectives on the Structure of the Service-Delivery Network and Responses to Service-Delivery Questions.

Service-Delivery Questions	Perspectives on the Structure of Service-Delivery Network	
	Closed System	*Open System*
Where shall authority and control rest?	Coordination	Citizen participation
Who carries out different tasks?	Role attachments	Professional disengagement
What will be the composition of the delivery system?	(Existing mix of units in the service network remains unchanged.)	Purposive duplication Specialized access structures

ture of the service network and planner assumptions regarding the functions of professionalism in generating these orientations is illustrated in Table 5–3.

We remind the reader that these orientations are ideal types represented in the table as the functions of two dichotomous variables, as theoretical polarities. But in reality there are innumerable variations of each of these orientations, one not clearly distinct from the next. We shall describe briefly each of these ideal types.

Professional/bureaucratic.   With this orientation the policy planner is committed to the administrator who "runs a tight ship," who assures that lines of authority within the system are clear and hierarchical. A high degree of reliance is placed upon professional expertise as demonstrated by both credential and performance, and upon the rationality of bureaucratic organization. At the extreme, this orientation directs planners to seek solutions to service-delivery problems that will maximize the professional's ability to do what it is believed he is competent to do within an organizational framework; such strategies will enhance the relationships of professionals within and between agencies. The organization and the professional are viewed as mutually supporting entities. When each is committed to the values of the other they constitute a formidable system of institutional control.

Egalitarian/bureaucratic.   Here the policy analyst's view of the importance and the power of the principles of organization are the same as

TABLE 5–3
Orientations to Service-Delivery as a Function of Theoretical Perspectives.

Perspectives on Structure of the Service-Delivery Network	*Perspectives on Functions of Professionalism*	
	Service	*Self-Enhancement*
Closed system	Professional Bureaucratic (*Coordination*)	Egalitarian Bureaucratic (*Role attachments*)
Open system	Professional/ Activist (*Professional disengagement*; *Special access structures*)	Egalitarian Activist (*Citizen participation*; *Purposive duplication*)

above. He will seek solutions that are based on a belief that whatever is done should be rationalized and brought under organizational control. However, under this orientation the policy planner does not believe that professionals are better equipped than anyone else to do the job of service delivery—linking clients to resources. Professionals are likely to be viewed as concerned primarily with developing methods and esoteric skills rather than with delivery. Thus, the attachment of nonprofessional role functions is likely to be advocated.

Professional/activist. The policy analyst who operates with the professional/activist orientation tends to rely heavily upon "outreach" types of strategies, sometimes referred to as "aggressive casework," "casefinding," or "health education," depending upon the functional area of service. In our schema such approaches fall in the categories of special access and professional disengagement. Here the belief in the ability of professionals to do the job is strong; it is the organization that is believed to be confining. With this orientation the proper role for administrators and professionals is "enabling"; professionals can provide good services, and the function of the organization is to develop the most effective means to help consumers use them, even at the cost of organizational power and control.

Egalitarian/activist. This orientation is the polar opposite of the professional/bureaucratic orientation since it is based upon a rejection of professionalism and embraces an open-system perspective of organization. Neither the organization nor the professionals are to be relied upon. One must turn to entirely different sources for legitimacy, wisdom, and policy. These sources may be the currently popular "alternative institutions" (e.g., free clinics, cooperative schools) which duplicate existing agencies, or they may be the recipients of services designated "the people," "the community," "the poor." And these constituencies may be defined ethnically, geographically, or in any other way that suits the ideological tastes of the planner. In the extreme, this orientation is similar to Rousseau's doctrine of the "general will" with its implied reduction of government to a mere agent of the community's corporate personality.[58] The answer, with this orientation, to all of the service-delivery questions is: Ask the people what they want and help them to get it. The overriding view of the ideal that should guide the role behavior of administrators and professionals in service-delivery is "advocacy."

Concluding Comments

Is there an orientation of choice? As we have indicated, each of the strategies may mitigate some service-delivery problems and exacerbate others. There is no calculus for computing all of the social costs and benefits. Any service network, whether it is "establishment" or "people-run," may operate as a system that is too closed and unable to deal efficiently with elements in its task environment, or too open and unable to deal efficiently with internal functioning. Any service network, whether it is a highly centralized one with firm boundaries or a diffuse, loosely structured, community-run enterprise may be too weighed down by the methods and doctrine of professional personnel or may lack sufficiently clear professional standards of behavior and conduct for its workers.

No orientation is ipso facto superior to another. In selecting service-delivery strategies policy planners are influenced by a combination of circumstantial factors, social values, empirical evidence, and theoretical viewpoints. At best, their choices are infused with much uncertainty.

In articulating how orientations toward strategy choices are informed by the interplay of their perspectives on the structure of service networks and the functions of professionalism, we have sought to illuminate the contributions made by competing theoretical viewpoints to the development of strategies to organize the delivery of social services. Accordingly, if there is a more immediate purpose to be served by this analysis, it is to heighten recognition of this fact: to fixate on any one strategy as a panacea for service-delivery problems is to foreclose prematurely the options on other strategies which are largely untested and which may have untapped potential. Given the present state of knowledge about the design and consequences of service-delivery strategies, efforts to exercise fully all of the available options appear to be the more practical policy course.

Notes

[1] Alfred Skolnik and Sophie R. Dales, "Social Welfare Expenditures, 1970–71," *Social Security Bulletin,* Vol. 34, No. 12 (December 1971), 3–16.

[2] Harry G. Bredemeier, "The Socially Handicapped and the Agencies: A Market Analysis," in *Mental Health of the Poor,* eds. Frank Riessman, Jerome Cohen, and Arthur Pearl (New York: Free Press, 1964); Richard Cloward and Frances F. Piven, "The Professional Bureaucracies: Benefit Systems as Influence Systems," in *The Role of Government in Promoting Social Change,* ed. Murray Silberman (New York: Columbia University, School of Social Work, 1966); Alfred J. Kahn, "Do Social Services Have a Future in New York?" *City Almanac,* Vol. 5, No. 5 (February 1971), 1–11; Irving Piliavin, "Restructuring the Provision of Social Service," *Social Work,* Vol. 13, No. 1 (January 1968); William Reid, "Interagency Coordination in Delinquency Prevention and Control," *Social Service Review,* Vol. 38, No. 4 (December 1964); Martin Rein, *Social Policy: Issues of Choice and Change* (New York: Random House, 1970); Gideon Sjoberg, Richard Brymer, and Buford Farris, "Bureaucracy and the Lower Class," *Sociology and Social Research,* Vol. 50, No. 3 (April 1966), 325–37.

[3]Robert R. Mayer, "Social Change or Service Delivery," in *Social Welfare Forum* (New York: Columbia University Press, 1970), pp. 99–116. See also Robert R. Mayer, *Social Policy and Social Change* (Englewood Cliffs, N.J.: Prentice-Hall, Inc., 1972).

[4]Clark describes these forms of coordination in terms of bureaucratic and interorganizational patterns, in Burton R. Clark, "Interorganizational Patterns in Education," *Administrative Science Quarterly,* Vol. 10 (September 1965), 224–37.

[5]Richard Titmuss, *Commitment to Welfare* (New York: Pantheon, 1968), p. 80.

[6]Herbert H. Simon, *Administrative Behavior* (2nd ed.) (New York: Free Press, 1965), p. 238.

[7]Peter Townsend, *et al., The Fifth Social Service: A Critical Analysis of the Seebohm Report* (London: Fabian Society, 1970).

[8]Townsend, *et al., The Fifth Social Service;* Peter J. Hitch, "Organizational Problems and Concepts in the Development of a Unified Social Service Department," *Applied Social Studies,* Vol. 3 (1971), 21–28.

[9]James D. Thompson, *Organizations in Action* (New York: McGraw-Hill, 1967); and Reid, "Interagency Coordination in Delinquency Prevention and Control."

[10]Roland L. Warren, "The Interorganizational Field as a Focus for Investigation," *Administrative Science Quarterly,* Vol. 12, No. 3 (December 1967), 396–419.

[11]Reid, "Interagency Coordination in Delinquency Prevention and Control."

[12]Neil Gilbert, *Clients or Constituents* (San Francisco: Jossey-Bass, 1970), pp. 79–81.

[13]Reid, "Interagency Coordination in Delinquency Prevention and Control."

[14]Robert A. Dahl and Charles E. Lindblom, *Politics, Economics, and Welfare* (New York: Harper & Row, 1953), p. 238.

[15]Sherry Arnstein, "A Ladder of Citizen Participation," *Journal of the American Institute of Planners,* Vol. 35, No. 4 (July 1969).

[16]Hans B. C. Spiegel *et al., Neighborhood Power and Control: Implications for Urban Planning* (New York: Columbia University, Institute of Urban Environment, 1968), p. 157.

[17]Ralph M. Kramer, *Community Development in Israel and the Netherlands* (Berkeley: University of California Press, Institute of International Studies, 1970), p. 127.

[18]Gilbert, *Clients or Constituents* p. 145; and Arthur B. Shostak, "Promoting Participation of the Poor: Philadelphia's Anti-Poverty Program," *Social Work,* Vol. 11, No. 1 (January 1966).

[19]Ralph M. Kramer, *Participation of the Poor* (Englewood Cliffs, N.J.: Prentice-Hall, 1969), p. 127.

[20]There is some evidence that local citizen elections may improve over time. Brager and Specht indicate that voter turnouts in Model Cities elections, while usually low, tend to be higher than turnouts for earlier elections sponsored by the Economic Opportunity Program. For example, nearly 30 percent of eligible voters participated in Trenton's Model Cities election in 1968. George Brager and Harry Specht, *Community Organizing* (New York: Columbia University Press, 1973).

[21]Harold Weissman, *Community Councils and Community Control* (Pittsburgh: University of Pittsburgh Press, 1970).

[22]Neil Gilbert and Joseph Eaton, "Who Speaks for the Poor?" *Journal of the American Institute of Planners,* Vol. 36, No. 6 (November 1970).

[23]Sjoberg, Brymer, and Farris, "Bureaucracy and the Lower Class."

[24]S. M. Miller and Frank Riessman, *Social Class and Social Policy* (New York: Basic Books, 1968), p. 207.

[25]George Brager, "The Indigenous Worker: A New Approach to the Social Work Technician," *Social Work,* Vol. 10, No. 2 (April 1965).

[26]Robert Pruger and Harry Specht, "Establishing New Careers Programs: Organizational Barriers and Strategies," *Social Work,* Vol. 13, No. 4 (October 1968), 23–24.

[27]David A. Hardcastle, "The Indigenous Nonprofessional in the Social Service Bureaucracy: A Critical Examination," *Social Work,* Vol. 16, No. 2 (April 1971), 63.

[28]Charles Grosser, "Manpower Development Programs," in *Nonprofessionals in the Human Services,* eds. Charles Grosser, William E. Henry, and James G. Kelly, (San Francisco: Jossey-Bass, 1969), pp. 136–37.

[29]Gerald Levy, "Acute Workers in a Welfare Bureaucracy," in *Social Problems and Social Policy,* eds. Deborah Offenbacher and Constance Poster (New York: Appleton-Century-Crofts, 1970); see also Harry Wasserman, "The Professional Social Worker in a Bureaucracy," *Social Work,* Vol. 16, No. 1 (January 1971), 89–95.

[30]Piliavin, "Restructuring the Provision of Social Service," p. 35.

[31]Piliavin, "Restructuring the Provision of Social Service."

[32]Robert Pruger, "The Good Bureaucrat," *Social Work,* Vol. 18, No. 4 (July 1973), 27.

[33]Alfred J. Kahn, "Perspectives on Access to Social Service," *Social Work,* Vol. 15, No. 2 (March 1970), 99.

[34]Rein, *Social Policy.*

[35]For a description of this method, see P. Nelson Reid, 'Reforming the Social Services Monopoly," *Social Work,* Vol. 17, No. 6 (November 1972), 44–54.

[36]Richard Cloward and Frances Piven, "The Case against Urban Desegregation," *Social Work,* Vol. 12, No. 1 (January 1967).

[37]Edward J. O'Donnel and Marilyn M. Sullivan, "Service Delivery and Social Action through the Neighborhood Center: A Review of Research," *Welfare in Review,* Vol. 7, No. 6 (November/December 1969), 95–102.

[38]O'Donnel and Sullivan, "Service Delivery and Social Action through the Neighborhood Center."

[39]Marshall Kaplan, Gans, and Kahn, and The Research Group, Inc., *Integration of Human Services in HEW: An Evaluation of Services Integration Projects,* An executive Summary of a Study for the Social and Rehabilitation Service of the Department of Health, Education, and Welfare (1972), p. 11.

[40]For an insightful analysis of the vital functions that may be served by duplication within systems, see Martin Landau, "Redundancy, Rationality, and the Prob-

lem of Duplication and Overlap," *Public Administration Review,* Vol. 29, No. 4 (July/August 1969), 346–58.

[41]Philip Kramer, "The Indigenous Worker: Hometowner, Striver, or Activist," *Social Work,* Vol. 17, No. 1 (January 1972).

[42]Ernest Greenwood, "Attributes of a Profession," *Social Work,* Vol. 2, No. 3 (July 1957).

[43]Greenwood, "Attributes of a Profession," p. 50.

[44]Greenwood, "Attributes of a Profession," p. 53.

[45]Harold Wilensky and Charles Lebeaux, *Industrial Society and Social Welfare* (New York: Russell Sage, 1958), p. 330.

[46]Matthew Dumont, "The Changing Face of Professionalism," *Social Policy,* May/June 1972, p. 31.

[47]Marie R. Haug and Marvin B. Sussman, "Professional Autonomy and the Revolt of the Client," *Social Problems,* Vol. 17, No. 2 (Fall 1969), 153–61; and Miller and Riessman, *Social Class and Social Policy.*

[48]As Eaton found in a study of professional employees in two treatment-oriented organizations, one of the difficulties of service evaluation stems from the reluctance of professionals to make interpretations of evaluative research data and their disinclination to communicate the findings of evaluative research. Joseph Eaton, "Symbolic and Substantive Evaluative Research," *Administrative Science Quarterly,* Vol. 6 (March 1962), 421–42.

[49]Haug and Sussman, "Professional Autonomy and the Revolt of the Client."

[50]Everett C. Hughes, "Professions," *Daedalus,* Vol. 92, No. 4 (Fall 1963).

[51]Richard Cloward and Irwin Epstein, "Private Social Welfare's Disengagement from the Poor: The case of Family Adjustment Agencies," *Social Welfare Institutions,* ed. Mayer Zald (New York: John Wiley & Sons, 1965), pp. 628–29.

[52]Talcott Parsons, "The Professions and Social Structure," *Social Forces,* Vol. 17 (Fall 1939), 457–67.

[53]Alvin W. Gouldner, "Organizational Analysis," in *Sociology Today,* eds. Robert K. Merton, Leonard Broom, and Leonard S. Cottrell, Jr. (New York: Harper & Row, 1959), pp. 404–5.

[54]Thompson, *Organizations in Action.*

[55]Thompson offers a creative synthesis of these two models by suggesting that organizations be viewed dynamically as open systems striving for the rationality, control, and certainty of a closed system. (Thompson, *Organizations in Action,* p. 10.)

[56]Thompson, *Organizations in Action,* pp. 27–28.

[57]William Dill, "Environment as an Influence on Managerial Autonomy," *Administrative Science Quarterly,* Vol. 2 (March 1958), 409–43.

[58]Harry Specht, "The Deprofessionalization of Social Work," *Social Work,* Vol. 17, No. 2 (April 1972).

Mode of Finance: Sources of Funds

Money speaks sense in a language all nations understand.
APHRA BEHN,
The Rover

But it is pretty to see what money will do.
SAMUEL PEPYS,
Diary, 21 March, 1667.

6 As the aphorisms of Behn and Pepys indicate, money talks in a universal tongue, and it is indeed "pretty" to see what it can do. But first, the money must be obtained. And in the realm of social welfare this is a difficult and complicated process to comprehend. Our objective in this chapter and the next is to explore some of the basic policy choices that enter into arrangements for financing social welfare and to sensitize students to the implications of different funding sources and different systems of transfer. For in social welfare the things that money can *do* are influenced by *how* it is obtained.

In the description of the framework for policy analysis (Chapter 2) we said that "funding choices involve the various sources through which social provisions flow, usually in the form of cash, and the conditions placed upon this movement up to the point that it reaches distributors." Essentially, then, these choices refer to the varied arrangements of relationships among the funders and the deliverers of social welfare services.

Questions related to mode of finance tend to be of greater interest to administrators and planners than to direct-service practitioners. Administrators and planners are concerned with how to get the resources needed to sustain the programs they want to operate. They therefore must understand the kinds of programs funders will support. Funders (e.g., legislators or trustees and executives of both public and voluntary funding organizations) are concerned with making choices among competing interests and programs to achieve their goals. In the negotiations for program support, both funders and those seeking funds will address the questions considered in the last three chapters—Who should be eligible? What is it they should receive? How should the delivery system be organized?

The direct-service practitioner is usually less attentive to questions involving the mode of finance than to other dimensions of policy choice. This is because choices in this dimension of policy are more remote from the activities of day-to-day practice, and the effects of these choices upon the welfare of clients are more difficult to comprehend than the other dimensions of choice we have discussed. Funding decisions for almost any kind of social welfare program, whether for community mental health, housing, or community action is likely to involve "big" government somewhere along the line. Most contemporary programs of significance require either the money, approval, or surveillance of one or more levels of government higher than the unit of government that operates the program. The direct-service practitioner is likely to think that questions related to mode of finance are not within his influence. Certainly the thought is based on a good deal of reality. Funding arrangements are complex, and frequently the final decisions are made by individuals and groups many steps removed from where service is given and received.

Yet all professionals concerned with social welfare should have at least a working knowledge of the major issues, concepts, and values involved in the mode of finance. While the vast majority of professionals will not participate directly in decision-making on the allocation of funds for services, they certainly can have an effect upon how decision-makers think, most generally through their social action as citizens, as members of professional associations and as employees of their agencies. In addition, considerations of funding arrangements may enter into reports and evaluations of programs. As mentioned in Chapter 1, because of their status as professionals, practitioners will be called upon to discuss and interpret the meaning of alternative modes of finance.

It is not unreasonable to expect that professionals, regardless of their specific job, should be able to respond thoughtfully to questions such as: Should public agencies "purchase" services from voluntary agencies, and if so, under what circumstances? Is revenue sharing preferable to categorical funding? What are the constraints of voluntary financing? What are the assumptions that support the use of contributory schemes and fee-charging arrangements? What are the redistributional implications of different taxes for financing social welfare? In what types of programs are open-ended or closed-ended funding arrangements more appropriate?

There are two interrelated sets of choices fundamental to the mode of finance dimension of policy design. These are choices pertaining to:

1. *The source(s) of funds.* Issues here involve whether financial support is derived directly from recipients in the form of user charges and certain earmarked taxes, from taxes that make up general revenues, from voluntary contributions, or some combination thereof.

2. *The system of transfer.* Issues here have to do with arrangements for the flow of money from sources to distributors, the different levels of review between sources and distributors, and the types of conditions that may be placed upon the transfer.

We will discuss various choices that inform the design of systems of transfer in the next chapter, but here we will examine the alternative sources of funding and their implications.

Sources of Funds

Funds to pay for social welfare services may be obtained either publicly or from voluntary sources. The term *voluntary social services* is frequently used to refer to those supported by funds obtained "voluntarily" through private contributions rather than "involuntarily" through the tax system. The notion of "voluntary" financing becomes somewhat confused by the fact that the term "private" is sometimes used to describe this sector of social welfare. In our discussion we will use the term *voluntary* to refer to nonprofit organizations and agencies that provide social welfare services and are financed mainly by private voluntary contributions. The term *private* will be used in reference to the personal choices of individuals in purchasing social and health services on the open market. As the reader shall see, in the actual financing of social services, "private," "voluntary," and "public" choices are frequently confounded.

Voluntary agencies are sometimes referred to as "public institutions." This is because voluntary organizations that devote all of their resources to education, science, religion, art, culture, or charity without pecuniary advantage to individuals or special groups are perceived as serving the public interest, even though they are not publicly administered. Thus, voluntary agencies may be conceived of as *privately administered public institutions*. Public programs and services supported by governmental funds are often referred to as "statutory," "governmental," and "legislative" programs because they must be enacted in law.

In this section we will describe the general scope of each of these sources of funds and some implications of the shifting balance between public and voluntary financing for the development of social welfare.

Issues of public versus voluntary financing for social welfare programs are important, especially in light of the phenomenal growth of public allocations in recent years. For example, public expenditures for health, education, and welfare services were over twenty-five times greater in 1967 than in 1929,[1] and this increase reflects a greater expansion of the role of the federal government than of other levels of government. The proportion of public over voluntary and private expenditures for these programs has grown continuously in the last forty years. In 1950, for example, voluntary and private expenditures for health, education, and welfare nationally were estimated to be 34 percent of the total of 49 billion dollars spent; public expenditures accounted for 66 percent of the total. By 1967 total expenditures had risen to 146 billion dollars and public expenditures then accounted for 68 percent of this greater total.[2] And, if we exclude consideration of costs of medical care, which are still largely private, the proportion of public expenditures for education and social welfare account for 85 percent of all expenditures.[3]

Since public allocations for social welfare are proportionately far greater than voluntary allocations, readers may underestimate the significance and scope of voluntary services. During these last forty years of burgeoning growth in the public services, the voluntary sector has also increased in size, although not as rapidly. This increase is reflected both in amounts of dollars and number of agencies.

National and regional voluntary agencies whose primary purpose is health and welfare increased from 15 in 1940 to close to 150 in 1972. The number of United Funds and Community Chests increased from 552 in 1940 to over 2,200 in 1970. In 1970, United Funds and Community Chests alone raised 834 million dollars.[4] In addition to the more than 100,000 voluntary health and welfare agencies soliciting funds either individually or through Community Chests, there are another 100,000 fraternal, civic, and veterans organizations, and 300,000 churches, many of which offer various types of health and welfare services as part of their programs.

The private foundation—a unique creation of private enterprise capitalism in the United States—is probably the fastest growing of all of the types of voluntary agencies. It was estimated that in 1969 there were over 26,000 foundations, most of them small, with approximately 150 new ones forming each month.[5] (This includes community foundations, company- and family-sponsored foundations, and general foundations.[6]) In 1969 it was estimated that the 5,454 foundations with assets of over one-half million dollars had capital assets totalling approximately 24 billion dollars and that they dispensed approximately 1.258 billion dollars per year for health, education, and welfare purposes.[7] Obviously the voluntary sector of social welfare is not an insignificant one.

Still, by 1972 the federal government emerged as the undisputed major source of funds for health and welfare services. Of 268 billion dollars spent on these programs from all sources (representing 25 percent of the gross national product), 29.2 percent came from voluntary and private sources, 31.9 percent from state and local governments, and 38.9 percent from the federal government.[8] The phenomenal increase in the amounts of monies spent for social welfare services over the last decades has been marked by a shift from private to public financing.

Such changes in the amounts and sources of support for social welfare services in this century have made for great changes in both the process and context of policy formulation in social welfare.[9] First, they have increased the degree to which social welfare policy choices are political rather than a matter of private consumption or voluntary philanthropy. Second, issues of social welfare policy and program have become inextricably tied to problems of large-scale bureaucratic organizations. And third, these shifts and increases in sources and sizes of social welfare expenditures reflect the emergence of the federal government as the major supporter of services.

Kramer describes the impact of this great expansion of the public sector upon domain and functions of the voluntary service organization:

> It becomes increasingly difficult to distinguish voluntary service organizations from their governmental and profit-making counterparts, and to justify the compelling and unique nature of their function. Many services perform the same function for society and the consumer regardless of the type of sponsor, and it is no longer easy to answer the question: What is it that voluntary service organizations do that cannot be done as well by government or the market?[10]

The increased federal role in financing social welfare programs in the social and political context of policy formulation has magnified the influence of extracommunity systems in social welfare policy decision-making. That is, policy formulation has become less a matter of the local community alone (or what Warren calls "horizontal" decision-making structures) and more a matter of the interests of several levels of government attempting to compete or coordinate with one another, as the case may be (or what Warren calls "vertical" decision-making structures).[11]

Historically, American individualism has supported a general American reluctance to rely upon government as a mechanism for meeting social welfare needs. As a result, Americans frequently tend to be suspicious and critical of the state's role in social welfare. While Americans may be reluctant about social welfare, the United States is unique among industrial nations in respect to the degree to which it has experienced an elaborate development of both the voluntary and public sectors of social welfare.

The parallel development of the voluntary and the public social welfare sectors has made the American social welfare system both dynamic, in its ability to change and innovate, and difficult to manage and control. In this chapter we will, therefore, give approximately equal emphasis to the characteristics of both sectors of welfare despite the differences in proportions of financial resources devoted to each of them.

However, the discussion of systems of transfer in the following chapter will be devoted largely to public programs. The practical reason for this allocation of space is that once the reader has grasped the nature of the relationship between the voluntary and public sectors, he must be able to deal with the fact that systems of transfer, whether for voluntary or public programs, will usually involve different levels of government.

Before examining some of the characteristics of voluntary and public financing, we will discuss one other source to which both voluntary and statutory programs sometimes turn for funds—the recipient of the benefits given.

Contributory Schemes and Fee Charging

Recipients of social welfare benefits may be asked to participate directly in financing programs in two ways: by contributions to statutory social and health insurance programs, and through fees paid for services rendered (rather than indirectly through the general tax system). The type of programs we are concerned with here would not be categorized as "private." That is, they do not operate according to the general rules of exchange in the open marketplace. Rather, the conditions of exchange are regulated by government; the exchange reflects recipient need as well as contribution and does not allow for private profit. Fee-for-service arrangements may, of course, operate privately, but these arrangements fall outside the purview of this discussion.

The social security program (OASDHI) is the outstanding example of a contributory system in the United States. The basic principle is that all those who receive benefits at the time that they withdraw from the labor force will have paid "insurance premiums" into the system during their working years, and, like any other insurance system, their investments "earn" entitlements to benefits. However, social security is not like "any other" insurance system. First, it is an involuntary tax on earnings (for employees) and payroll (for employers); both workers and employers contribute to the system. It is estimated that approximately 95 percent of the work force is covered by a combination of the social security system and other governmental retirement systems as a legal requirement. Some groups of workers who are not required to participate may arrange to enter the system voluntarily.[12]

Unlike a private insurance system, OASDHI benefits are not paid on the basis of a contract between private parties (i.e., the contributor and the insurance company). Benefits are determined by Congress and change from time-to-time. As we shall explain in more detail below, while there is some relationship between contributions and benefits, Congress is free to alter these relationships, and benefits are awarded on the basis of need as well as on the basis of contributions.

In fee-charging systems, services are provided publicly or by voluntary organizations on a nonprofit basis with a "user-charge" arrangement. Under these arrangements, fees are often calculated on sliding scales according to the user's economic circumstances and they rarely cover the entire cost of services rendered. This kind of system also can be introduced into contributory programs. For example, under Medicare (the Health Insurance (HI) program which is part of the contributory social security system), beneficiaries may opt to pay $60 per year to participate in Part B of the program which provides for payment of physicians' fees. In addition, there is a deductible charge of $72 for hospital care under Part A which means that the recipient must pay this amount of his bill first before the program covers any costs. In some health plans (such as Britain's National Health Service) members may be required to pay a fee that covers part of the cost for each use (e.g., for each visit to a dentist or for prescribed medication).

Psychological and behavioral consequences are included among the assumptions underlying the use of contributory and fee-charging schemes as sources of finance. From the psychological point of view, it is argued, recipients of benefits (whether financial grants, or goods, or services) are less likely to feel any sense of stigma or indignity about being a recipient when they have contributed their own money to the program even though the benefit may represent a greater number of dollars than the recipient contributed. At the same time, the act of contributing is believed to enhance the individual's sense of social responsibility. This has been one of the major arguments for continuing to operate the social security program on a contributory basis.

The behavioral rationale for contributory schemes and fee-charging, as it applies to service-giving programs, is that contributions from recipients will restrain overutilization. That is, even if recipients have to pay only small amounts for visits to the doctor or therapist the fee will discourage unnecessary and excessive use.

There is little empirical evidence to support or reject the psychological and behavioral arguments for fee-charging and contributory taxes. Recipients of social security benefits appear to feel a greater sense of entitlement to benefits than in some other programs, but what part of this attitude is due to having made contributions to the program and what part is due to general public acceptance of the program is not clear. There are other publicly accepted programs in which the recipients of benefits do not make direct contributions (e.g., unemployment insurance, public education, veterans' benefits), and yet recipients seem to develop the same sense of entitlement.[13]

Sense of entitlement can be based on factors such as compensation or general public commitment to the program. Wolins points out that recipients of Old Age Security in California (one of the federal categorical public assistance programs) receive much better benefits, feel more entitled to their benefits, and are socially perceived as being more entitled to them than recipients of Aid to Families of Dependent Children (another federal categorical public assistance program).[14] Thus, while contributory schemes may have some effect on sense of entitlement, they are by no means determinative by themselves.

Similarly, it is not entirely clear whether contributions and user-fees have an effect upon consumption of benefits. Some policy analysts have pointed out that charging a user-fee for services rendered tends to restrain excessive use on the part of service consumers. But, even small fees may discourage utilization by the neediest segment of the population to whom even a nominal fee can make a great deal of difference in the family budget. Naturally this defeats the distributive purpose of the program.[15]

As Burns points out, contributions and fee-charging are likely to have a responsibility-inducing effect only in small units where individual members can perceive the relationship between the organization's operations and the money they pay in contributions or fees. However, she also notes that because of these contributions the recipient's "belief that he has paid for whatever benefits he gets may . . . work in the opposite direction from that intended by those who view the contributory requirement as a brake upon unreasonable benefit increases or extensions."[16]

Voluntary Financing: Not Entirely a Matter of Private Charity

"Voluntary" financing of social welfare services is not quite as private nor as much an act of philanthropy as we might think at first. Voluntary financing includes programs financed through a variety of organizations: foundations, community chests, and individual agencies, such as the American Cancer Society and Planned Parenthood, that may subsist on contributions, bequests, earnings, and government payments for services and programs.[17]

Essentially, with the exception of government payments, monies used by these kinds of organizations are funds that the government agrees not to tax if the individual taxpayer chooses to contribute them to nonprofit organizations engaged in health, education, welfare, religious, scientific, or cultural activities. In the higher income brackets (i.e., over $200,000 a year), money that is given to nonprofit organizations would be subject to a tax rate of 70 percent if it were not designated as tax-exempt by the government. One way, then, of viewing voluntary welfare funds is as money that has "escaped" from the public treasury.[18]

Thus, it has been said that our "painless" system of private philanthropy, which costs the taxpayer "nothing," is like a "painless dentist." It is hardly ever painless and afterwards something is missing. We would have to go too deeply into the intricacies of tax law to explain these matters much further, but voluntary contributions may not always be motivated entirely by charitable instincts. And under certain conditions (especially in the past when maximum income tax rates were as high as 91 percent), wealthy contributors can even use the system to their economic advantage.[19]

In addition to some doubts about the charitable spirit, there is also question of just how "voluntarily" some private contributions may be given. Community pressures to "give," whether "at the office" or elsewhere, may exert sufficient social coercion so that the choice not to give can only be exercised at great cost to the individual's prestige and economic and social relations. Such pressures, of course, do violence to the whole idea of voluntarism.

Functions of Voluntary Services

Another side to voluntary financing could easily be overlooked if we focused only on the notion of voluntary dollars as funds that "escape" from the public treasury. In one study of the relationship between tax exemption and voluntary giving, 96 percent of donors of large sums said that they would reduce their contributions by an average of 75 percent if tax benefits were removed.[20] Because "tax deductions are a monetary ointment to salve the strains of charity," they provide an incentive for individuals to support nonprofit services of their choice.[21]

Ideally, this arrangement encourages the development of pluralism in community services and provides opportunities for the religious, ethnic, and cultural interests of individuals and groups to flourish without direct government intervention. This is what Kramer refers to as the "value guardian" function of the voluntary agency, which allows for the expression of particularistic and sectarian values in social welfare.[22] In its role of value guardian, the voluntary organization is one of the major social devices for mitigating many of the strains that exist in American political life. The history of successive groups of minority peoples who have been assimilated into American society can be written as a biography of their organizational life.[23]

Charles Henderson, writing in 1895, characterized voluntary organizations as social units that are less permanent and rigid than formal institutions, and are thus better able to meet the needs of a particular class or social category. Of course, many voluntary organizations do evolve into large bureaucratic agencies, a phenomenon that is one of the subjects of interest in the study of social movements and voluntary associations.[24] Henderson's comments on the functions of voluntary associations are still relevant today.

> [Voluntary associations] may be compared to the tenders which ply between the port and the great ships which are more at home on the deep sea than in the shallow harbor or to the skirmish lines which are thrown in advance of the main army . . . It is said that these societies dissipate social energy, rival the home, sap the resources of the church, and multiply like a plague of locusts. Unquestionably, the objection is partly justified by facts. There are too many societies, especially too many bad ones. They overlap, duplicate, and interfere with each other. Some of them seem to be organized simply to advertise the benevolence of the executive secretary . . . But the severest judgment of an abuse leaves the normal use untouched. The voluntary associations require criticism and regulation but the principle of their life is legitimate.[25]

In addition to supporting diversity and pluralism in community life, voluntarily financed services provide an important vehicle for implementing new and possibly unpopular ideas that might not find advocacy in an agency of government. The flexible and changing characteristics of some voluntary agencies make them uniquely suited to this "vanguard" function.[26] This function is exemplified by the Ford Foundation's sponsorship of the Grey Areas Projects, the demonstration program that laid the theoretical base and paved the way for the programs of the President's Committee on Juvenile Delinquency, the Economic Opportunity Program, and the Model Cities Program.[27] But, this is not to imply that governmental agencies are incapable of innovation and experimentation. To the contrary, most of the funds used for research, experimentation, and innovation in social welfare services come from public sources.[28]

Voluntary agencies may also function as "improvers" and "supplementors" of public services.[29] They can serve as critics and "watchdogs" to assure the quality of public services and they can support programs to meet needs that public agencies are unable or unwilling to undertake.

The case of the Family Service Association of America (FSAA) provides a general illustration of the supplementary function performed by a voluntary agency.[30] When the Social Security Act was passed in 1935, the federal government undertook relief-giving functions for special categories of needy individuals. FSAA abandoned the "quantitative" job of providing income relief to the poor and undertook the "qualitative" task of providing highly skilled family casework services. By 1953, FSAA had developed a "family-oriented" casework approach for dealing with social problems and, for a while, the difference between public and FSAAs voluntary services seemed clear. But with the 1956 amendments to the Social Security Act the public assistance program took on a family orientation and states were encouraged to grant assistance and "other services" to needy children and parents and relatives "to help maintain and strengthen family life." The 1958 and 1962 amendments to the Act further strengthened this orientation in the public services. By the mid-1960s, agencies like FSAA began once again to reassess their functions vis-à-vis public services. While there were no doubt many other reasons for the change, in 1971 the Community Service Society of New York City which had been a veritable bastion of family casework services for most of this century announced its intention to abandon this particular program, and concentrate instead on community organization for neighborhood self-improvement.[31] And in 1973 member agencies of the FSAA in Chicago and Minneapolis began to emphasize social advocacy services.

Problems and Issues in Voluntary Financing

Several problems arise in financing social welfare services through voluntary funds. First, there is the question of the criteria to use in deciding which community activities should remain private and voluntary. This question reflects the conflict between cultural pluralism and social equality. For example, should contributions to ethnically or religiously exclusive educational and social welfare agencies be tax-exempt? Should the government provide at least some direct support for those activities of religiously or ethnically exclusive agencies that meet community requirements and standards (e.g., for the strictly educational activities of parochial schools)? Do these actions by government violate constitutional guarantees separating church and state?

The issue becomes even more complex when there is "mixing" of voluntary and public funds. This may take place through a variety of arrangements. *Subsidies* to voluntary agencies are lump sum grants that the government makes to support agency programs. Subsidies have come to be considered poor government policy because, as an essentially "agency-oriented" means of financial support, they commit government to support-ing *all* of the goals and purposes of an organization.[32]

Purchase of service is an arrangement whereby the government pays for services (e.g., foster care) rendered to needy individuals by voluntary agencies. This form of fund-mixing is apparently used extensively. In a 1961 survey of 407 sectarian agencies in twenty-one states, Bernard Coughlin found that 71 percent of the agencies were involved with gov-ernment in some form of purchase of service.[33] In addition, governmental units develop contracts with private and voluntary agencies (both profit and nonprofit) to perform specific services such as development and opera-tion of programs, social planning, research, demonstrations, and training.

The major virtue of these forms of subvention to private and voluntary organizations is that they provide a varied means for starting government programs quickly. They avoid the rigidities of civil service and bureau-cracy. Such characteristics are advantageous for public programs for small special groups of clients and for experiments or demonstrations.

For the voluntary agency, the obvious advantage of these arrangements is access to the public coffers as additional sources of income. But they pay a price. To the extent that voluntary agencies are supported by government funds, they forfeit some degree of autonomy. Consequently, these agen-cies are limited in their ability to function as agents for the expression of new or unpopular ideas, as critics of public services, and as the guardians of pluralistic values. In the extreme, voluntary agencies may simply become an instrument of government policy. As Wickenden suggests, the degree to which governmental constraints upon voluntarism may be im-posed depends in part on the method of financing that is employed, whether indirectly through tax concessions, directly through subsidies or purchase of specified services, or through some other means of government support.[34]

The issue of government involvement places voluntary agencies in a paradoxical situation. On the one hand, government control and influence are seen as undesirable and dysfunctional for the special roles of voluntary agencies. On the other hand, lack of formal mechanisms of accountability to the public also poses a problem. This lack of accountability, or "power without responsibility" as Marris and Rein phrase it, constitutes some-thing of a dilemma for voluntary agencies.

> The dilemma of philanthropy arises from its lack of a base within the political structure from which to organize reform. It must work dis-cretely through those who have, easily finds itself at cross-purposes with its allies, and has little power to assert policy once its grants are committed.[35]

Historically, charitable trusts have been held as "in the public interest" and therefore subject to a degree of government regulation.[36] It is on this basis that voluntary funds can be restricted and some degree of control can be exercised over them. Tax-exempt organizations must be chartered by state governments, and the states may require various kinds of accounting procedures and impose standards of practice upon private agencies. Probably the most important limitation placed on voluntary agencies is that "no substantial part" of the agencies' activities may consist of efforts to influence legislation.[37] This restriction accounts, in part, for the reluctance of many voluntary welfare agencies to become engaged in social action.

Public concern regarding the accountability of voluntary organizations, particularly philanthropic foundations, developed during the 1960s and finally found expression in the Tax Reform Act of 1969. Though it is not as severe as many critics of voluntary organizations desired, the Act does impose several important limitations on voluntary organizations. Almost one-third of the Act is concerned with foundations and establishes new policies regarding investment of funds, public reporting, and the amount of income they may receive on assets. In addition, the Act requires that such organizations pay a 4 percent excise tax on their income and that they dispose of at least 5 percent of their capital annually.[38]

The problems of establishing accountability of voluntary agencies can be understood in relation to a much older and more general notion known as "charitable immunity." Originating in centuries-old English law, this concept holds that charitable trusts cannot be held responsible for dereliction of duties to clients (e.g., negligence and neglect), since without such immunity government intervention might eventually violate the intentions of the donors and limit the functions of voluntary charity.[39] The questions of charitable immunity and the extent to which bequests may be altered by action of government is not insignificant. In 1970 alone, 1.4 billion dollars was bequeathed to charitable organizations,[40] and the accumulation of these funds, as capital assets of non-profit organizations runs into tens of billions of dollars.

Thus, for many years charitable bequests and legacies have been protected by this concept of immunity, sometimes referred to as "the dead hand," and allowed to carry out original purposes which often become outdated. In time, some of these outdated purposes come to appear frivolous and others seriously discriminatory and socially harmful. Whimsical examples from recent history include the following: a trust fund for providing Christmas dinners ("one bushel of oats or a half bushel of corn chops") for hungry horses in Kansas City; Smith Charities of Northampton, Mass., which had a trust fund for providing "marriage portions" for poor young women about to be married; a Bryn Mawr legacy provided "a baked potatoe at each meal for each young lady at Bryn Mawr."[41]

A more serious illustration is the case of Girard College. In this instance the United States Supreme Court decided, after the matter had been under adjudication for many years, that the charitable bequest involved could not be used for tax-exempt purposes if the activities of the enterprise supported discrimination against minority groups, and thus conflicted with the public interest.[42]

Here, the grip of "the dead hand" was loosened by another important legal concept, the *cy pres* doctrine (i.e., "as near as may be"). This doctrine holds that the court may modify bequests to be "as near as" possible to the original intent of the giver in light of social changes that have taken place in the community.[43]

There is another side to the issue of accountability that concerns voluntary agency relationships not with government but with different social classes of the population. Tax-exempt funds for support of nonprofit social welfare activities are distributed unequally within the population. Some people have more money to contribute voluntarily than others, and those with more have greater say in what is to be done with the money. Nielsen, in his analysis of foundations, describes the fundamental contradiction of voluntary philanthropy:

> In the great jungle of American democracy and capitalism, there is no more strange or improbable creature than the private foundation. Private foundations are virtually a denial of basic premises: aristocratic institutions living on the privileges and indulgence of an egalitarian society; aggregations of private wealth which, contrary to the proclaimed instincts of Economic Man have been conveyed to public purposes. Like the giraffe, they could not possibly exist, but they do.[44]

Voluntary agencies are an important part of the policy-making system for social welfare. These agencies, like many others, become organizational vehicles for their professionals, board members, and volunteers to participate in the policy-making system and to become spokesmen of social welfare from the voluntary sector, an important role in American political life. Consequently, voluntary social welfare activities, to the extent that they are accountable to some source, tend to answer to and gravitate toward the interests of the economically advantaged segment of the community. This is no longer an acceptable conception of the public's purpose for supporting voluntarily organized public services.

Elling and Halebsky argue that, at least in part, voluntary social welfare and health services function to meet the needs of higher status groups in society. In a study that compares public hospitals with voluntary hospitals they found that the governmental institutions were generally rated less favorably on several criteria. They draw the following conclusion from their findings:

> In a democratic society, the political system, far from being the power instrument of the capitalist ruling class, as Marx maintained, has often been a major means of control and representation available to ordinary citizens. As changes in medical technology have encouraged the use of the hospital by all elements of society, "upper" elements have preserved the class structure of the community by organizing their own facilities outside of control of the masses and to some extent beyond their participation.[45]

In the last decade there has been great concern about community participation in planning and decision making in all forms of social welfare services. Voluntary as well as public agencies have been criticized and attacked for their failures to provide adequate representation of the interests of the poor and minority groups. In response to criticism and pressure, some voluntary agencies have taken steps to increase the representation of low-income and minority-group people on their boards, and some have begun to review their allocation and program policies in light of these criticisms.[46]

However in recent years the major impetus for more diverse participation in planning social welfare services has come, not from voluntary organizations, but through governmental support of community action programs. The Community Action Program of the Economic Opportunity Act of 1964 required that there be "maximum feasible participation" of the poor in the planning and implementation of programs. (See Chapter 4, pp. 92 to 99). Although the exact meaning of this requirement was not very clear at the time the legislation was passed, it resulted in Community Action Agencies devoting significant resources to fostering participation by many groups that had not previously had the opportunity to do so. Since 1964, most social welfare legislation has required that there be broadly based participation of relevant community groups in social welfare planning and program development.

In effect, government has begun to provide resources to assure that opportunities for voluntary participation in community planning and problem solving are equally available to all. To be sure, citizen participation in community action supported by government funds is a proposition fraught with dangers and filled with contradictions all amply demonstrated in the stormy and colorful history of the War on Poverty. Nonetheless, it represents one of the potentially significant changes that will have taken place in the process of community decision-making in this century.

And this change has put the government into the service of a cause which, traditionally, has been considered in the functional preserve of voluntary agencies.

Public Financing

Public financing refers to *programs supported by units of government with the power to levy taxes.* The units of government and the kinds of taxes they collect are varied. And these variations account, in part, for many of the differences in publicly supported welfare programs. Although the principal purpose of the taxing power is to defray the costs of government, tax law may serve many purposes, one of which is an expression of social welfare policy.

Not Entirely a Public Matter

We have indicated that voluntary financing is not completely a matter of private philanthropy. And public (or governmental) financing of social welfare services is not quite as public a business as it may initially appear. Tax exemptions for charitable contributions are one set of means whereby the community uses its taxing powers to support certain voluntary efforts. There are other "private" uses of the tax system, as illustrated by the federal income tax which provides deductions for medical expenses, and deductions for special groups such as children, the aged, and the blind. All of these are instances of publicly supported means to finance privately implemented social welfare objectives.

When means such as tax exemptions and credits are used by government to achieve social welfare purposes, a high degree of freedom of choice is left to individuals in the consumption of social welfare benefits. In addition, there are also organizational and technical advantages that may lie in social provisions offered through tax exemptions and tax credits compared to provisions offered through subsidies, vouchers, and financial grants. The former requires relatively no administrative apparatus beyond the existing structure for tax collection, while vouchers and grants usually require the development of extensive additional bureaucratic machinery for implementation.

Types of Taxation

Public taxes change the distribution of resources in our society. But redistribution is accomplished by means of a double-edged sword—by taxation and by allocation. We have discussed the allocative end of redistribution in the chapters dealing with the basis of allocation and the nature of the provision. Now we want to look at some of these choices from the fund-raising viewpoint in more detail, specifically at choices concerning the types of taxes levied and the unit of government levying them.

One way to distinguish among types of taxes is to consider their redistributional effects in terms of a regressive-progressive continuum. At the progressive end of the continuum are taxes that are based on individuals' incomes and that are proportionally higher for the wealthy than for the poor. The federal graduated income tax, one of the most progressive taxes in the United States, is an example. Theoretically, in 1972 individuals with incomes below a certain level paid no taxes; those who had incomes of between $12,000 to $14,000 after allowable deductions paid taxes at the overall rate of 22 percent on their income up to $12,000 and at the rate of 29 percent on their income above $12,000. Individuals with taxable incomes of more than $100,000 paid taxes at the overall rate of approximately 53 percent on their income up to $100,000 and at the rate of 70 percent on their income above $100,000.[47] If social welfare programs are financed by the income tax, the *source* of funding is progressive. Provisions thus financed are therefore potentially redistributive, depending upon the economic status of the major beneficiaries.[48]

The primary example of a *regressive tax* is the sales tax, under which everyone is taxed at the same rate regardless of income. The result of such a tax is that the poor pay proportionately higher amounts of their income than the wealthy. For example, consider the differential effects of a 5 percent sales tax on food items. The U.S. Department of Labor estimates that a family of four with an income of approximately $6,500 per year spends approximately $1,800 on food, while a family of the same size with an annual income of approximately $14,500 spends approximately $2,800 on food.[49] On the basis of the 5 percent sales tax the first family is taxed $90 or 1.4 percent of their total income, and the second family is taxed $140 or .9 percent of their total income. Thus, although the wealthier family spends more on food, it still pays a sales tax that represents *proportionately* about one-third less than that paid by the poor family.

If social welfare programs are financed by sales taxes the *source* of funding is regressive. Hence, the program is not likely to have a strong redistributive effect, though there may be a degree of redistribution introduced at the allocative end of the program. The programs that achieve the most redistribution are those that are financed through progressive taxes and then allocate greater benefits to lower-income groups than to higher-income groups.

Other taxes may fall somewhere between the extremes of progressiveness and regressiveness represented by the graduated income tax and the sales tax. The payroll tax used to finance the social security system is a good example.[50] The tax rate is regressive in that all workers pay the *same* 5.85 percent on the first $10,800 of their *earnings* (not *income*). Thus, workers who earned $10,800 a year paid the same annual social security tax of $631.80 as those earning $100,000 a year. (This was the rate in 1973. It will increase to 6.25 percent of the first $12,000 of earnings by 1986.)

But the social security system is redistributive on the allocative end of the equation. That is, the benefits to those who contributed the smallest amounts are proportionately more generous than to those who contributed at higher levels. Some people may receive social security benefits without having made any contributions to the system. For example, all people over seventy-two years of age are entitled to a minimum benefit whether they contributed to the system or not. Medicare began in 1966 and until 1968 operated under the rule that all those over sixty-five years of age could receive all of the medical benefits even if they had made no contributions to the program. However, this rule was temporary and is to be gradually phased out. It is expected that most of the work force will come to be included in the program on the basis of their contributions. In the future, all those over sixty-five may participate in Part A (the hospital insurance) regardless of contributions, but participation in Part B (physicians' fees) will eventually require a minimum of forty quarters of contributions. The social security system is also redistributive between generations because payments to those presently in retirement come from the social security fund, which is supported by the current generation of workers.

Nonetheless, the regressive features of this tax system make it considerably less effective than the income tax as a means for redistribution. Unlike the income tax, the social security tax does not apply to total income, it is not graduated, it does not take account of family size and extraordinary family expenses such as those for medical care and child care. To add to these regressive aspects, tax experts point out that the employer's contributions to social security payroll taxes is most likely to be passed on to the consumer, further nullifying the redistributive effects of the program.[51] Thus, many social welfare policy analysts have supported the view that it would be desirable to finance the social security system at least partially through income tax rather than through the payroll tax.[52]

The payroll tax used for the social security system is one of many "earmarked" taxes. That is, taxes may be classified as "general revenues" (e.g., the income tax) or they may be special purpose taxes, which means they are earmarked and can only be used for purposes designated in legislation. Special purpose taxes are raised by all kinds of governmental units, including units like boards of education, sanitation districts, recreation districts, and so forth.

Earmarking taxes places the burden for supporting a specific program upon a clearly identifiable source of payment. We have already noted some of the general implications of this arrangement for contributory programs where the taxpayer is also a recipient of benefits as in social security. In other programs where the taxpayer is not necessarily a recipient of benefits there are potential advantages and disadvantages to earmarking, depending upon the relationship between the tax and the program it supports. In certain cases, taxpayer resistance may be allayed by the creative linkage of specific taxes to programs. As Burns observes, "on occasion some states have financed their aid to the blind programs by taxes on amusements, for psychological reasons, and the practice of others of using an earmarked tax on meals in restaurants to finance old-age assistance probably relies on the same kind of emotional appeal to the taxpayer."[53]

In addition to the progressive-regressive characteristics of taxes, the unit of government through which taxes are imposed has an important bearing on the design of redistributive programs. Generally speaking, redistributive programs must be financed by progressive taxes that are levied by large governmental units. Only the federal government can levy taxes in all jurisdictions at once, although states can levy almost all of the same kinds of taxes as the federal government. (In 1971 forty-two states had an income tax.) But like other units of government below the federal level, there is a restraining force on the taxing power of the states because they must be concerned about competition from other units of government and about the possible loss of taxpayers who may choose to "escape" excessive taxes. That is, smaller units of government are in constant competition with one another to attract revenue-producing residents or enterprises to their jurisdictions. A unit that levies high taxes may find that industry or more affluent taxpayers move elsewhere.[54] Only the federal government has the taxing power to implement programs that aim at large scale redistribution of wealth.

Additional Considerations:
Taxes and the Stabilization Goals of Government

In considering choices among the alternative sources and amounts of financing that are both possible and desirable, there are other policy concerns that public officials must take into account in addition to redistributional objectives and the social and psychological impact on the taxpayer. The choices in public financing of social welfare programs cannot be realistically stated in the simple terms of, "What are its differential costs and benefits to various economic groups, and will the voters buy it?"

One of the most important concerns of policy makers involves the stabilization goals of government.[55] *Stabilization goals* are those which join monetary policy, manpower policy, fiscal policy, social welfare, and other policies to manipulate the level of aggregate demand for goods and services and thus avoid extremes of inflation, unemployment, and a low balance of payments. The consideration of stabilization goals means that designs for financing social welfare programs must also be analyzed in terms of their effects upon the larger social system, specifically with reference to the functioning of the economic market.

Thus, schemes for financing social welfare programs will be evaluated against such questions as:[56]

1. Should contributory tax rates for social insurance be increased during economic upswings and decreased during downswings to enhance the countercyclical effects of this program?

2. What effects will an increase in social security benefits have upon withdrawal rates of the elderly from the work force?

3. What are the economic implications of distributing the costs of a program over longer periods by basing payments on the accumulation of a reserve fund (which withdraws monies from consumers) as compared to pay-as-you-go financing?

4. To what extent does financing unemployment compensation through employer contributions that vary according to their firms' employment record (taxes based on experience rating) encourage the employer to stabilize employment in his firm?

Although there are limits to the extent to which the economic effects of different financing arrangements can be predicted, policy makers are attentive to these considerations. While students of social welfare policy tend to emphasize the distributional characteristics of alternative modes of public financing, it is important that they remain aware of these additional considerations relating to stabilization goals of government.

Notes

[1]Pearl Peerbloom, "Major Trends in Health, Education, and Welfare," in *Trends, 1966–67* Edition: Part I, National Trends, U.S. Department of Health, Education, and Welfare, (Washington, D.C.: Government Printing Office, 1967), p. 22.

[2]Wilbur J. Cohen, "The Public–Private Venture in Health, Education, and Welfare," in *Trends, 1966–67* Edition, pp. 32–33. The estimates of amounts of money spent by different sources for social welfare services vary, depending upon what items writers include in their estimates, particularly on what items constitute the voluntary/private parts of the equation. For example, Cohen mixes both "volun-

tary" and "private" monies in his estimates of "private" expenditures. Herman Levin, in "Voluntary Organizations in Social Welfare," *Encyclopedia of Social Work*, Vol. II, ed. Robert Morris (New York: National Association of Social Workers, 1971), pp. 1518–24, estimates that 1967–68 expenditures for health and welfare totalled 116.7 billion dollars, 62.6 percent of which came from public funds. However, the overall trends in the balance of public vs. private funding patterns appear to be similar among the different sources we cite.

[3]Cohen, "The Public–Private Venture in Health, Education, and Welfare," p. 35.

[4]*Giving U.S.A.* (New York: Association of Fund Raising Counsel, Inc., 1971).

[5]Marianna O. Lewis, et al., eds., *The Foundation Directory, Edition 4* (New York: Columbia University Press, 1971), p. viii; for a current analysis of American foundations, see Waldemar A. Nielsen, *The Big Foundations* (New York: Columbia University Press, 1972).

[6]For a detailed description of types of foundations, see Warren Weaver, *U.S. Philanthropic Foundations* (New York: Harper & Row, 1967), pp. 57–59; and Nielsen, *The Big Foundations*.

[7]Lewis, *The Foundation Directory*, p. viii.

[8]Alfred M. Skolnik and Sophie R. Dales, "Social Welfare Expenditures, 1971–72," *Social Security Bulletin*, Vol. 35, No. 12 (December 1972), 3–17.

[9]These changes are discussed in greater detail in George Brager and Harry Specht, *Community Organizing* (New York: Columbia University Press, 1973), Chapter 1.

[10]Ralph M. Kramer, "The Future of Voluntary Service Organization: An Organizational Perspective" (Berkeley: School of Social Welfare, University of California, 1973), mimeographed.

[11]Roland L. Warren, *The Community in America* (Chicago: Rand MacNally, 1963), pp. 240–44.

[12]Social Security Administration, *Social Security Programs in the United States*, U.S. Department of Health, Education, and Welfare (Washington, D.C.: Government Printing Office, 1968).

[13]For an analysis of public views toward OASDHI and unemployment insurance, see Michael E. Schiltz, *Public Attitudes Toward Social Security 1935–1965* (Washington, D.C.: Government Printing Office, 1970).

[14]Martin Wolins, "The Societal Function of Social Welfare," *New Perspectives*, Vol. 1, No. 1 (Spring 1967), 12.

[15]Richard Titmuss, *Essays on "The Welfare State"* (London: Unwin University Books, 1963), p. 138.

[16]Eveline M. Burns, *Social Security and Public Policy* (New York: McGraw-Hill, 1956), p. 157.

[17]For example, see Levin, "Voluntary Organizations in Social Welfare"; and *Giving, U.S.A.*

[18]For a more detailed discussion of tax-deductible philanthropic contributions, see C. Harry Kahn, *Personal Deductions in the Federal Income Tax* (Princeton: Princeton University Press, 1960), Chapter 4.

[19]Willard L. Thorp gives the following example: "Suppose a man in the 91 percent income tax bracket holds a security now valued at $10,000 for which he paid $2,000. If he sells it and pays 25 percent capital gains tax, he is left with $8,000 cash on hand. But if he gives the security to a charitable institution, he can deduct the full amount and thus reduce his income tax by $9,100. Not only is he better off by $1,100 but he has the credit for being a generous donor!" (See Thorp, "The Poor Law Revisited," in *Philanthropy and Public Policy* ed. Frank G. Dickinson (New York: Columbia University Press, 1962), p. 142.

[20]Gordon Manser, "The Voluntary Agency–Contribution or Survival?" *Washington Bulletin*, Vol. 22, No. 20 (October 1971), 107; *Voluntary Giving and Tax Policy* (New York: National Assembly for Social Policy and Development, 1972).

[21]One interesting note on tax-exempt contributions in this context is that the majority of taxpayers only contribute a small proportion of the funds that could be given as tax free. In studies of patterns of philanthropic giving it has been found that most taxpayers, including those reporting exceedingly high annual incomes, do not contribute anywhere near the percentages of the resources for charitable purposes that would be allowable under the exemption system. Kahn, *Personal Deductions in the Federal Income Tax,* and William S. Vickrey, "One Economist's View of Philanthropy," in Dickinson, *Philanthropy and Public Policy.*

[22]Kramer, "The Future of Voluntary Service Organization."

[23]For example, see Oscar Handlin, *The Uprooted* (New York: Grosset and Dunlap, 1951); and Milton M. Gordon, *Assimilation In American Life* (New York: Oxford University Press, 1964).

[24]For example see C. Wendell King, *Social Movements in the United States* (New York: Random House, 1956); and David L. Sills, *The Volunteers* (New York: Free Press, 1957).

[25]Charles Richard Henderson, "The Place and Functions of Voluntary Associations," *American Journal of Sociology,* Vol. 1 (November 1895), pp. 334–39.

[26]Kramer, "The Future of Voluntary Service Organization."

[27]Peter Marris and Martin Rein, *Dilemmas of Social Reform: Poverty and Community Action in the United States* (New York: Atherton, 1967). For a dramatic account of how foundations undertake projects that the government may abjure because of political considerations, see Thomas C. Reeves, *Freedom and the Foundation: The Fund for the Republic in the Era of McCarthyism* (New York: Alfred A. Knopf, 1969).

[28]Alvin L. Schorr, "The Tasks for Voluntarism in the Next Decade," presented at the Centenary Conference on Voluntary Organization in the 1970s, sponsored by the Family Welfare Association, University of Sussex, Brighton, England (June 1969). Schorr cites five pioneering ventures of the 1960s which he notes were largely inspired and set in motion by government: the juvenile delinquency programs; community action; amendments to the Social Security Act; community care of the mentally ill; and the Model Cities Program.

[29]Kramer, "The Future of Voluntary Service Organization."

[30]This example is based on the article by Herman Levin, "The Future of Voluntary Family and Children's Social Work: A Historical View," *Social Service Review,* Vol. 38, No. 2 (June 1964), 164–73.

[31]"Social Work Unit Changing Tactics," *New York Times*, January 29, 1971, p. 1.

[32]Arlien Johnson, "Public Funds for Voluntary Agencies," *Social Welfare Forum, 1959* (New York: Columbia University Press, 1959).

[33]Bernard J. Coughlin, S. J., *Church and State in Social Welfare* (New York: Columbia University Press, 1965).

[34]Elizabeth Wickenden, "Purchase of Care and Services: Effect on Voluntary Agencies," in *Proceedings of the First Milwaukee Institute on a Social Welfare Issue of the Day* (Milwaukee: School of Social Welfare, July 1970).

[35]Marris and Rein, *Dilemmas of Social Reform*, p. 130.

[36]Austin W. Scott, "Charitable Trusts," *Encyclopedia of the Social Sciences, Vol. III*, eds. Edwin R. A. Seligman, *et al* (New York: Macmillan, 1937), pp. 338–40.

[37]The Tax Reform Act of 1969 made the prohibition on social and political action even more stringent for organizations classified as "private foundations" by removing the qualifying word, "substantial."

[38]See, *General Explanation of the Tax Reform Act*, 9162, H. R. 13270, Public Law 91–1972 (Washington, D.C.: Government Printing Office, 1970), pp. 48–49.

[39]For a detailed discussion of the concept of charitable immunity, see George W. Keeton, *The Modern Law of Charities* (London: Sir Isaac Pitman and Sons, Ltd., 1962).

[40]*Giving U.S.A.*, p. 8.

[41]Warren Weaver, *U.S. Philanthropic Foundations* (New York: Harper & Row, 1967), pp. 11, 23; see also Julius Rosenwald, "Principles of Giving," *The Atlantic Monthly*, May, 1929; and Wilmer Shields Rich, "Community Foundations in the U.S. and Canada" (New York: National Council on Foundations, 1961).

[42]For a detailed history of the Girard College case see Milton M. Gordon, "The Girard College Case: Desegregation and a Municipal Trust," *The Annals of the American Academy of Political and Social Science*, March 1956, pp. 53–62.

[43]For further discussion of *cy pres* see Keeton, *The Modern Law of Charities*, and Edith L. Fisch, *The Cy Pres Doctrine in the United States* (New York: Matthew Bender and Co., 1950), pp. 141–42. On the general controlling legal principle as applied to Girard College, see "Validity and Effect of Gifts for Charitable Purposes Which Exclude Otherwise Qualified Beneficiaries Because of Race or Religion," in 25 ALR 3d 736 (1969).

[44]Nielsen, *The Big Foundations*, p. 32.

[45]Ray H. Elling and Sandor Halebsky, "Support for Public and Private Services," in *Social Welfare Institutions*, ed. Mayer N. Zald (New York: John Wiley & Sons, 1965), p. 329.

[46]For example, see the following: United Bay Area Crusade, *New Directions Report*, San Francisco, Ca. (June 1971), United Community Fund of Greater Toronto, *Reexamination Project*, Toronto, Ontario, Canada (May 1971), United Foundation, *Priorities Study*, Detroit, Mich. (April 1971), United Community Services of San Diego County, *UCS Implementation Program* (November 1971), and

Bertram M. Beck, "The Voluntary Social Welfare Agency: A Reassessment," *Social Service Review*, Vol. 44, No. 2 (June 1970), 147–54.

[47]The income tax system is complicated and allows for many different kinds of deductions, some of which mitigate its theoretically progressive character. For a discussion of various means used by the wealthy to evade tax on large amounts of income, see Gabriel Kolko, *Wealth and Power in America* (New York: Praeger, 1962).

[48]For an assessment of the redistributive effects of public income distribution programs, see Robert J. Lampman, "How Much Does the American System of Transfers Benefit the Poor?" in *Economic Progress and Social Welfare*, ed. Leonard H. Goodman (New York: Columbia University Press, 1966), pp. 125–57.

[49]U.S. Department of Labor, *Three Budgets for an Urban Family of Four Persons, Preliminary Spring 1969 Costs Estimates* (Washington, D.C.: Government Printing Office, 1969).

[50]This tax ranks as the third largest federal tax, coming after the individual income tax and corporation income tax.

[51]Joseph A. Pechman, *et al., Social Security: Perspectives for Reform* (Washington, D.C.: Brookings Institution, 1968), pp. 175–78.

[52]Pechman, *Social Security;* Burns, *Social Security and Public Policy;* and Titmuss, *Essays on 'The Welfare State.'*

[53]Burns, *Social Security and Public Policy,* p. 173.

[54]Walter W. Heller, "Reflections on Public Expenditure Theory," in *Private Wants and Public Needs,* ed. Edmund S. Phelps (New York: W. W. Norton, 1965).

[55]Heller, "Reflections on Public Expenditure Theory."

[56]For a detailed analysis of these and other issues concerning the relationship between public finance arrangements and stabilization goals, see Margaret A. Gordon, *The Economics of Welfare Policies* (New York: Columbia University Press, 1963).

Mode of Finance:
Systems of Transfer

*In general, the art of government consists in taking as much
money as possible from one class of citizens to give to the other.*
                                                    VOLTAIRE
                                    Dictionnaire Philosophique

7 The complex political system of the United States divides
power among the executive, legislative, and judicial branches
by a system of checks and balances that exists at several levels
of government. There are, of course, variations in the system at
the municipal, county, state, and federal levels, not to mention other
specialized units of government such as regional districts, authorities, and
boards. In 1967 it was estimated that there were approximately 105,000
units of government in the United States, and this count does not include
many kinds of semi-autonomous units and agencies.[1]

Jurisdiction over programs and services to meet social welfare needs is
distributed among these levels of government in various ways. One program (e.g., public assistance) may be under the exclusive administrative
authority of the state in some states and under state and county authority
in other states. The powers of a particular government may vary from
program to program (e.g., states share authority with the federal government in public assistance, have almost complete authority for unemployment insurance, and have practically no authority in the social security or
the Model Cities Program).

There are in this complex system of division of powers and checks and
balances a limitless number of arrangements that can be made for the

transfer of allocations for social welfare programs from the source of finance to the point of delivery. The choices made in regard to the system of transfer are affected by, and will affect, the other dimensions of choice. Two examples illustrate this point.

The first example comes from the public assistance program. When the federal government adopted the policy of separating the delivery of services and income in public assistance (thereby affecting choices in the nature of the provision and the delivery system) several innovations in the system of transfer were introduced to implement the policy. The federal government provided financial incentives for states to reorganize the delivery of service and cash provisions. In addition, the federal government reorganized its own operations so that states had to report financial grants to one office and services to another office, thus making it not only economically unrewarding but operationally uncomfortable for the states to maintain a unified system. Specifically, in 1967 HEW was reorganized internally with the creation of the Social and Rehabilitation Service Administration assuming responsibility for (and holding state and local agencies accountable for) services, and the Assistance Payments Administration assuming responsibility for the money-payments aspects of the public assistance program.

For a different example, we shall briefly compare the legislation that established the Office of Economic Opportunity (OEO) with the legislation creating the Model Cities Program. The War on Poverty was based in an "office" (OEO), while the Model Cities Program was established in the Department of Housing and Urban Development (HUD) under the Model Cities Administration. Being part of HUD, the organizational resources of the Model Cities Administration were greater than those of the OEO, but the commitments of HUD to all of the constituencies served by its various programs were greater in comparison to the uncommitted OEO. Thus, the Model Cities Administration could bring greater organizational resources to bear in the Model Cities Program, but was bound by HUD's commitments to its various constituencies. OEO could be much more freewheeling but had less in the way of organizational resources to back up its policy goals.

OEO was able to respond to a wide variety of arrangements for transferring money to the local level because the Community Action Programs (CAPs), the local vehicles for implementation, could be constituted by different kinds of public or private groups. (This freedom was reduced somewhat by the Green Amendment to the Economic Opportunity Act in 1967). In the Model Cities Program, HUD did not have this freedom. The legislation that created the Model Cities Program stated clearly that the City Demonstration Agency (CDA), the local vehicle for implementation, was to be established by the local governing body of the city or county.

The effect of these differences was that OEO often bypassed established government and developed new constituencies in the cities. HUD, on the other hand, could not implement the Model Cities Program without the approval and cooperation of established local government. The details of the costs and benefits of the different systems of transfer in OEO and Model Cities are more complex than this, but even this minimal description should make it clear that the choice of the hands through which money for a program is to pass has an effect upon other aspects of policy.

These examples of financing arrangements in public assistance, OEO and HUD, point up two major features of the system of transfer which we will consider: (1) how the money flows, and (2) the conditions attendant to the transfer. Readers should bear in mind that these features apply equally to publicly and voluntarily financed programs, although the political nature of these decisions is usually not as obvious in voluntary programs as they are in public programs.

How the Money Flows

In *federated* systems (like our federal government) allocations of money flow like water—downward. In *confederated* systems, where the smaller units have greater power than the larger unit (as in Canada), the flow of money is less clearly unidirectional from central government down to the local community. While there are some confederated systems among private agencies in the United States, our discussion will deal primarily with the downward flow of money since that is the direction in which it usually goes in our country.[2]

Although the federal government has preeminence in revenue-raising ability over the states, and the states over yet smaller units, there is much support in the United States for the general belief that programs are better implemented and administered by smaller units than by larger units. While increasingly larger proportions of funds to support programs emanate from the federal or state levels, there remains a strong impulse toward community control and self-determination at the local level, and this impulse is probably stronger in regard to health, education, and welfare services than others.

Power to implement and administer programs carries with it some degree of control over the choices regarding the nature of provisions, basis of allocations, and system of delivery. However, this devolution of power has implications beyond choices for designing the program that is funded, since the transfer of program funds to a unit confers upon it the ability to dispense benefits to a constituency, to hire and appoint staff, and to award contracts. Apart from programmatic choices, the transfer of funds among units represents the exchange of important political resources and there is strong competition among units of government to control these resources.

Social welfare agencies and programs are established by a combination of law, tradition, and experience and come to be supported by an organizational and institutional apparatus. Hence, they do not change as quickly as political coalitions do. But the arrangements for transferring funds that are made in the formulation of policy are likely to reflect current political coalitions.

The example of OEO and Model Cities legislation, discussed above, illustrates how political coalitions are a consideration in transfers. Both OEO and Model Cities are programs directed at urban areas. In OEO the system of transfer reflected desires of the incumbent Democratic federal administration to link itself with the newly developing voting blocks in the cities, particularly with minority groups. Model Cities represents a variation on this theme, for in that program the federal administration was pushing for the development of new coalitions between low-income and minority residents and city hall. We will point out in the next chapter how later developments in the Model Cities Program reflect the interest of the federal government in increasing the power of executive-centered government in cities.

Revenue-sharing proposals in the early 1970s offer a final example of how the system of transfer reflects political coalitions. The thrust toward revenue sharing with the states is, not surprisingly, an interest of a Republican national administration. The Republicans inherited OEO and the Model Cities Program from their Democratic predecessors. Because these programs were established by law, tradition, and experience and were supported by an organizational and institutional apparatus, the Republicans had to live with them temporarily, later containing and modifying them with an eye to ultimately eliminating them. The low-income and minority groups in urban areas do not represent a major segment of the Republican constituency. State governments and city-wide government are more likely to reflect Republican interests and to represent important parts of the Republican constituency. Therefore, some forms of revenue sharing with the states and cities is of greater interest to Republicans than to Democrats.

We have described the flow of money as though it is a simple and clear-cut exchange between two parties, but this is not always the case. Several actors may be involved, and the benefits to each may vary. For example, the OEO legislation required that funds to a local CAP have the approval of the state's governor. (However, the 1967 amendments to the Act gave the national director of OEO authority to override the governor's veto.) Thus, although he did not receive the money, the governor could exercise some control over the transfer. In the Model Cities Program, it was required that funds for the CDA "pass through" the city, thus giving the city some control over expenditures. In both programs the "guidelines" (i.e., the rules set down on the basis of administrative discretion) required "sign-offs" from various local, state, and federal agencies, meaning that funding required their general approval.

While political considerations may influence choices concerning the units to which funds will be given, some degree of scientific analysis also enters into these decisions. That is, technically, there are some identifiable characteristics of units that can be utilized in selecting the one that is most appropriate to receive funds. These characteristics would include the degree of expertise and the resources required of the local unit to administer a program; the appropriate size of the unit given the substantive nature of the program; and the nature of the problem for which a programmatic solution is being sought. However, application of these technical considerations requires the utmost care and scrutiny. Often, for each logical reason given to vest a program in one unit (e.g., "They will be more efficient") another equally compelling reason can be found to vest it in another unit (e.g., "They are more committed to these policy goals," or "They are closer to the problem").

Moynihan's observations on a report by the Task Force on Jurisdiction and Structure of the State Study Commission for New York City illustrate how technical considerations apply to the allocation of program responsibility between different units. Regarding the allocation of services the Task Force suggests that rat control services should be a central function, while service centers to provide information on poison control should be a local responsibility. In both cases Moynihan argues that the reverse arrangements are technically superior. As for rat control services he notes:

> Given stable food and harborage, the model urban rat lives and dies in an area extending at most a few hundred feet . . . the urban rat is preeminently a neighborhood type, preferring when possible, never even to cross the street. As for rodent control, opinion is universal (as best I know) that the fundamental issue is how homonids maintain their immediate surroundings. I cannot conceive a municipal service more suited to local control, nor one which more immediately calls on those qualities of citizenship which the Task Force describes as constituting in some degree a "quasi-governmental responsibility" toward the community. It comes down, alas, to the question of keeping lids on garbage cans. What better issue for Neighborhood Service Representatives to take up?[3]

On the other hand, Poison Control Centers provide services that require great knowledge about the chemical nature of different substances that people may have ingested as well as possible antidotes in cases where the chemicals are poisonous. Quick access by day or night to a tremendous bank of information is required. In light of these requirements, Moynihan suggests:

> At very least it should be a City function, although a good case could be made for making it regional, or perhaps national: one telephone number anywhere in the Nation, putting the doctor through to a laboratory/computer facility that would provide the most information fastest. The idea that such a function could be broken down into thirty to thirty-five separate centers, in New York City alone, each to be manned day and night is . . . not persuasive.[4]

Finally, a major consideration in flow of funds is whether lesser units should operate a program for which they do not have financial responsibility. Here, the issue is how responsible the unit will be in spending funds that they do not have to raise, and whether they will act in the financial interests of the granting authority. For example, one general critique of financing in the public assistance program is that the federal government gives almost a blank check to the states by paying major costs of a program in which the basic determinants of costs—the number of recipients and level of benefits—are left to the control of the states.[5]

Not all transfers of monies between units result in a loss of control over major decisions by the larger unit. In the next section we will discuss some of the means that are used to assure that grantees meet conditions specified by the granting authority.

Conditions Attendant to the Transfer

The conditions that attach to the transfer of funds among units refer to the means by which funders attain compliance with the goals and purposes of the program they are supporting. These conditions may range from grant requirements that detail the purposes funds may be used for to those that leave specification of purpose to the discretion of grant recipients. At the first extreme the grantee may be figuratively bound hand and foot in a tight contractual arrangement, accounting for each nickle spent and held to spending it as directed by the grantor. A "fee-for-service" program is the best example of how fees-agreed-upon-in-advance are paid for specified services or goods provided by the receiving unit. General revenue sharing is a good example of the other extreme, where larger units transfer funds to smaller units for "general" purposes, leaving the grantee free to spend the money in almost any way he chooses.

Between these two extremes lie a number of possible variations such as categorical grants, block grants, and special revenue sharing, which we will discuss in the next section. But even in fee-for-service funding, there are several choices. With the "capitation" principle, the individuals or organizations are paid "by the head"; that is, they receive a fixed sum for each client served regardless of the specific services given. With a "cost" basis of payment the individuals or organizations providing service are paid for the unit of service given to the client. Advantages and disadvantages to each of these forms of payment vary with the program. Capitation is helpful in predicting costs and maintaining economy and efficiency, especially when the size of the eligible service population is known. However, when the service given the client is fixed in advance by the "per head" amount, providers may be tempted to scrimp on what is given since their fee is fixed regardless of their costs. This principle is useful when the service is very specific (e.g., giving vaccinations). The cost principle is best used when services are complex and charges are difficult to calculate in advance.

However, it is generally harder to maintain budget control with the "at-cost" principle since providers may offer, and users may request, services that are unnecessary. One effect of an at-cost fee-for-service system may be to encourage providers to "charge what the traffic will bear." Recent studies in Canada suggest that the liberal use of an at-cost fee-for-service mechanism in health insurance allows medical practitioners to render the most expensive services regardless of need. A policy paper on health insurance produced for the cabinet of Manitoba finds that "The effect of [the at-cost] system is to encourage the doctor to resort, in a given case, to the procedure that offers him the highest return."[6] Programs funded on an at-cost fee-for-service basis must usually be bound by detailed guidelines and reporting and evaluation procedures in order to maintain control of both quality of service and financing.

One of the fundamental dilemmas that inheres in choice of conditions attached to the transfer is, as Burns has pointed out, that the more detailed the defining standards the more control and autonomy is removed from the units responsible for service-delivery. In part this condition defeats the very rationale for delegating programs to these units, yet the less definite the conditions of the grant the less assurance there is to those who pay the bills that they are getting what they paid for.[7]

This dilemma has become an increasingly difficult one to resolve as our society becomes more complex and the interdependence of units increases. Consider the growth in the "grants economy" (i.e., the transfers of money from private organizations or government to individuals, organizations, or other units of government) over the last decades. Kenneth Boulding estimates that in 1929 grants came to about 5 billion dollars, approximately 1/20 of our gross national product at that time. By 1966, grants constituted about 1/7 of our gross national product and came to about 100 billion dollars. The number of units of government, agencies, and organizations involved in these exchanges is quite substantial.[8] For example, in 1970–71 the federal government alone had approximately 500 different kinds of categorical grant programs which provided 29.2 billion dollars to smaller units of government. Slightly more than 72 percent of this amount, 21.1 billion dollars, was allocated for programs with social welfare purposes.[9]

Bear in mind that there are differences in the legislation establishing these programs, in the jurisdictions which administer them and to which they apply, in the formulas for distributing funds, and in other conditions that attach to the grants. From this we can understand why many smaller units are unable to even maintain an inventory of categorical programs operating within their jurisdictions, much less be able to plan and coordinate programs on a rational basis.[10] The federal government has responded to this situation by attempting to increase local capacity for planning (e.g., the Model Cities Program and the Allied Services Bill of 1972) or by revenue sharing and other measures which simplify the process of transferring money.

Marris and Rein sum up the federal government's problems in managing the grants economy in their history of the poverty program:

> [American] society guards against abuse of power by diffusing and fragmenting it. Any authority to direct change is necessarily confined within a single jurisdiction. . . . The administrative and political structure of the United States explicitly intends no power, at any level of government, shall claim an authority broad enough to control all institutions of a community . . . and this principle is upheld by radicals and conservatives alike. . . . [11]
>
> The dilemma of federal government arises from the multiplicity of overlapping agencies, each with its own political constituency, through which its policies must be implemented. A coherent plan for reform depends upon coordination. But the instrument of coordination rarely finds its authority accepted, and tends to become yet another agency competing for power, adding still further to the confusion of the rival jurisdictions.[12]

Within this context, funding agencies attempt to achieve compliance with their goals in a number of ways. These efforts can be categorized broadly in terms of *grant requirements, timing, and reporting procedures* that may be statutory (i.e., written into the legislation) or left to the discretion of the program's administrator (at the funding end).

Grant Requirements

Smaller units may receive money under several conditions. The requirement that there be "matching" funds for a program means that the smaller unit must make a contribution (in cash or kind) to the financing. The funding agency may require matching funds as a means of assuring that the smaller unit assumes responsibility for achieving economy and efficiency in their operation. Matching is also used to redirect the allocations of resources in smaller units. Frequently, programs may be financed on a decreasing basis. For example, in the Community Action Program, the plan was for the Office of Economic Opportunity to pay 90 percent of expenses for first-year operations and less for each succeeding year, the aim being to entice local governments into supporting the program by giving a generous federal boost at the start.

A negative consequence of the matching method is that smaller units may tend to invest their resources in programs that attract the most federal dollars and to ignore others. This has been the case in income-maintenance programs. For example, smaller units invest far greater resources in Old Age Assistance where the federal matching formula gives them a very good return for their investment, and comparatively little in General Assistance where there is no federal matching.

More significantly, the matching grant requirement tends to exacerbate inequalities that exist among different units. Units that are poor and cannot afford to put up their matching share receive little or nothing, while wealthier units are able to pyramid their resources by raising large sums to be matched by the funding agency. The fact that poorer units usually have greater social welfare needs further compounds the maldistribution of resources resulting from this grant requirement. Thus, matching grant arrangements are often modified by the introduction of additional variables into the funding formula, such as size of population, proportion of work force unemployed, and per capita income of residents within the political unit to which the program will apply. With such variables under consideration, formulas may be developed whereby poorer units are required to contribute a smaller proportion of matching funds as, for example, in the case of states matching share for public assistance discussed in Chapter 2 (p. 34).

Funding agencies may exercise considerable leverage in achieving compliance with their objectives through grant requirements addressed to the purpose of the program being funded. In this regard, we have already indicated that a large measure of the control by the funding agency is gained through fee-for-service arrangements (capitation or at-cost) and that the least control over how funds are used is obtained through general revenue sharing. Between these two extremes there are three representative funding arrangements, as illustrated in Figure 7–1, that vary in terms of the degree to which the specific purposes for which funds may be used are a requirement of the grant.

Categorical grants refer to funding arrangements that specify with some exactness who is to be served, what benefits they are to receive, and how the delivery system is to be organized. For this reason, the public assistance program is often referred to as "the categorical program," although the term applies to many others. Categorical programs may specify any number of conditions, including requirements regarding certification and licensing of personnel who are hired, how recipients are to be interviewed, and the appeals machinery that smaller units must set up. This method of funding insures that the unit of government that raises revenue has substantial control over its expenditure. The categorical method usually requires that the recipient unit contribute matching funds and that, prior to funding, program plans for grant use be approved by the funding unit.

Block grants are funding arrangements that consolidate a number of related categorical grants into lump-sum grants that may be used for general purposes *within* designated functional areas, such as law enforcement, education, and public health. Similar to categorical funding, the block grant method usually requires matching funds and prior project approval. But block grants allow recipient units more latitude than categorical grants in determining the specific allocation of funds to programs within functional areas. In block grant funding the balance of control over basic policy formulation is shifted from larger/central units to smaller/local units.

Special revenue sharing is a variation on the block grant funding method that allows for virtually unrestricted use of funds within specified functional areas. Since special revenue sharing arrangements do not require matching funds or prior project approval, this method affords almost complete control to recipient units over the use of funds within functional areas.[13]

TABLE 7–1

Funding Arrangements	Specification of Purpose
Fee-for-service	Most specific
Categorical grants	↑
Block grants	
Special revenue sharing	↓
General revenue sharing	Least specific

Timing

The duration of programs is another variable factor in funding that may be used by funding agencies to introduce controls over units that receive grants. Programs funded on a year-to-year basis are under continual pressure to maintain the political support required to sustain their operation. For time-limited programs (e.g., demonstrations) this is less of a problem but it is of considerable concern for programs that are expected to be ongoing. For example, OEO was funded in this way until 1969 and as a result personnel had to confront Congress and justify their operations each year in order to be refunded. In 1969 OEO funding was put on a two-year basis which provided somewhat more security and which required somewhat less expenditure of organizational resources for self-maintenance. Programs can be funded for almost any period of time. Those which are funded "permanently" may never be subject to Congressional review until there is an attempt to change the legislative basis of the program.

Records and Reports

Maintaining records and reporting information about program operations is one of the ways in which funding agencies develop judgments about the outcomes of the programs they are supporting. They can set conditions that describe what records the grantees will maintain and what they will report. Funders may not want all recording reported to them. Instead, they may do occasional audits of or take samples of agency records.

Probably no other grant condition placed upon smaller units excites more outrage and resentment than reporting requirements. Detailed report forms submitted in quadruplicate on a monthly basis to some central body is a fact of bureaucratic life that action-oriented practitioners find stifling. At the same time, these requirements may be no less frustrating to the funders. While in large and complex systems, funding agencies must depend upon reporting procedures to determine the extent to which the goals of a program are achieved, it is often difficult to determine in advance what "important" items of information are necessary to fulfill this purpose.

Generally speaking there are limits to the utility of reporting requirements as a mechanism to maintain control over expenditures, especially in large programs with ambitious objectives. In the Model Cities Program, for example, CDAs were able to report their financial expenditures. But it was nearly impossible to develop a reporting system that could inform HUD of what the CDAs were actually doing and accomplishing. Attempts to

develop an information system to do this bogged down because of the
uncertainty inherent in a complex, multifaceted program where much
latitude was given to local initiative. What items of information should be
counted to actually measure the program's progress? How much weight
should be given to the numbers of individuals or agencies participating in
planning, or the quality of the process, or the outcome of the process?
What criteria are indicative of the quality or relevance of programs
planned? All of these factors are related to the goals of the Model Cities
Program, but the goals as stated in the legislation are so vague, global, and
comprehensive that in many respects they defy measurement. In addition,
there are several other qualifying factors that must be reconciled to understand how the program worked (such as race and income of participants,
size of city, and other programs operating in the city). Thus the problem
of developing a meaningful reporting system was unmanageable in the
early stages of the program. As a result, reporting of Model Cities Programs, like many other social welfare programs, remained a source of
frustration to funders and receivers alike.[14]

Centralization versus
Decentralization of Authority

In the United States there are over 25,000 school districts which respond
to different needs and local traditions. The two biggest cities in the country
each have populations that are as large as and more varied in ethnic
composition than Sweden's. Given such size and diversity in a federated
system, the balance between centralization and decentralization of authority is a perennial issue.

In the design of social welfare policy, values and assumptions related to
centralization and decentralization are expressed in a number of ways,
foremost among which are the choices made concerning the degree of
public or voluntary financing, the flow of money between units and the
conditions placed upon the transfer. When the money flows only to large
central units on the federal or state level, or when central funding to small
local units is accompanied by rigid guidelines and restrictions, the freedom
of local units to define their own social welfare objectives is impinged
upon.

"Community control," "self-determination," "participatory democracy," and "local initiative" are catch-words that convey the strong feelings vested in the value of decentralization. The presumed virtues of
decentralization may be summarized as follows: Local governments are
more knowledgeable about problems in their areas; they are more responsive to the special needs of their constituencies; and they function more

directly in line with "the consent of the governed" than large centralized units. In addition, small decentralized units can more easily experiment because if they fail, all is not lost; instead, the losses suffered through the failure of one unit's experiment may be compensated for by the spillover of successful experiments of other small units. Finally, there is an existential quality about small decentralized units that is appealing. They lend themselves more readily to visions of the Gemeinschaft marked by warm, meaningful relationships and a sense of belonging to the community in contrast to the bureaucratic-alienation of large centralized units.[15]

Yet, there is another side to the existential quality of localism that is parochial and oppressive. Privacy and freedom may find more secure shelter in the cold impersonality of large centralized units. As McConnell argues:

> Impersonality is the guarantee of individual freedom characteristic of the large unit. Impersonality means an avoidance of arbitrary official action, the following of prescribed procedure, conformance to established rules, and escape from bias whether for or against any individual. Impersonality, and the privacy and freedom it confers, may be despised, and the human warmth and community concern for the personal affairs of individuals characteristic of the small community preferred. Nevertheless, the values involved are different, and are to a considerable degree antagonistic.[16]

The defense of minority interests within small decentralized units is often more difficult to achieve than within the larger unit. In small units it is easier to weld a cohesive majority that may disregard the interests of other groups or that bring great pressure for conformity to bear upon these groups. Further arguments for centralization are made on the grounds that the larger centralized unit tends to be more progressive and commands greater resources to attract and support administrative expertise than smaller units. Moreover, some problems are clearly beyond the scope of local initiative.

Thus, the sovereignty of local units is not without potential limitations and abuses, and the centralization of authority has some potential virtues. Further arguments can be made in the abstract to support one or the other of these arrangements, but it is clear that in practical matters most groups support different degrees of centralization or decentralization in regard to specific social welfare policies. The political left, for example, traditionally supports centralization of income-maintenance programs. Currently, the political left also supports an extreme form of decentralization (e.g., "community control") of certain services such as education, health, and law enforcement.[17] Opposition to this form of decentralization tends to come from the political right, although it is traditionally decentralist in inclination. The political right, however, would subscribe to perhaps the most extreme form of decentralization of services which involves the government providing grants directly to individual consumers in the form of vouchers for service.[18]

Finally, it is possible to find parties supporting both centralization and decentralization *at the same time* because different system levels are involved in either choice. For example, it is possible to support decentralization of programs at the federal level and centralization at the state or municipal level. We shall illustrate this in detail in the next chapter.

Notes

[1]U.S. Department of Commerce, *Statistical Abstract of the United States* (Washington, D.C.: Government Printing Office, 1969), pp. 405–6.

[2]For an analysis of the organizational effects of unitary vs. confederated systems, see Martin Rein and Robert Morris, "Goals, Structures, and Strategies for Community Change," in *Readings in Community Organization Practice*, eds. Ralph M. Kramer and Harry Specht (Englewood Cliffs, N.J.: Prentice-Hall, 1969), pp. 188–201.

[3]Daniel P. Moynihan, "Comments on 'Re-Structuring the Government of New York City'," in *The Neighborhoods, the City, and the Region: Working Papers in Jurisdiction and Structures* (New York: State Study Commission for New York City, 1973), p. 15.

[4]Moynihan, "Comments on 'Re-Structuring the Government of New York City'," p. 16.

[5]Eveline M. Burns, *Social Security and Public Policy* (New York: McGraw-Hill, 1958), p. 230.

[6]" 'Fee for Service' Abuses Leading to MDs on Salary," *Victoria Times,* August 7, 1972, p. 5.

[7]Burns, *Social Security and Public Policy*, p. 235.

[8]Kenneth E. Boulding, "Grants Versus Exchange in the Support of Education," *Federal Programs for the Development of Human Resources,* Subcommittee on Economic Progress of the Joint Economic Committee, Congress of the United States, Vol. 1 (Washington, D.C.: Government Printing Office, 1968), p. 232.

[9]Sophie R. Dales, "Federal Grants to State and Local Governments, 1970–71," *Social Security Bulletin,* Vol. 35, No. 6 (June 1972), 29–38.

[10]See, for example, San Francisco Federal Executive Board, *An Analysis of Federal Decision-Making and Impact: The Federal Government in Oakland,* Oakland Task Force, Oakland, Ca. (August 1968, two volumes); Advisory Commission on Intergovernmental Relations, *Special Revenue Sharing: An Analysis of the Administration's Joint Consolidation Proposals* (Washington, D.C.: Government Printing Office, December 1971), pp. 19–20.

[11]Peter Marris and Martin Rein, *Dilemmas of Social Reform* (New York: Atherton, 1967), p. 137.

[12]Marris and Rein, *Dilemmas of Social Reform,* p. 130.

[13]For a more detailed analysis of revenue sharing arrangements, see Melvin Mogulof, Neil Gilbert, and Harry Specht, "Allocating Funds for Social Welfare Services: The Prospects and Problems of Special Revenue Sharing," Warner Modular Publications (forthcoming); and John C. H. Oh, "How Good Federalists Can Take Advantage of Revenue Sharing," *Human Needs,* Vol. 1, (April-May 1973), 8–12.

[14]Some of the difficulties in devising performance measures as means of maintaining accountability to federal funders are discussed by Alice M. Rivlin, *Systematic Thinking for Social Action* (Washington, D.C.: Brookings Institution, 1971), pp. 122–144.

[15]For a creative and lively explication of the decentralist's position, see Paul Goodman, *People or Personnel* (New York: Vintage Books, 1968).

[16]Grant McConnell, *Private Power and American Democracy* (New York: Alfred A. Knopf, 1966), p. 107.

[17]Proposals along these lines are discussed in Milton Kotler, *Neighborhood Government: The Local Foundations of Political Life* (Indianapolis: Bobbs-Merrill, 1969).

[18]For an analysis of these different forms of decentralization see Alice Rivlin, *Systematic Thinking for Social Action,* pp. 120–44.

Who Plans?
Choices in the Process of
Policy Formulation

The dispute between the modern planners and their opponents is not a dispute on whether we ought to choose intelligently between the various possible organizations of society; it is not a dispute on whether we ought to employ foresight and systematic thinking in planning our common affairs. It is a dispute about what is the best way of so doing. The question is whether for this purpose it is better that the holder of coercive power should confine himself in general to creating conditions under which the knowledge and initiative of individuals are given the best scope so that they *can plan most successfully; or whether a rational utilization of our resources requires* central *direction and organization of all our activities according to some consciously constructed "blueprint."*

FRIEDRICH A. HAYEK,
The Road to Serfdom

8 In the preceding chapters we have examined a series of choices that inhere in the design of social welfare policies. Generally speaking, these choices address questions of what is to be done, what alternative courses of action can be taken to fulfill social welfare objectives, and what their implications are, with the analytic focus upon the product or plan. In this chapter our attention shifts to a dimension of choice that is found, not in the design of the product, but in the process of policy formulation. While we have emphasized policy issues that relate to the product, it is important for the beginning student not to lose sight of the point that the arrangements governing how decisions are made are as significant a policy issue as questions pertaining to the substantive content of the decisions.

Hayek, writing in 1944, claimed that the dispute between "modern planners and their opponents" is not around the desirability of planning per se, but about the merits of alternative planning arrangements and the degree to which they allow for expression of individual interests as opposed to the collective will. This issue may be expressed in the question, Who plans? Specifically, the question is whether smaller units of society —individuals and groups—are directly involved in planning for their own interest or whether plans in the public interest are centrally determined. It was the latter course that Hayek perceived as the "road to serfdom."[1]

In recent years this dispute appears to have lost some of its edge. There are a number of modern planners who (along with Hayek) would critically question the desirability of unitary, centrally determined plans. As Paul Davidoff, an influential member of the professional planning community, puts it:

> A practice that has discouraged full participation by citizens in plan making in the past has been based on what might be called the "unitary plan." This is the idea that only one agency in a community should prepare a comprehensive plan; that agency is the city planning commission or department. Why is it that no other organization within a community prepares a plan? Why is only one agency concerned with establishing both general and specific goals for community development, and with proposing the strategies and costs required to effect goals? Why are there not plural plans?[2]

Pluralistic planning occupies a middle-range position somewhere between the laissez-faire, highly individualistic approach to planning that Hayek advocates and the highly collectivist approach of the centralized unitary plan. The pluralistc approach conceives of planning as a contentious process involving the clash of different interests in the community but emphasizes the group (or micro-collective) rather than the individualistic nature of these competing interests.

There is considerable distance on the spectrum of political thought between the nineteenth century laissez-faire liberalism of Hayek and the twentieth century liberalism of Davidoff. And, to be sure, their positions contain disparate views on various aspects of the social planning enterprise. Yet their convergence of thought on two fundamental points is interesting. First, as indicated above, they favor diversity in planning arrangements in place of the centrally produced unitary plan. On this point Hayek's views are stronger and more extreme in the sense that they are inclined towards laissez-faire and the diversity of individual choices. Davidoff's position favors pluralistic planning and the diversity of group choices. Second, they tend to emphasize similar conceptions as to the nature of the public interest. That is, both Hayek and Davidoff hold the view that the common good is arrived at out of contending individual and group interests.[3]

The Planner's Role

There are other conceptions of the public interest that call for different answers to the question of who plans. Before discussing these relationships, however, we would like to clarify the planner's role in the planning enterprise. The policy issue might be put to rest simply by saying that the planner plans. But in so doing he is more or less influenced and directed by his own values, knowledge, and inclinations as well as by the values, knowledge, and inclinations of other relevant parties in the planning environment. The issue with which we are concerned turns on the degree to which planning decisions are more or less influenced by the planner in comparison to the influence exerted by other relevant parties. Thus, "who plans?" is a relative matter that depends upon the organizational arrangements among planners, political and bureaucratic leaders, and consumer publics. To whom is the planner primarily accountable? Whose values and interests guide the planning choices that are made? Efforts to answer these questions confront policy planners with major policy choices that govern the planning process and the development of organizational arrangements for how to decide what is to be done.

Role refers to the ways in which responsibilities, expectations, and commitments are structured in regard to the planner's job. There is some body of knowledge, skill, and expertise that all planners who claim "professional" status are supposed to have mastered. But obviously, in any given professional position there are specific tasks the worker must do, there are expected ways in which he must behave and there are people to whom he must be accountable. And these vary from job to job. The policy-planning professional is not an independent operator. In addition to a guiding set of professional ethics there is some sponsor, usually an agency, to whom he is accountable, and clients and/or constituents to whom he is also accountable. The competing claims of his profession, his sponsor, and his client frequently constitute a great source of strain and sometimes conflict for the planner since their demands upon and expectations of him may be contradictory.

The profession may place great importance on "professional standards" of practice and award recognition, as well as status to practitioners who observe and defend these standards (e.g., seeing that only properly credentialed people perform professional tasks). The sponsor may have more interest in economy and efficiency than in standards and therefore constrain the planner to find the least expensive way of doing things. Clients or constituents will tend to evaluate the planner in terms of what he produces for them and are not likely to have as great an interest in maintenance of professional standards or in economy. (This is not to say, of course, that professional standards, economy, and effectiveness are necessarily contradictory.)

The social context of the planner's role, then, is one of the factors that determines the kind of process he can engage in successfully. His relationships with these other actors, his sponsors and clients, play an important part in determining the values and interests that will be uppermost in his work. To a large extent he is both committed to and limited to working in certain ways by the nature of these relationships. The professional who is involved in policy planning should be cognizant of the features of the social context that bear upon his work.

The planner's role requires the integration of knowledge and skill to deal with both interactional and analytic functions. As noted in Chapter 1, the planning process is frequently discussed and analyzed according to two perspectives: planning as a socio-political process and planning as a techno-methodological process. Perlman and Gurin and Kramer and Specht suggest that these perspectives are different sides of the planning coin—both equally required to bring the process to fruition. These authors use the notions of "analytic" and "interactional" tasks to describe the techno-methodological and socio-political aspects of the planning process.[4] Analytic tasks (or techno-methodological considerations) involve data collection, quantification of problems and analysis in light of these data, ranking priorities, specification of objectives, program design, and the like. The interactional tasks (or socio-political considerations) involve the development of an organizational network. This requires the structuring of a planning system within which communication and exchange of information among relevant actors takes place and planning decisions are made. The ways in which these interactional tasks are completed are the means of resolving the question of who plans. The distinction between techno-methodological and socio-political aspects of the planning process may be illustrated by examining the planning requirements for the Model Cities Program.

An Example:
Planning in the Model Cities Program

Briefly, the Model Cities Program was run as follows: All cities were invited by the Department of Housing and Urban Development (HUD) to submit applications for planning grants. In these applications the cities described their characteristics, social problems, and their "plan for planning." In the first application period which ended May 1, 1967, 193 cities had sent in applications. After a careful and complex scrutiny of the applications and the applicants, 75 cities were selected to receive planning grants.[5] Announcements of the grants were made on November 16, 1967. A similar process was used in the following year to select another 73 cities bringing the total to 148 cities given grants over the two-year period.[6] The Model Cities experience for any given city was planned to last approximately six years (the first for planning and the next five for implementation).

With regard to the analytic and interactional sides of the planning coin, the HUD guidelines for the Model Cities Program participants were quite clear and firm on techno-methodological approaches and rather vague and loose on the socio-political aspects of planning.

Techno-Methodological Approaches

The HUD planning model stipulated that cities follow a predefined, rational, analytic process in developing their Comprehensive Demonstration Plans (CDPs). Intitially, this entailed a three part CDP framework:

> *Part I* was to describe and analyze problems and their causes, to rank these problems in order of local priorities, and to indicate objectives, strategies, and program approaches to solving these problems. This document was to be submitted to HUD two-thirds of the way through the planning year. Based on these documents HUD was to provide appropriate feedback to the City Demonstration Agencies (CDA's) that would be useful for the completion of Parts II and III.
>
> *Part II* was to be a statement of projected five-year objectives and cost estimates to achieve these objectives. This document was to be submitted at the end of the planning year with Part III.
>
> *Part III* was to be a detailed statement of program plans for the first action year, the costs involved, and administrative arrangements for implementation. This document was to be a logical extension of the analysis, strategies, and priorities outlined in Part I.[7]

Toward the end of 1969 this framework was simplified by the elimination of the Part II document and changing Part I to a Mid-Term Planning Statement (limited to seventy-five pages) that was to be submitted midway in the planning year and then revised and merged with what was previously designated as the Part III document for the final submission—the CDP.

The extent to which cities were able to satisfy the methodological requirements of the planning process is detailed in some of the studies we have cited.[8] In general, as noted in Chapter 4, the cities made considerable effort to follow the guidelines, but few were able to do more than approximate the ideal process prescribed by HUD. In part this is because the demands were strenuous even for those cities that could command the required technical expertise. Their causal analyses of problems had a tendency toward infinite regress, and the problem analysis approach often proved to be a frustrating and unilluminating exercise to the participants in the planning systems. Given the limited planning resources that were available, five-year projection plans could hardly demand the investment of time, effort, and commitment that planning for the following year's programs received; and in fact, the Part II CDP submission was often the most superficial document prepared by the cities. Moreover, many cities simply did not have the staff expertise to do comprehensive planning according to HUD's model. This is strongly suggested by data from a nationwide study which indicates that 64 percent of the cities used private consulting firms to provide technical assistance during the planning period.[9]

Socio-Political Approaches

While the technical requirements of the planning process for the Model Cities Program were spelled out in detail, the socio-political aspects of the process were left largely to the determination of local groups. The major prescription HUD offered was that ultimate administrative and fiscal responsibility for the program be vested in the local chief executive. Beyond this, the guidelines left considerable latitude for the types of linkages and relationships among groups that might develop to imbue the decision making around CDPs with an element of social choice as well as technical procedure. The first Program Guide states it as follows:

> [The CDA] should be closely related to the governmental decision-making process in a way that permits the exercise of leadership by responsible elected officials in the establishment of policies ... It should have sufficient powers, authority, and structure to achieve the coordinated administration of all aspects of the program ... It should provide a meaningful role in policy making to area residents and to the major agencies expected to contribute to the program.[10]

While "a meaningful role in policy-making to area residents" is an innocent enough statement, the HUD administrative staff responsible for the

Model Cities Program were philosophically inclined to favor substantive citizen participation and vigorously sought the realization of citizen influence in the decision-making process. (The Model Cities Administration was staffed largely from outside of HUD. A number of Office of Economic Opportunity (OEO) personnel had transferred to the Model Cities Program anticipating that this program was where the Administration would concentrate its urban thrust.) Various case studies indicate that first-round planning grant awards were often accompanied by stipulations that the city spell out or strengthen its provisions for resident participation in Model Cities planning.[11] Further evidence of this is found in data from a study of the Planning Grant Review Project. The Planning Grant Review Project was the means used by HUD to select the cities that were to be funded for first-round planning grants. In the Project, federal staff rated each city's success potential based upon information provided in their applications. Results of the study of the Project indicate that the federal staff gave highest ratings to those cities that later proved to be most successful at achieving high degrees of citizen participation. However, there were either no correlations or negative correlations between these ratings of success potential and other measures of performance.[12]

Though citizen influence in the planning process was emphasized, the guidelines for its achievement and the structure of relationships between professional planners, political leadership, and citizen groups were relatively vague compared to guidelines for the technical aspects of the planning process. Overall, a number of planning arrangements emerged in which planners were accountable, in varying degrees, to different parties.[13] In general terms these different patterns of relationships among planners, political leadership, and citizen groups are associated with the ways in which the "public interest" is defined.

Conceptions of the Public Interest

One justification for any form of social planning is that the decisions arrived at and the choices made will serve the common good or the ends of the whole public. This is true whether the planner is primarily accountable to himself, to political or bureaucratic leaders, or to the consumer public. It is true whether planning is done under public auspices or by private agencies. Take, for instance, the United Community Funds and Councils of America. This private organization explicitly disclaims that the community planning activities under its direction reflect the special interests of its member agencies. Thus, the Council literature prescribes:

There are valid and compelling reasons why policy decisions and program determination of a Council should be vested basically in the hands of lay citizens. A true planning body should be a citizens' organization. It should not be a creature of agencies nor a federation of agencies. *The board of directors of a Council should view health and welfare needs from a total community point of view; they must be able to look beyond agency structure and issues of agency territorial rights or aspirations.*[14] (Emphasis added.)

But the problem with claims that planning activities serve the public interest is that there are different conceptions of precisely what constitutes the common good and the means by which it is served. It is a matter of opinion whether, for practical planning purposes, "a total community point of view" is attainable or for that matter even desirable as a means for defining the public interest. Depending upon how the idiom is interpreted, planning *pro bono publico* may be expressed through several sociopolitical processes, each of which involves different relationships between planners and relevant parties in the planning environment. To illustrate let us examine three conventional meanings of the "public interest" as described by Banfield: these are the *organismic, communalist,* and *individualistic* conceptions.[15]

The Organismic View

According to this conception there is an ideal public interest that transcends the specific preferences and interests of the individuals of which the public body is composed. The public body is viewed as a unitary organism whose interests are greater or different than the sum of its parts. Thus, for example, in community planning the community is believed to have certain anthropomorphic needs and interests that are essential to its health: its arteries must be able to sustain a sufficient flow of goods and services; its tax base must be sufficient to nourish growth and maintenance costs; and police are needed to protect, social services to mend, and sanitation agencies to cleanse its parts. To stretch the analogy a bit further, given this view, the planner's relationship to the community is akin to that of doctor to patient. In diagnosing the community's interests the planner is guided primarily by his own values and technical expertise. While he may be working out of a public or a private agency, the planner's primary accountability is to the profession. In essence this conception of the public interest in its purest form gives rise to *technocracy*.

The Communalist View

According to this conception there is a unitary public interest composed of the interests that all members of the public share in common. This single set of common ends is viewed as more valuable in calculating the public interest than are the unshared ends that individuals and groups may hold. The public's common ends are embodied in political leaders and community institutions. This view of the public interest is associated with a planning process that includes, as Rothman notes, "legislators or administrators who are presumed to know the ends of the body politic as a whole and to strive in some central decision-making locus to assert the unitary interests of the whole over competing lesser interests."[16] In this context the planner is accountable primarily to political or bureaucratic leadership. Planning choices are guided by the values and interests these leaders express.

The Individualist View

According to this conception, there is no unitary public interest, only different publics with different interests. The unshared ends that are held by individuals and groups are seen as of more consequence than shared ends in determining the common good. In this view the public interest is a momentary compromise arising out of the interplay among competing interests; it is constantly shifting as new groups are able to make their interests known and respected. Individualistic conceptions of the public interest are associated with *advocacy planning,* an arrangement in which the planner is accountable to a specific group whose values and interests guide planning choices. The objective is to increase this group's participation and influence in the competitive process through which definitions of the public interest are achieved.

Each of the conceptions of the public interest implies socio-political processes that involve different planning roles and different relationships among planners, political and administrative leaders, and consumer publics. Along the continuum of possibilities three modal types emerge that may be summarized as follows:

1. The planner as a *technocrat* accountable primarily to the profession and operating with a view of the public interest derived from the special skills and knowledge in his possession

2. The planner as a *bureaucrat* accountable primarily to the political and administrative hierarchy and operating with a view of the public interest derived from institutional leadership

3. The planner as an *advocate* accountable primarily to the consumer group that purchases his services and operating with a view of the public interest derived from consumer group preferences

These modal types represent the logically consistent planning arrangements corresponding to organismic, communal, and individualistc conceptions of the public interest. We indicate that they range along a continuum because reality sometimes intrudes upon conceptual distinctions such as these in a disconcerting manner.[17] And students of social planning will find that inconsistencies are incorporated in the operations of individuals and organizations engaged in the social planning enterprise. As Banfield explains:

> An institution may function as a mechanism which asserts at the same time different, and perhaps logically opposed, conceptions of the structure of the public interest. The members of a citizen board, for example, may endeavor to explicate the meaning of some very general ends which pertain to the body politic or *ethos* while at the same time—and perhaps inconsistently—seeking to find that compromise among the ends of individuals which will represent the greatest "total" satisfaction.[18]

Alternative views of the public interest are sometimes held simultaneously because of the dynamic interplay of competing social values that are associated with these views.

Three Competing Values: Participation, Leadership, and Expertise

There is a continuing cycle of competition among three values that govern the management of community affairs, and that affect the degree to which different conceptions of the public interest are emphasized. These are the values of participation, leadership, and expertise. All three are prized values that compete for ascendency in community life. These values and their significance for social planning have been noted and described in the literature.[19] Our particular interest here is to point out the dialectical relationship among these values and how it affects the community planning process. Each value, when it is maximized, contains the seed of its own undoing and generates conditions which will, in turn, encourage another of the values to emerge. While policy plannners have relatively little control over these dynamics, there is benefit in understanding the dialectical process.

Participation is a value that extols the virtue of each and every man joining meaningfully and directly in making decisions that affect his welfare. In the extreme it supports the vision of a participatory democracy and vigorously champions schemes for community control and decentralization. It is celebrated in the slogans "Power to the people" and "One man —one vote." Theoretically, this value is supported by findings from small group experiments and industrial psychology which indicate that when people participate directly in the decisions that impinge upon their lives, they are more likely to feel a part of their community. Decisions arrived at by participation are more likely to be binding, and alienation and apathy are reduced.[20]

Countervailing theory contends that an urban industrialized society is too large and complex to allow the value of participation to operate in the extreme. Rather, participation must be organized and expressed through a representative system. The New England Town Meeting might have been an appropriate decision-making device for eighteenth century small-town America, but modern society needs electoral machinery for selecting representative leaders of organized interests.

The value of participation in the management of community affairs always exists, though at some times and places it is more prominent than at others. For example, the Jacksonian era, which followed the Revolutionary War, and the Populist period of the late 1880s were times when issues of participation were paramount. In terms of governmental forms, the value of participation finds expression most directly in county government which, because of its rural, small-town heritage, has been disposed to value neither leadership nor expertise. County government is the personification of Emerson's view on the general functions of government—"the less, the better."

Participation becomes the primary value in governing community affairs when leadership or expertise are perceived as unresponsive to those being led or served. Under these circumstances, movements for change will grow around dissatisfactions with the ways community institutions are run by their custodians. Decentralization, localism, and constituency satisfaction are likely to be the major programmatic goals of planning. Major evaluative concerns about programs will derive from the central question: Do the people like it?

Leadership as a value is the antithesis of participation. Because complex decisions must be made continuously and in great number, and authority must somehow extend to their implementation, leadership becomes important in any organized collectivity. In a heterogeneous society like ours where a swarm of competing claims to the public interest descend upon a complex framework of levels and types of government, community decision-making is bound to generate a hopeless drone of discussion and debate unless citizens can find leaders whom they trust, whom they can hold responsible, and who have the ability to mitigate conflict and regulate competition with equity and dispatch. Unless the executive committee, the board of directors, the officers—in short, leadership—undertake these tasks for the community, chaos will reign. The extreme example of leadership in government is the boss system and the political machine. Historically, both the nineteenth century movement against the "long ballot" and the twentieth century charter reform movement aimed to strengthen the power of governors and mayors.

When leadership emerges as the prime value in community life, centralization and growth become the major programmatic goals of planning. The major evaluative question is: Does it work? But the capacity to rule and lead does not ensure the capacity to plan and implement. Leaders searching for ideas, concerned and constrained to rule with economy and efficiency, eventually turn to the repository of another set of values—the experts—for assistance.

Expertise is a value that makes rationality the supreme criterion for decision-making. Theoretically, experts choose among programmatic alternatives on the basis of merit rather than politics. Expertise is an antidote to corruption and waste in government. Historically, expertise in government, whether in the form of civil service, the merit system, or the city manager, often appears on the scene to undo or restrain the ravages of leadership. Because he is presumably insulated from the vagaries of politics, the expert is free to bring knowledge and skill to bear on the problem-solving process, enabling leaders to make the most sensible decisions for the community.

As the expert's role gains primacy, the major concern in the planning enterprise moves to the touchstone of professionalism—technique. Refinement of professional skill, experimentation, coordination, and the attainment of improved methods of executive intervention become the major planning interests. Evaluative concerns deriving from this perspective focus on information about how and why different programs operate.

However, experts often succumb to their own ambitions. They may be inclined to preserve the status quo and to protect their privileged positions, whether as *eminences grises* to the ruling coalition, as the vanguard of an emergent technocracy, or entrenched administrators of planning "empires." In time, experts may suffer from "hardening of the categories" and become a major obstacle to innovation and change. The synthesis then transforms to a new thesis in the dialectic process. Technocracy may be challenged and community renewal brought about by new efforts to mobilize the dissatisfied public, to organize the disadvantaged and from their ranks to draw fresh leadership. Sooner or later, these leaders will call upon the experts for advice—and the cycle recurs.

The Cycle of Values

The political scientist, Robert Michels, saw this dialectic in the great European socialist political parties earlier in this century. His "Iron Law of Oligarchy" was based on the doctrine that history is a record of a continuous series of struggles over values, all of which culminate in the creation of new oligarchies that eventually fuse with the old, "representing an uninterrupted series of oppositions ... attaining one after another to power and passing from the sphere of envy to the sphere of avarice."[21] His insights into this process are timely.

> The democratic currents of history resemble successive waves. They break ever on the same shoal. They are ever renewed. This enduring spectacle is simultaneously encouraging and depressing ... Now new accusers arise to denounce the traitors; after an era of glorious combats and inglorious power, they end by fusing with the old dominant class; whereupon once more they are in their turn attacked by fresh opponents who appeal to the name of democracy. It is probable that this cruel game will continue without end.[22]

Contemporary experience suggests the ways in which the dialectic of social planning operates. In the years following World War II, the technician emerged as the central figure in community welfare planning. The notion of a community "master plan" developed by professionals achieved broad support. In the 1950s dissatisfaction grew with this process of planning and its effects. Citizen participation, as a check on the professional planners, was a significant ingredient of the Seven-Point Workable Program for urban renewal contained in the Housing Act of 1954. Initially, this participation involved the appointment of a city-wide advisory committee, generally composed of civic leaders, to work with planners; representation of the poor, who were usually most affected by renewal activities, was neither mandatory nor commonplace. As experience with resident opposition to renewal increased, agencies began to give greater consideration to the involvement of neighborhood residents, although as various studies and observations indicate citizen participation in urban renewal was modest.[23]

Other efforts in the late 1950s and early 1960s gave citizens an increasingly active role. These included the Grey Area Projects, the planning programs spawned by the President's Committee on Juvenile Delinquency, and the War on Poverty. All gave increasing emphasis to the value of participation vis-à-vis leadership and expertise. (It is interesting to note that at their inception, *all* community planning programs seem to invoke all three values, though this kind of *tout ensemble* never comes off very well. One of the values is sooner or later elevated above the rest.) By the mid-1960s the value of participation reigned; the expertise of professionals was rejected or disrated in favor of the direct visceral experiences of neighborhood residents who were called upon to "tell it like it really is."[24] Meanwhile, leadership fretted, floundered, and failed to achieve consensus.

An Example:
Planned Variations as a Blueprint for Leadership

The Model Cities Program followed the direction set by the earlier Economic Opportunity Act and other federal legislation in calling for a rapprochement among the three values. As suggested by the Program Guide, elected officials were to exercise leadership, area residents were to have a meaningful role, and the planning agency was to exercise powers and authority in the planning process. In the early stages of this program, community participation was emphasized as the guiding value. Federal, regional, and local interests and energies were almost completely occupied with questions about resident organizations, proportions of resident representatives, and the allocation of funds to facilitate participation. That technicism and expertise received short shrift is evident in early reports on the program.[25] However, by mid-1970 interest in participation had begun to subside on all levels. As the federal investments in efforts to achieve widespread citizen participation were retrenched, a new era opened in which concerns for building the capacities of local executive leadership became prominent.

From the early 1970s the federal government drifted from fostering community participation toward supporting and building local political leadership. The drift, though most evident in policies developed in Washington, D.C., reflected some of the changing currents in all of American society. We shall explore this change by examining Planned Variations, a HUD program designed to enhance the authority of local executive leadership.

Planned Variations is one program among several that reflects a policy emphasis on strengthening local competence which began to develop in the late 1960s and early 1970s. Others include the Office of Management and Budget's "A-95" project notification and review system, the Office of Economic Opportunity's policy governing local checkpoint procedures, and the Department of Health, Education and Welfare's arrangement for certification sign-off by CDA directors on grants for programs impacting on Model Cities neighborhoods. Each of these mechanisms allow local political leaders varying degrees of influence on independent agency applications for federal grants.[26] On a broader scale these mechanisms may be viewed as pilot efforts in the national adminstration's strategy to enhance local leadership and autonomy through revenue sharing.[27]

In 1973, the "drift" became a tiderace. The abandonment of community action programs like OEO and Model Cities was announced as official federal policy with the publication of the 1974 federal Budget.[28]

Announced in 1970, Planned Variations was a pilot effort to shift the locus of allocative decision-making within the federal urban grant system. Combined into one package, the Variations offered a preview of the Nixon administration's "new federalism" by breaking ground for revenue sharing via what approaches a system of block grants to Model Cities Programs at the local level. Later on in 1973, revenue sharing was touted as the Nixon administration's method for communities to fill the gaps left by the 1974 budget cuts.[29]

In early statements on the program the HUD secretary, George Romney, announced that the major Variations would (1) eliminate all but statutorily defined federal reviews concerning the use of supplemental and categorical funds in cities; (2) permit development of Model Cities plans and programs for entire cities rather than just specific neighborhoods; and (3) grant local chief executives the right to review, comment, and sign-off on all federal agency categorical programs prior to use in their cities.[30]

Fifteen months later, the program's objectives had expanded from three to eight, as follows:

PLANNED VARIATION PROGRAM OBJECTIVES

1. Develop comprehensive plans for the entire city, not just the original and new Model Neighborhood Areas (MNAs), by using administrative, planning, and evaluation funds on a citywide basis.

2. Coordinate the planning of federal programs through the local chief executive by utilizing the Chief Executive Review and Comment (CERC) procedure on major federal program activities.

3. Build the capacity of the local chief executive to budget resources and determine priority needs on a city-wide basis by using administrative, planning, and evaluation funds on a city-wide basis.

4. Extend the impact of the Planned Variations funds to New Target Areas.

5. Increase local control of federal programs by reducing federal reviews and requirements and encouraging cities to request waivers.

6. Improve procedure for applying state resources and technical expertise to local needs by establishing State–Local Task Forces.

7. Develop a comprehensive and coordinated federal response to local needs by encouraging use of Regional Councils for Coordinating technical assistance and project funding.

8. Coordinate the delivery of HUD categorical programs to the locality in accordance with local priorities by negotiating an Annual Arrangement with each Planned Variation city.[31]

Of these eight objectives, the two principal ones are clearly Chief Executive Review and Comment (CERC) and city-wide planning. The intention of eliminating all federal review had dwindled to a more or less hortatory statement that reviews would be limited. In any case, the limited review concept applied to all Planned Variation cities; there were no cities for which *all* federal review of plans and projects had been eliminated, even experimentally.

The major import of the Variations is to shift the locus of allocative decision-making along two dimensions of the federal grant system, as indicated in Figure 8–1. On the horizontal plane the changes designated are *within* the levels and on the vertical plane they are *between* levels.

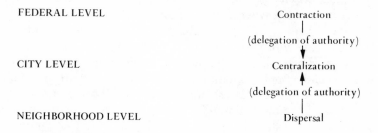

FIGURE 8–1
Planned Variations Impact on Allocative Decision Making.

Limited federal review reduced the number of agency criteria used to assess grant applications and reduced the number of reviews to which an application is subject. Typically, an application is reviewed six to ten times as it moves through local, regional, and federal layers of agency and interagency review committees. This cumbersome, extended system involves extensive coordination. Clearly, since coordination had proven less effective than was hoped, the federal government was ready to experiment with new forms of centralized decision making in CERC and city-wide planning.

If the multiplicity of federal reviews was to be replaced by the one overall decision of whether to fund or not to fund ("go—no go," in bureaucratic parlance), then allocative decision-making would be contracted at the federal level with more discretion and authority over detailed reviews channeled down toward the local level. But in the meanwhile, the thrust of Planned Variations was upon strengthening the mayor.

On the city level, increased centralization is brought about by the mayor's sign-off Variation which requires the chief executive's review of local applications for federal assistance. The mayor could make written comments on each application prior to its submission. Before this shift the procedure was such that numerous local private and public organizations received federal grants over which local chief executives had no control and little influence.

There are now over 500 federal categorical grant programs.[32] Most large city mayors find it a formidable task just to keep abreast of the amounts, locations, and purposes of these grants. As the mayor's sign-off becomes a requirement for an increasing number of federal grants, the mayor's office is transformed into a clearinghouse for local applications for federal funds. While the mayor's review and comment do not constitute a formal veto power, it does have that effect in practice. The intent of this procedure is both to give the mayor an opportunity to influence and regulate the flow of funds into his city and to have the grantee agency take the mayor's priorities into account when drawing its application. With skillful operation, a mayor can employ this mechanism to adjust the flow of federal funds to coincide with local needs.

Aside from substantially increasing the administrative workload of the mayor's office, the implementation of this Variation requires special staff competence to review and assess projects within a broad planning framework, to create a modus operandi for planning between the mayor's office and local agencies (a delicate matter, as agency autonomy is compromised under these new arrangements), and to initiate project applications when a need exists that is not currently being met. Most cities now lack the staff capacity to effectively use the mayor's sign-off as a central planning mechanism. Larger, more competent staffs are likely to be established in the mayors' offices to vitalize the nascent central planning functions inherent in mayoral sign-off.

As suggested earlier, the exercise of leadership tends to generate a demand for supportive expertise. A model that is put forth to fulfill this demand is the kind of structure that evolved in Butte, Montana, one of the twenty Model Cities participants selected to take part in the Planned Variations. With HUD's full approval, the Butte City Demonstration Agency, renamed "Office of Programming and Management," serves a staff function in the mayor's office.

This evolution is not unique to the urban scene. Over the last decade cities have used urban renewal programs not only to secure federal funds for themselves but also to create, outside the city's regular departmental structure, a cadre of professional talent that could be employed in various capacities. "The best local renewal authorities," Wilson observes, "became generalized sources of innovation and policy staffing and their directors became in effect deputy mayors (and sometimes more than that)."[33] The move, as in Butte, to incorporate these functions under the formal jurisdiction of the mayor's office has the effect of centralizing planning under the chief executive's leadership.

On the neighborhood level, the impact of Planned Variations is to experiment with the relegation of allocative decision-making to city hall. This relegation is inherent in the "City-Wide Variation" which encourages Model Cities plans and programs to be developed on a city-wide basis instead of for a subarea (i.e., Model Neighborhood Area) as under the original Model Cities requirements. This Variation also increases the number and variety of groups who may claim a stake and seek a voice in the program's outcome. As the program opens to the whole city, there are more opportunities for planning on functional bases that transcend neighborhood boundaries. One would expect the emergence of new interest groups and a dispersal of resident influence on Model Cities Program development.

This dispersal of influence is likely to result in decreased resident cohesion and increased competition among would-be beneficiaries. Thus the overall impact of Planned Variations is to centralize authority in city hall. As indicated above, this is accomplished by limiting discretionary review at the federal level and by dispersing citizen inputs at the neighborhood level. While allocative decision-making authority is siphoned off at these two levels, the mayor is provided with power in the form of the "mayor's sign-off" variation to encourage the exercise of his authority.

There are, of course, certain obstacles to the realization of these objectives. As Banfield points out, organized beneficiaries of the categorical grant system are prone to be unenthusiastic about any changes that deprive them of their special status, such as dissolving their identities in a mass of supplicants through grant consolidation.[34] Congressmen, too, have a special affinity for categorical grants that can be tailored to suit particular groups of constituents. Moreover, the rhetoric of local control notwithstanding, it is unclear exactly how anxious mayors are to assume authority and responsibilities that may prove politically awkward when the foil of federal control is removed.

However, the blueprints of Planned Variations, executed even on a moderate scale (and the message of the 1974 federal budget suggests that the scale is more likely to be quite grand) will distinguish urban planning in the seventies from urban planning in the sixties in at least two ways. First, mayors will be held increasingly accountable by their constituencies for plans and programs in their cities. Mayors often claim that they cannot keep track of all federally assisted programs coming into their cities, or that they have no authority over the agencies receiving federal funds, or that if they do have authority over the local agencies, they must comply with federally designed program guidelines. In each case, accountability that is impaired by the exigencies of the categorical grant system would be enlarged under Planned Variations.

Second, citizen participation characterized by grass-roots organizations, created in Community Action and Model Cities neighborhoods to assist in planning and implementing these programs, will be emphasized less in federal requirements for grant assistance. As programs are designed for a broader urban constituency, the influence of neighborhood groups will diminish. Instead, the focus of political activity on the neighborhood level is likely to shift from elected neighborhood councils to the formal city-wide political apparatus—perhaps injecting a new vitality into urban politics.

Social Welfare Planning:
By Drift or Design

Where does the policy planner fit into all this? Does he conveniently gravitate towards executive leadership for the authority to plan when leadership is in the saddle, and "back to the people" when the impulse for participation arises? Is there any meaning for professional planners in what we describe as the dialectical relationship among the values of participation, leadership, and expertise beyond, perhaps, the recognition that planning is an awfully complex business?

In response to the last question, Rein suggests that conflicting values such as participation, leadership, and expertise invest the planning enterprise with insoluble dilemmas.[35] From the dialectical perspective, however, the competition among participation, leadership, and expertise is not a dilemma but a dynamic, necessary, and continuously unfolding process that sustains the pulse of democracy in the planning endeavor. Policy planners should encourage rather than avoid the dialectical relationship among these values, so that no single value becomes the professional's polestar. This implies that the planner regard the contradictions among these values as a healthy stimulant to his profession and be prepared to keep each value salient as emphases in the community change.

To conclude, we should like to emphasize our own view about the values described in this discussion. Shifts in the values that guide social planning bear careful scrutiny. In the short run, a change from participation to leadership will be welcomed by many members of the planning profession who experienced some of the turbulence and frustration of citizen participation in the Community Action and Model Cities Programs. They may be inclined to embrace the value of leadership warmly. And as leadership perpetually looks to expertise, planners in general may expect to be well received.

But planners should be mindful that as local executives extend their spheres of authority and the numbers of planners on their staffs increase, the executive's ability to control his planners is reduced, laying the ground for technocracy. Instead of being an advocacy planner for the poor as he was in the sixties, the planner-technocrat of the seventies could become exceedingly remote from the would-be beneficiaries of his enterprise. Only by continuing to work with representatives of different groups, including consumer publics, can this estrangement be avoided.

A central challenge to social planners at any time is to avoid drifting on the currents of change towards whatever value happens to be in favor; rather they must chart an independent course of action—one designed to facilitate the dialectical process and enliven the clash of values that seems fundamental both to democracy and to social welfare.

Notes

[1] Friedrich A. Hayek, *The Road to Serfdom* (Chicago: University of Chicago Press, 1944), pp. 32–42.

[2] Paul Davidoff, "Advocacy and Pluralism in Planning," in *Community Organization Practice*, eds. Ralph M. Kramer and Harry Specht (Englewood Cliffs, N.J.: Prentice-Hall, 1969), p. 440.

[3] Hayek, *The Road to Serfdom*, pp. 56–65; and Davidoff, "Advocacy and Pluralism in Planning," pp. 438–50.

[4] Robert Perlman and Arnold Gurin, *Community Organization and Social Planning* (New York: John Wiley & Sons, 1971), pp. 52–75; and Ralph M. Kramer and Harry Specht, *Readings in Community Organization Practice* (Englewood Cliffs, N.J.: Prentice-Hall, 1969), pp. 8–9.

[5] For a detailed description of this process see Neil Gilbert and Harry Specht, *Planning for Model Cities: Process, Product, Performance, and Predictions* (Washington, D.C.: Dept. of Housing and Urban Development, Government Printing Office, forthcoming).

[6] For further details on the Model Cities Program legislation, guidelines, and operational procedures, see the following: Gilbert and Specht, *Planning for Model Cities; Improving the Quality of Urban Life: A Program Guide to Model Neighborhoods in Demonstration Cities*, U.S. Department of Housing and Urban Development, HUD PG-47, December 1966, and HUD PG-47, December 1967 (Washington, D.C.: Government Printing Office); Marshall Kaplan, *Model Cities and National Urban Policy* (Chicago: American Society of Planning Officials, 1971); Marshall Kaplan, Gans, and Kahn, *The Model Cities Program: A Comparative Analysis of the Planning Process in Eleven Cities* (Washington, D.C.: Dept. of Housing and Urban Development, Government Printing Office, 1970); and Roland L. Warren, "Model

Cities' First Round: Politics, Planning, and Participation," *Journal of the American Institute of Planners,* Vol. 35, No. 4 (July 1969), 245–52.

[7]Summarized from *Improving the Quality of Urban Life.*

[8]See footnote 6.

[9]Gilbert and Specht, *Planning for Model Cities.*

[10]*Improving the Quality of Urban Life,* p. 11.

[11]See, for example, Marshall Kaplan, Gans, and Kahn, *The Model Cities Program* and Warren, "Model Cities' First Round."

[12]Gilbert and Specht, *Planning for Model Cities.*

[13]For example, in the Marshall Kaplan, Gans, and Kahn study, *The Model Cities Program,* five types of planning systems are identified: staff dominant, staff influence, parity, resident influence, and resident dominant. Each of these systems is characterized by different sets of relationships among planners, political leadership, and citizen groups.

[14]*Essentials for Effective Planning* (New York: United Community Councils of America, 1962), p. 4.

[15]Martin Meyerson and Edward Banfield, *Politics, Planning, and the Public Interest* (New York: Free Press, 1955), pp. 322–29. These conceptions are similar, respectively, to the idealist view, the rationalist view, and the realist view of the public interest as analyzed by Glendon A. Schubert, *The Public Interest* (New York: Free Press, 1960).

[16]Jack Rothman, "Three Models of Community Organization Practice," in *Social Work Practice, 1968* (New York: Columbia University Press, 1968), p. 38.

[17]For an excellent analysis of the complexities and some variations in these planning relationships see Francine F. Rabinovitz, *City Politics and Planning* (New York: Atherton, 1969), pp. 79–117.

[18]Meyerson and Banfield, *Politics, Planning, and the Public Interest,* p. 329.

[19]For example, see Herbert Kaufman, *Politics and Policies in State and Local Government* (Englewood Cliffs, N.J.: Prentice-Hall, 1964); Martin Rein, "Social Planning: The Search for Legitimacy," *Journal of the American Institute of Planners,* Vol. 35, No. 4 (July 1967), 233–44; and George A. Brager and Harry Specht, *Community Organizing* (New York: Columbia University Press, 1973).

[20]For example, see Eric Fromm, *The Sane Society* (New York: Holt, Rinehart and Winston, 1955); Ralph White and Ronald Lippitt, "Leader Behavior and Member Reaction in Three Social Climates," in *Group Dynamics,* eds. Dorwin Cartwright et al. (Evanston, Ill.: Row, Peterson and Company, 1953); Jacob Levine and John Butler, "Lecture vs. Group Decision in Changing Behavior," *Journal of Applied Psychology,* Vol. 36 (February 1952), 29–33.

[21]Robert Michels, *Political Parties* (New York: Dover Publications, Inc., 1915), p. 319.

[22]*Ibid,* p. 408.

[23]Peter Rossi and Robert Dentler, *The Politics of Urban Renewal* (New York: Free

Press, 1961); James Q. Wilson, "Planning and Politics: Citizen Participation in Urban Renewal," in *Urban Renewal: People, Politics and Planning,* eds. Jewel Bellush *et al.* (New York: Anchor Books, 1967); and Scott Greer, *Urban Renewal and American Cities* (Indianapolis: Bobbs-Merrill, 1965).

[24]Neil Gilbert and Joseph Eaton, "Research Report: Who Speaks for the Poor?" *Journal of the American Institute of Planners,* Vol. 36 (November 1970), 411–16.

[25]Marshall Kaplan, Gans, and Kahn, *The Model Cities Program,* 1970; Warren, "Model Cities' First Round."

[26]A cogent analysis of these and other policies that have implications for the exertion of local leadership may be found in a study by Marshall Kaplan, *et al., Local Government Leadership in Federal Assistance Programs: Some Experience with Existing Planning and Coordination Mechanisms* (San Francisco: Marshall Kaplan, Gans and Kahn, 1971); and Melvin Mogulof, "Regional Planning, Clearance and Evaluation: A Look at the A-95 Process," *Journal of the American Institute of Planners,* Vol. 37, No. 6 (November 1971), 418–22.

[27]Marshall Kaplan, *et al., Local Government Leadership.*

[28]"Savings Expected to Be Made through Reductions and Terminations in Federal Programs in 3 Fiscal Years," *New York Times,* January 30, 1973, p. 20.

[29]"Excerpts from President Nixon's Budget Message as Presented to Congress," *New York Times,* January 30, 1973, p. 21.

[30]Department of Housing and Urban Development, *HUD News,* #70——723, "Statement by Secretary George Romney, September 30" (Washington, D.C.: Government Printing Office, 1970).

[31]Department of Housing and Urban Development, Office of Community Development, *Planned Variations Evaluation Report* (Washington, D.C.: Government Printing Office, 1971).

[32]See William Lilley, "Urban Report: Both Parties Ready to Scrap Grant Programs in Favor of 'City Strategy' Package of Aid," *National Journal,* Vol. 3, No. 6 (July 1971), 1391–97; and Advisory Commission on Intergovernmental Relations, *Special Revenue Sharing: An Analysis of the Administration's Joint Consolidation Proposals* (Washington, D.C.: Government Printing Office, December 1971), pp. 19–20.

[33]James Q. Wilson, "The Mayors vs. the Cities," *Public Interest,* Vol. 23, No. 3 (Summer 1969), 30.

[34]Edward Banfield, "Revenue Sharing in Theory and Practice," *Public Interest,* Vol. 23, No. 2 (Spring 1971), 33–45.

[35]Rein, "Social Planning."

Subject Index

Name Index